A Guidebook

REGULATING
SENSITIVE LANDS

A Guidebook

REGULATING SENSITIVE LANDS

by Jon A. Kusler
Attorney at Law

Environmental Law Institute   Washington, D.C.

Ballinger Publishing Company • Cambridge, Massachusetts
A Subsidiary of Harper & Row, Publishers, Inc.

This book was prepared with the support of the Resources and Land Investigations Program, U.S. Geological Survey, U.S. Department of the Interior. Any opinions, findings, conclusions, or recommendations are those of the author and do not necessarily reflect the views of the U.S. Department of the Interior.

International Standard Book Number: 0−88410−095−2

Library of Congress Catalog Card Number: 79−27684

Printed in the United States of America

Library of Congress Cataloging in Publication Data

Kusler, Jon A
  Regulating sensitive lands.

  Bibliography: p.
  Includes index.
  1. Land use−Planning−United States.
I. Title
HD205 1980.K87   333.73'15'0973   79−27684
ISBN 0−88410−095−2

FOREWORD

Many persons and agencies have contributed in varying degrees to the preparation of this book. In a sense, the book was begun more than ten years ago when I was employed by the University of Wisconsin to help develop manuals and model ordinances for county zoning of lake and stream shores. County zoning of unincorporated shorelands within 1000 feet of lakes and 300 feet of streams was required by the Wisconsin Shoreland Zoning Act of 1966. In the next decade this act served as a precedent for many state sensitive area programs.

I spent several years with this program under the excellent guidance of Professors Jacob Beuscher and Douglas Yanggen of the University of Wisconsin. Cooperative state/local land use regulation proved a new approach and there was little experience to draw on in Wisconsin or elsewhere. It became apparent that traditional land use controls were only partially suitable to address the interrelated institutional and scientific issues of resource management. Fortunately, several dozen scientists, lawyers, sociologists, planners, and economists volunteered their services to help develop new approaches. The author learned that theoretical nicety had to be tempered with strong doses of practicality and common sense.

During this project, I became interested in the needs and problems of managing all types of resource areas, not just shorelands. From 1968 to 1971 I was able to survey flood plain regulations on a national basis through a contract with the University of Wisconsin from the U.S. Water Resource Council, U.S. Department of Interior, U.S. Army Corps of Engineers, Tennessee Valley Authority, U.S. Department of Housing and Urban Development, and the U.S. Department of Agriculture. Hundreds of federal, state, and local agency personnel contributed invaluable information to this effort. Special appreciation is due the late Thomas Less for his contributions.

From 1971 to 1977 I conducted studies as a consultant and staff member for the University of Wisconsin and the University of Massachusetts concerning lakes, parks, coastal areas, wetlands, environmental impact analysis, water pollution control, and surface water regulation. Each study permitted further exploration of a specific aspect of sensitive area regulation. Differences were revealed between the issues and approaches for different types of areas, such as flood plains and wetlands, and between the needs of various states. But similarities in programs developed in isolation from one another were also striking. These similarities indicated that (1) certain issues and approaches were basic to resource regulations and (2) a somewhat coherent body of knowledge could be developed pertaining to sensitive area regulation. Information concerning common denominators in efforts proved of interest not only from academic and research perspectives. This data aided the design of regulatory programs simultaneously addressing several types of areas and the design of broader planning, data gathering, or other efforts with sensitive area regulatory components.

Despite the several dozen individual studies, their synthesis in the present book would not have been possible without further help. Initial studies dealing with three common denominator topics—sensitive area definition, data gathering, and standard setting—were funded by the University of Wisconsin Institute for Environmental Studies with support from the Sea Grant program. These funds were provided by the National Oceanographic and Atmospheric Administration. Later, assistance in preparation of this guidebook was provided by a grant from the Resource and Land Investigations (RALI) program, U.S. Department of Interior, to the Environmental Law Institute.

Many contributed to these final efforts. Graduate student assistants at the University of Wisconsin included Barbara Bedford, Terence Sawyer, and Jim Lingle. Others who gave time to review drafts and provide invaluable suggestions included Professors John Steinhart and Louis Echoles of the University of Wisconsin Sea Grant Program; Professor John Ross of the University of Wisconsin Institute for Environmental Studies, who served as supervisor (principal investigator) for the three University of Wisconsin studies; Professor Steve Born of the University of Wisconsin Department of Regional Planning; Eric Strauss, University of Wisconsin Institute for Environmental Studies; and Professor Bernard Niemann, University of Wisconsin Department of Landscape Architecture. Editorial assistance was provided by William Toner and Carl Nelson.

I greatly appreciate the funding, assistance, encouragement, and comments provided by each individual and agency. Particular appreciation is due Edgar Imhoff of the RALI program. Without his support and warm encouragement, this book would not have been completed.

Jon A. Kusler
September 1977

PREFACE

"The land belongs to the people . . . a little of it to those dead . . . some to those living . . . but most of it belongs to those yet to be born . . . ."[1]

"Buy land, they're not making any more," Will Rogers once advised, recognizing that land must meet not only present but future needs. The following report reduces to general principles a decade of state and local regulatory experience in managing lands with special natural resource values or natural hazards to meet both present and future needs. These regulatory programs form the main thrust of the quiet revolution in state land use control. They have been applied to hazard areas (flood, erosion, and seismic areas), recreation lands (parks, recreation areas, shorelands, and coastal areas), and environmental areas (wetlands, scientific areas, estuarine areas, shorelands, coastal areas, and scenic and wild rivers).

In this book, lands with special natural resource hazards and values are collectively referred to as sensitive areas.[2]

Sensitive area programs evolved from state and local efforts to establish priorities in allocating resources and managing lands. A growing society requires water, energy,

[1]Just v. Marinette Co., 56 Wis. 2d 7, 201 N.W.2d 761, 770 (1972). The court endorsed this quotation which apparently has an American Indian source.

[2]They are also commonly referred to as "critical areas." These terms are used interchangeably in this report.

food, fiber, minerals, wildlife, and other products derived from finite land resources. These same land and water resources must also meet demands for recreation, education, housing, commercial and industrial development, transportation, scientific study, and other uses. Competition and shortages result.

Identifying and regulating lands with special natural resource values and hazards can reduce shortages, prevent conflicts, and reduce losses from natural hazards. Sensitive area programs can also serve broader land and water management objectives. They can protect property values and tax bases and reduce the cost of public services.

This book surveys a broad range of existing sensitive area programs throughout the nation. Differences were encountered in program goals, natural resources (*e.g.*, flood plains versus mineral resource areas), governmental institutions, and state and local preferences. Nevertheless, striking similarities were observed in the issues and the programs developed to meet them.

The book also suggests future directions for conservation[3] of critical resources. It begins with an outline of goals to improve existing sensitive area programs and create new ones, followed by an overview of existing state programs. Parts two through nine set forth in greater detail (1) resource conservation goals, (2) general goals for program design and implementation, (3) definition of areas, (4) data gathering, (5) government roles in regulating areas, (6) legal restraints, and (7) the relationship of sensitive area programs to broader land use management efforts.

---

[3]The term "conservation" is used in the present report to mean wise and careful use rather than outright protection of resources.

TABLE OF CONTENTS

Table of Contents (continued)

LIST OF FIGURES

List of Figures (continued)

LIST OF TABLES

List of Tables (continued)

PROGRAM GOALS

This outline serves as a checklist of goals[1] and considerations for sensitive area program design and implementation. It provides an overview of topics considered later. Of course, a state or a locality may find it financially or politically impossible to meet all of the goals. Goals should be modified to reflect the physical circumstances and preferences.

Resource Management Goals[2]

Programs should be designed to serve several major resource conservation goals simultaneously. They should:

   1. Require that private and public resource decision-makers evaluate the short term consequences of activities on sensitive lands and waters, consider the reversi-

---

[1]Each of these goals and considerations is individually explored by later sections of the report. These goals apply both to new and existing programs. They are applicable to programs addressing a single type of area (*e.g.*, wetlands) and programs simultaneously regulating many types of areas.

[2]*See* Part Two.

bility of impact, and develop and consider alternative strategies for use of lands and waters. These evaluations can be required through environmental impact statement requirements and regulatory standards;

2. Shift incompatible uses to nonsensitive area sites through zone restrictions, setbacks, and other measures;
3. Prohibit uses which cause nuisances, threaten public safety, or violate air or water pollution standards;
4. Protect renewable and nonrenewable resources from incompatible uses through use and density restrictions;
5. Protect essential water resources and related ecological systems through use restrictions and performance standards;
6. Insure that activities in natural hazard areas do not threaten safety, cause nuisances, or result in public losses. This may be achieved through tight regulation of uses in severe hazard areas and requirements that hazard mitigation measures be applied in other areas;
7. Minimize the impact of permitted uses by regulating design, precise location, construction materials, method of construction and operation, tree-cutting, dredging, and other features of permitted uses;
8. Promote broader local, state, and national economic, social, and environmental goals by separating incompatible uses, requiring that developers provide public services, and requiring that uses be consistent with broader land and water management efforts.

General Goals for Program Implementation[3]

Programs must be politically and legally acceptable and capable of implementation with available or modest increases of manpower and budgets.
They should:

1. Build upon existing land use and resource management efforts, using them for sensitive area regulation or involving them in new independent program efforts;
2. Protect state and national interests while considering home rule by involving several levels of government in program design and implementation;
3. Balance the public interest in resources with private land use expectations and options through the application of use and density restrictions permitting some private uses and by applying performance standards;
4. Insure impartial treatment of landowners and expeditious review of permits through careful design of regulatory procedures;
5. Comply with statutory and constitutional requirements through strict compliance with regulatory procedures and a concern for fairness and reasonableness in all phases of program implementation;
6. Balance the interests of competing groups by involving them in program design. This can insure political acceptability.
7. Develop technically sound regulatory standards through expert data gathering and analysis;

[3]*See* Part Three.

8. Reflect administrative needs in program design;
9. Incorporate cost-saving techniques;
10. Involve and educate the public through workshops, public hearings, and other techniques;
11. Carefully allocate scarce funds and manpower by establishing funding priorities;
12. Develop tangible, incremental approaches to land use decision-making while dealing with the cumulative impact of development through application of performance standards;
13. Insure necessary expertise for program administration and enforcement by involving state and federal technical agency staffs, consultants, university personnel, and other experts;
14. Provide landowners with certainty in their use of land while providing flexibility in the consideration of individual uses and areas. This may be achieved through application of performance guidelines, combining both quantified and unquantified standards;
15. Insure acceptable levels of resource protection and use through careful monitoring and enforcement of regulations;
16. Coordinate and integrate sensitive area programs with broader land and water management efforts;
17. Combine regulatory and nonregulatory approaches.

Definition of Areas[4]

Efforts to define sensitive areas should:
1. Insure the practicality of definitions by reflecting the needs of specific implementation techniques;
2. Facilitate definition application by reflecting anticipated development standards;
3. Facilitate regulatory administration by defining areas in terms of features readily identifiable on the ground;
4. Insure soundness of definitions by applying a variety of definition tests appropriate to the type of area;
5. Facilitate regulatory standard-setting and administration by distinguishing, in some instances, between important and "critical" lands and identifying subzones and gradations within broader sensitive areas.

Development Standards[5]

Efforts to formulate and apply development standards should:
1. Provide a systematic approach to standard-setting by taking into account the physical circumstances of an area, the probable impact of uses in these circum-

[4]*See* Part Four.
[5]*See* Part Five.

stances, and the need to restrict uses in light of broader conservation and developmental goals;

2. Achieve the necessary degree of restrictiveness to achieve program goals by prohibiting uses with unacceptable impact and conditionally permitting other uses;
3. Consider the cumulative impact of development by taking into account existing impact and anticipating future uses;
4. Modify use restrictions at sites according to the actual physical characteristics and the impact of anticipated uses. This can be achieved through permit requirements combined with performance standards in areas with variable resource characteristics;
5. Prevent immediate harm to areas by applying interim restrictive standards;
6. Maximize political and legal acceptability by focusing primarily upon new uses;
7. Protect the essential features of highly sensitive areas by controlling non-structural as well as structural uses, such as fills in wetlands;
8. Regulate public as well as private uses;
9. Provide both certainty and flexibility in standards by combining quantified standards for subjects amenable to quantification and unquantified standards for other impacts;
10. Involve several levels of government in standard-setting to reflect local, state, and national interests through joint programs and a hierarchy of standards;
11. Insure that necessary expertise and data gathering capability are available during program administration. This can be achieved through careful program design involving several levels of government and the private sector;
12. Adopt administrable standards reflecting the practical limitations of impact evaluation methodologies;
13. Lend certainty to standards by specifying regulatory goals and procedures with particular care where quantified development standards are not adopted;
14. Facilitate the evaluation of special permits by carefully designing case-by-case data gathering and administrative mechanisms;
15. Facilitate speedy review of proposed development by employing combined permit processing procedures.

Data Gathering[6]

To maximize cost-effectiveness and improve resource decision-making, data gathering efforts should:

1. Emphasize data essential for program implementation such as detailed maps as opposed to broad-scale surveys;
2. Incorporate techniques to minimize data gathering costs;
3. Increase political, legal, and administrative acceptability by preparing maps at minimum scales of 1:24,000 for most rural areas and 1:12,000 for urban areas;
4. Facilitate use of data by decision-makers through careful design of data dissemination techniques;

[6]*See* Part Six.

5. Define zone boundary lines with relative precision and use field procedures to resolve boundary disputes;
6. Delineate gradations and subzones within some areas through mapping of soils, vegetation, and other features;
7. Provide quantified evaluation of hazards through statistical evaluation of hazard frequency and severity;
8. Optimize use of funds and manpower by mapping areas with development threats first;
9. Reduce costs by shifting data gathering cost to developers;
10. Reduce costs by maximizing use of existing federal, state, and local data;
11. Reduce costs by using air photos and air photo interpretation techniques;
12. Provide site-specific data through the use of field surveys to supplement air photos for sensitive area definition and the evaluation of development proposals on a case-by-case basis;
13. Facilitate monitoring and enforcement by gathering time-series information such as time sequence air photos;
14. Optimize the use of funds for site-specific decision-making by giving low priority to computerized information systems;
15. Improve overall program efficiency by coordinating sensitive area and broader data gathering efforts;
16. Reduce costs by involving local units of government and interested individuals through nomination procedures, workshops, and other techniques to tap local expertise and personnel knowledge.

Governmental Roles[7]

To maximize political and cost-effectiveness, programs should:
1. Build upon the strengths of both state and local efforts by involving both state agencies and local governments in most programs;
2. Use both the "carrot and stick" to encourage local efforts meeting state standards. States should establish standards for local regulation of most areas and provide technical assistance and incentives;
3. Protect statewide interests by applying direct state regulation to limited classes of uses (*e.g.,* large scale subdivisions) and areas with clear multijurisdictional impact (*e.g.,* floodways). States should also directly regulate areas where local units fail to adopt and enforce regulations meeting state standards;
4. Promote regional data gathering, planning, and technical assistance efforts by involving regional planning agencies in program implementation;
5. Promote special purpose data gathering, technical assistance, and nonregulatory land management functions by involving special districts, such as soil conservation districts, in program implementation.

[7]*See* Part Seven.

Legal Restraints[8]

To reduce legal problems, programs should:
1. Emphasize the multijurisdictional nature of areas and encourage local participation in program implementation to minimize home rule objections;
2. Clearly authorize local sensitive area regulations by amending local land use control enabling statutes;
3. Avoid due process challenges by carefully complying with statutory, ordinance, and administrative regulation procedures;
4. Avoid "taking" challenges by emphasizing protection of health and safety and prevention of nuisances;
5. Avoid claims of unreasonableness by tailoring use restrictions to variable resource characteristics and by applying performance standards and site-specific data gathering and analysis techniques;
6. Avoid claims of discrimination by impartial treatment for similar properties. This can be provided through systematic standards and even-handed application of program policies;
7. Avoid claims of inadequate standards by establishing clear goals and factors for the delegation and exercise of administrative powers;
8. Avoid the "taking" issue through a genuine attempt to balance public and private interests and efforts to relieve the burden of regulation through tax incentives and other techniques.

Relationship to Broader Land Management Efforts[9]

To integrate broader efforts while continuing to meet special needs, sensitive area programs should:
1. Consider interrelationships between sensitive areas and combining sensitive area programs with broader land use planning and management efforts;
2. Continue to operate on a priority area basis by addressing individual types of sensitive areas where a comprehensive approach is not acceptable;
3. Recognize the special needs of sensitive area regulations. To do this, they should distinguish sensitive area regulatory efforts from broader critical area programs and those governing developments of regional impact;
4. Improve coordination of individual sensitive area programs through adoption of lead agencies;
5. Improve the effectiveness of regulations through their combination with non-regulatory techniques such as coordinated government works and policies, acquisition of fee and lesser interests, and tax incentives.

[8]*See* Part Eight.
[9]*See* Part Nine.

Part **1**

AN OVERVIEW
OF PROGRAMS

1. BACKGROUND

While regulation of sensitive lands is relatively new, state and local natural resource management dates from the last century when park, wildlife, and forestry programs were established for lands in the public domain. Until the 1920's and 1930's, little effort was made to control the private use of land without outright acquisition. During this period, states authorized local units of government—cities, towns and counties—to adopt zoning and subdivision regulations.

In the 1950's, it became clear that the marketplace and exclusive local control of lands would not meet long-term state and national needs. The demand for land resulted in construction in flood plains, wetlands, slopes, and other areas traditionally considered unsuitable for development. Natural hazard losses mounted despite massive federal expenditures for protective works.[1] Areas needed for science, wildlife, and recreation uses were being destroyed at an alarming rate. Prime agricultural lands, forestry lands, and mineral resource areas were quickly subdivided for residential and second home use in both urbanizing and rural areas.

[1] A 1966 Task Force on Federal Flood Control Policy estimated that more than 7 billion dollars had been spent by the federal government alone on flood control work since 1936 and, despite these expenditures, flood losses continued to mount.

Local governments often did little to control these trends due to a combination of inadequate natural resource data, lack of expertise, inadequate budgets, inadequate geographical scope, and narrow interests.

These abuses led to the *"quiet revolution"* in land use control.[2] As shown in Appendix B, state legislatures during the 1965-1977 period adopted 94 statutes promulgating minimum development control standards for sensitive areas. These statutes usually directed local units of government to adopt and administer regulations meeting or exceeding state standards within a specified period of time.

If the local units failed to adopt the regulations, the state agency was itself authorized to administer and enforce regulations. Only two-fifths of the statutes authorized direct state regulation without local administration and enforcement. Thus the quiet revolution primarily involved a shift to cooperative state and local control. In response to federal and state initiatives and their own concern for dwindling resources, local governments adopted more than 1,000 wetland and 1,400 inland lake and stream protection programs. More than 17,000 local governments adopted, or indicated an intent to adopt, flood plain regulations as part of the national flood insurance program. Thousands of others adopted regulations for coastal areas, erosion control, seismic areas, steep slopes, prime agricultural lands, forestry areas, and mineral resource areas.

Since 1965, many state legislatures also considered more sweeping state planning and land use regulation statutes.[3] Comprehensive land use legislation was adopted in a few states, but failed to gain widespread support. In the Congress, a National Land Use Policy Act was considered and rejected in four separate sessions. Two types of programs were consistently adopted by state legislatures during this period. The first, sensitive land programs, usually emphasized the regulation of a single type of resource area.[4] The second, regulatory permit programs, governed special uses such as strip mining, large scale development, and utility plants.[5]

The success of sensitive land programs compared to broader proposals has sometimes been dismissed as opposition by conservatives to too much state or federal power. This factor played an important role, but more basic forces were at work.

First, comprehensive statewide planning and regulation pose complex data gathering, planning, standard-setting, and implementation issues not easily understood by legislators or the public. They suspect this complexity and the hidden value judgments implicit in most planning approaches. In contrast, an emphasis on resources focuses land use policies on basic, understandable issues. Performance-

---

[2]*See* F. Bosselman and D. Callies, *The Quiet Revolution in Land Use Control*, Council on Environmental Quality, U.S. Government Printing Office (1971); N. Rosenbaum, *Land Use and the Legislatures, the Politics of State Innovation*, The Urban Institute, Washington, D.C. (1976).

[3]*See* N. Rosenbaum, *Land Use and the Legislature, the Politics of State Innovation*, The Urban Institute, Washington, D.C. (1976) for a listing and analysis of these efforts. Dr. Rosenbaum notes on page 3: During their 1974 session, seven state legislatures—Idaho, Iowa, Michigan, New Hampshire, Ohio, South Dakota, and Wisconsin rejected proposals to expand state land use authority. In four states, Colorado, Maine, Maryland, and North Carolina, where new land use legislation was passed in 1974, the powers given state governments were far weaker than those provided in the legislation of the pioneering states.
At the present time only Hawaii has adopted statewide zoning.

[4]*See* Appendix B.

[5]*See* N. Rosenbaum, *Land Use and the Legislatures, the Politics of State Innovation*, The Urban Institute, Washington, D.C. (1976). A number of states also required local units of government to adopt zoning and subdivision controls during this period although most established no mechanism for direct state regulation in the event local units of government failed to adopt and enforce adequate regulations.

oriented controls linked to natural resource values and hazards have an obvious logic.

Second, sound comprehensive planning and regulation are time-consuming and expensive. Lacking money, manpower, and time, planning efforts are superficial and of little value. In contrast, a focus on resource areas establishes clear priorities for data gathering, planning, and implementation and also provides a rational basis for later planning. The term "critical" has commonly been applied to these areas to indicate their importance to society and their need for immediate attention through allocation of scarce manpower and monies.

Third, comprehensive planning and regulation at the state level threatens local home rule. Resource programs are less a threat where they address selected sensitive areas with clear regional and statewide interest. Further, sensitive areas are precisely the areas where local governments lack the expertise or motivation for adequate control. State regulation can be linked to traditional state resource protection roles, such as the protection of the public trust in navigable waters.[6] These interests have visibility and strong public support in many instances.

The merits of state or local land use programs which focus on sensitive lands alone can be overemphasized. Transportation, economic development, and housing needs, for example, cannot be resolved with a sensitive area focus. But it is clear that all needs of man depend upon land, water, and mineral resources. Serious shortages will occur without careful utilization of renewable and nonrenewable resources.

2. MOTIVATION FOR PROGRAMS

A major motivation for adopting sensitive area programs has been the protection and management of state waters and aquatic life. These concerns have resulted in shoreland, wetland, coastal, flood plain, and some broader comprehensive critical area programs. They form the majority of existing sensitive area efforts. For example, the threat of water pollution led to the adoption of lake and stream shore zoning programs in Wisconsin and Maine; fills in lakes led to the enactment of the Washington shoreline zoning statute; erosion problems along Lake Michigan prompted the adoption of the Michigan shoreland program; a water shortage led to adoption of the Florida state planning and critical area act; destruction of spawning grounds prompted coastal wetland protection in Georgia; and severe floods prompted flood plain legislation in Nebraska and Minnesota.

Federal legislation has proved another major motivating factor. (See table 1.) The National Flood Insurance Act, requiring the regulation of the 100-year flood plain, was a direct motivation for adoption of state flood plain programs in New York, Texas, Alabama, and other states. Similarly, the Coastal Zone Management Act, requiring the definition of coastal areas of "particular concern," prompted coastal legislation in North Carolina. National scenic and wild rivers legislation has encouraged many state scenic and wild river programs.

In a broader sense, sensitive area programs reflect deep public concern with natural resources and the environment. A variety of statutes evidence this concern. They require environmental impact statements, authorize citizen suits for environmental degradation, regulate large-scale development, control air, water, and noise pollution, and establish statewide land resource inventories and planning.

---

[6]*See* Sax, "The Public Trust Doctrine in Natural Resource Law: Effective Judicial Intervention," 68 Michigan Law Review 491 (1971).

Table 1

Federal programs encouraging or requiring sensitive area protection efforts.*

Program/Agency Statute	Area Affected	Standards	Experience
National Flood Insurance Program, The Department of Housing and Urban Development. 42 U.S.C. §§4001, 4128	Area flooded by a once in 100 years probability flood. H.U.D designates flood areas and provides profiles and maps.	Local governments or states must adopt regulations consistent with H.U.D. guidelines in order for property owners to qualify for federally subsidized flood insurance. Regulations require control of development and subdivision in 100 year flood plain, the maintenance of floodway areas, and elevation or other protection for new structures to the 100 year flood elevation.	More than 17,000 communities are now participating in the flood insurance program. The total number may increase to 20,000.
Permits for the Discharge of Materials into the Waters and Wetlands of the U.S. The U.S. Army Corps of Engineers, The Environmental Protection Agency. 33 U.S.C. §§401-466, 1251-1376	Waters of the U.S. including all wetlands.	The Corps—with the advice of E.P.A. and the Fish and Wildlife Service—evaluates individual permit applications for consistency with statutory and administrative criteria. Five types of permits include: (1) navigation permits, (2) blanket or general permits, (3) special purpose permits, (4) national permits, and (5) non-permits called letters of no objection. National and general permits set general criteria and remove the necessity of separate permits for every action. Regulations require that Corps field personnel evaluate the impact of individual permits. Corps permits are not granted where proposed activities are prohibited by state or local regulations.	The Corps has evaluated individual permit applications for fills, dredging, and structures in navigable water since 1899. However, jurisdiction over wetlands dates from the 1972 Water Pollution Control Act Amendments. The Corps has implemented this broader permitting power in three phases, gradually extending jurisdiction to most wetlands and water. The Clean Water Act of 1977 authorizes the Environmental Protection Agency to approve state regulatory programs for a portion of the waters under Corps jurisdiction.
Coastal Zone Management Act, The National Oceanographic and Atmospheric Administration 16 U.S.C. §1454	The "coastal zone" is defined by each state and includes coastal waters and adjacent shorelines.	Each coastal and great lake state is required to define its coastal zone to qualify for program development and implementation grants. It must also identify coastal zone areas of "particular concern" such as flood plains and wetlands. It must formulate coastal zone protection and development policies and identify regulatory procedures for implementation. Once NOAA has approved a state coastal zone plan, federal activities must be consistent with this plan. NOAA also provides grants-in-aid to fund state acquisition of estuarine sanctuaries.	Thirty-three of 34 eligible "coastal states" have applied for and received program development grants. Washington state's coastal zone management plan has been approved, entitling the state to management grants. Three estaurine sanctuaries have been established to date—one in Coos Bay, Oregon, one in Sapelo Island, Georgia, and the third in Waimanu Valley, Hawaii.
Land and Water Conservation Fund, Bureau of Outdoor Recreation	Recreation lands, wetlands, flood plains, scientific areas, and other	Funds are made available on a matching basis (up to 50%) to aid state and local acquisition of recreation and open space areas. To qualify, a state	All 50 states participate in this program. Funds are allocated according to population. Fiscal 1977 ap-

*This only lists major programs. Many other federal programs play some role such as EPA "208" water quality protection efforts, HUD "701" planning efforts, NOAA coastal energy impact and beach access programs.

Table 1 (continued)

Program/Agency Statute	Area Affected	Standards	Experience
16 U.S.C. §§4601-4 to 4601-11	open space.	must prepare a comprehensive outdoor recreation plan. The state establishes criteria for funding local projects.	propriations were $17,516 million. Forty percent of these monies funded federal acquisition projects, the rest state and local. States and localities have usually used the funds to acquire park and other recreation lands. However, funds have also been used to acquire wetlands, flood plains, and other open space areas.
Federal Aid to Wildlife Restoration (Pittman-Robertson Act), Department of the Interior 16 U.S.C. §§669-669(i)	Wildlife areas, wetlands	Funds derived from federal taxes on sale of firearms, shells, and cartridges is apportioned to states to cover up to 75% of the cost of projects for acquisition, restoration, and maintenance of wildlife areas and research into problems of wildlife management.	More than $800 million in tax revenues have been disbursed under this program since 1937 with more than 75% spent for wildlife restoration. Revenues in fiscal 1975 totaled $63,046,646. By 1975 states had acquired more than 3.48 million acres.
Federal Aid in Fish Restoration (Dingell-Johnson Act), Department of the Interior 16 U.S.C. §§777-777k	Wetlands, fisheries	This act is essentially identical to the Pittman-Robertson Act described above except it provides federal assistance to states to cover 75% of fish restoration and management projects. Funds are derived from federal excise tax on fishing equipment.	Fiscal 1975 revenues under this act totaled $21,894,197. By 1975, states had acquired 95,678 acres for fish restoration under this act.
Water Bank Program for Wetlands Preservation, U.S. Department of Agriculture 16 U.S.C. §§1301-1311	Wetlands serving as migratory waterfowl and breeding areas	The Secretary of Agriculture is authorized to enter into 10 year renewable agreements with landowners who are paid an annual fee for not destroying important wetlands. The Agriculture Stabilization and Conservation Service is authorized to select lands in cooperation with state and county committees that may qualify.	In 1975 the program operated in 73 counties in 13 states and encompassed 130,000 acres. Most acreage was in Minnesota, North Dakota, and Wisconsin. Fiscal 1977 appropriation was $10 million.
Rare and Endangered Species Conservation Act, U.S. Fish and Wildlife Service, Department of the Interior 16 U.S.C. §§1531-43	Habitat for rare and endangered species	Project grants are available to state fish and wildlife agencies which have entered into a cooperative agreement concerning rare and endangered species with the Secretary of Interior. Grants pay up to 2/3s of the costs to develop and implement programs to protect rare and endangered species. Grants are also available to purchase rare and endangered species habitat.	
Wild and Scenic Rivers Act, U.S. Department of the Interior, U.S. Depart-	Scenic, wild, and recreation rivers	The 1968 Act establishes general criteria for scenic, wild, and recreation rivers and specifically designated eight rivers. Congressional approval	Congress has added four new rivers to the system and state legislatures have added four others. In addi-

Table 1 (continued)

Program/Agency Statute	Area Affected	Standards	Experience
ment of Agriculture 16 U.S.C. §§1271-1286		is required for the addition of new rivers except where a state legislature requests that a state scenic, wild, or recreation river be admitted directly to the system with the approval of the Department of the Interior. With such a procedure, the legislature must assure that the river will be permanently administered without expense to the federal government. Direct federal land acquisition funds are available for Congressionally approved rivers. Acquisition funds may be available for state designated rivers through the Land and Water Conservation Fund. Any river accepted into the system is protected from federal water resources projects.	tion, many states have adopted their own scenic, wild, and recreation river systems. The use of waters and adjacent shorelands is controlled through regulations, acquisition, or some combination.
Surface Mining and Reclamation Act, U. S. Department of the Interior 30 U.S.C. §§1201 et seq.	Surface coal mining areas.	Under the 1977 Act, states must establish a planning process to identify areas unsuitable for surface coal mining operations. These may include fragile, historic, renewable resource, natural hazard, and other types of lands.	The Department of Interior is presently developing standards and criteria to implement this section.

3. OVERVIEW OF REGULATORY APPROACHES

Areas with special natural resource values and hazards are found on both public and private lands. Regulations may be adopted at federal, state, or local levels, for both types of lands, although most efforts to date have focused on private lands.

The federal government is playing an increasingly important role in protecting sensitive areas on the one-third of the nation's land which is federally owned.[7] This includes more than 755 million acres of land managed by the Bureau of Land Management, the U.S. Forest Service, the Department of Defense, the Army Corps of Engineers, the Bureau of Sport Fisheries and Wildlife, the Bureau of Reclamation, the Tennessee Valley Authority, and the National Park Service. Protection takes the form of resource inventories, management planning, and, in some instances, regulation of private activities such as grazing, mining, and recreation. (See figure 1.)

States and local units of government also plan and manage public lands such as parks and forests. Private activities other than outdoor recreation are tightly regulated.

State regulation of privately owned sensitive areas takes two forms: direct state regulation and state standard-setting for local regulation. (See table 2.) Approximately two-fifths of the state regulatory statutes authorize some direct state control of uses. These include most of the wetland, some floodway, and several coastal

[7]A strong federal resource assessment and land management role was recommended by the Public Land Law Review Commission, *One Third of the Nation's Lands,* U.S. Government Printing Office (1970).

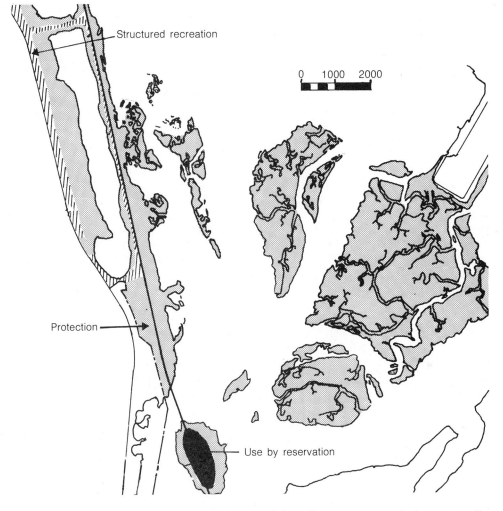

Figure 1

Management zones at the Jamaica Bay Wildlife Refuge, Gateway National Recreation Area, illustrate a proposed federal land management plan. (Source: National Park Service, Discussion Draft, *General Management Plan, Gateway National Recreation Area,* **National Park Service, Washington, D.C., 1976.)**

statutes. (See Appendix B). Statutes authorizing direct state regulation generally require permits from a state regulatory agency for proposed structural uses and some nonstructural uses such as dams and fills in navigable waters. States usually map sensitive areas and adopt specific administrative regulations controlling particular uses.

Administrative regulations, like their statutory counterparts, usually contain a statement of goals and policies. They often include more precise critical area definitions along with minimum standards pertaining to lot sizes, building setbacks from roads and waters, use of septic tanks, and flood protection elevations. Administrative regulations usually apply to all lands of a particular type within the state. For example, general standards are adopted for all flood plains requiring protection of structures to the 100-year flood elevation and preserving floodway areas. However, some agencies have established several sets of standards with

Table 2

Steps in sensitive area regulation.

Direct State Regulation	**Cooperative State/Local Regulation of Enabling Statute**

1. Legislative Adoption

The legislature adopts a statute authorizing a state agency to define, map, and directly regulate a type of area. The statute usually contains specific definition criteria and requires permits for uses in mapped areas.

The legislature adopts a statute authorizing a state agency to define and map one type of sensitive area and to adopt minimum standards for local zoning, subdivision control, or other regulation. Local units are required to adopt regulations meeting minimum state standards by a fixed date or within a specified period after state mapping. The agency is directed to provide technical assistance and, in some instances, grants-in-aid to local units. The agency regulates directly if local units fail to adopt and enforce regulations meeting state standards.

2. Mapping or Other Identification of Areas

The regulatory agency adopts more specific definitions and either directly maps areas or assists federal mapping efforts. Subzones and gradations may be mapped. State permits are required within mapped areas. The agency usually has considerable discretion with regard to map scale and procedures. Some statutes require that areas be designated through "orders" preceded by written notice to landowners and formal hearings.

The regulatory agency more precisely defines and maps areas in cooperation with federal agencies and local units of government. In some programs, local units, regional planning agencies, interested individuals or other agencies may "nominate" candidate areas. After an area is mapped, local units are required to adopt regulations meeting state standards within a specified period.

3. Establishment of Land Use Control Standards

The regulatory agency adopts administrative regulations supplementing statutory standards. General "administrative" rules may be adopted which apply to all areas throughout a state. In some instances, the agency also adopts special rules or orders for particular areas. Both general and special rules typically include performance standards.

The regulatory agency adopts administrative regulations establishing minimum standards for local zoning, subdivision control, and other regulations. General rules are often adopted simultaneously with specific definition criteria and may, therefore, precede mapping. Setbacks from road and water, minimum flood protection elevation, and other standards are common. Local units then adopt zoning, subdivision, or other controls meeting or exceeding state standards. These may be adopted as separate regulations or as part of broader local land use control efforts.

4. Administration and Enforcement of Regulations

The regulatory agency applies development standards, through procedures established in the enabling statute, to permit applications. A public hearing is usually held on each application. Site inspections are common. Developers are often required to submit environmental impact statements or other data. After evaluation is completed, the agency denies, permits or, most often, conditionally permits uses. A wide range of conditions may be attached to minimize development impact. Monitoring and enforcement is carried out through field inspections and court suits. Appeals may be provided to an appeals board or, more commonly, to the courts.

Local units of government permit, deny, or conditionally permit uses in light of statutory, administrative rules, and ordinance criteria. A public hearing is usually required on each permit. Developers are often required to submit environmental impact statements or other data. Appeals may be taken to a local board of appeals, a state appeal board or, more commonly, directly to the courts. The state regulatory agency may directly regulate areas if local units fail to adopt and administrate regulations consistent with state standards.

varying degrees of restrictiveness for a particular type of area. In Minnesota, the shoreland and zoning program classifies lakes and establishes different shoreland use restrictions for each category.

Most state critical area enabling statutes authorize state standard-setting for local regulation rather than direct state control. The state regulatory agency typically adopts administrative regulations establishing minimum standards for local zoning, subdivision controls, and, less frequently, minimum standards for building codes, sanitary codes, or other types of regulations. Local governments are usually required to adopt regulations that meet or exceed state standards within a specified time period. This period generally begins when the state agency formally maps the sensitive area. The state regulatory agency is authorized to regulate development in the event local units fail to adopt and enforce satisfactory controls.

Prior to 1972, sensitive area statutes were adopted solely on an individual area basis for particular types of areas such as flood plains. Since then Florida, Minnesota, Wyoming, Oregon, Maine, North Carolina, Virginia, Maryland, Nevada, and Colorado have authorized a single agency to define and map several types of areas. However, these statutes place primary regulatory responsibility at the local level.[8]

Local regulations continue to play a dominant role in controlling sensitive area development. They are typically adopted pursuant to broader zoning, subdivision control, and building code enabling statutes. Statutes authorize cities to adopt zoning and subdivision regulations in all states except Hawaii and Alaska, where counties and boroughs have zoning powers.[9] Counties are authorized to zone and adopt subdivision regulations in all but a few states. Towns and townships are authorized to zone and exercise subdivision control powers in most states. Cities, counties, towns, and townships are authorized to adopt building codes in many states. A number of these general enabling acts contain specific resource protection provisions.

In addition, special enabling acts authorize local sensitive area regulations in some states.[10] Special statutes authorizing flood plain regulations have been adopted in Alabama, Texas, and Kansas; shoreland regulations have been authorized in Minnesota, Wisconsin, Maine, and Vermont; and wetland regulations have been authorized in Connecticut, Virginia, and Massachusetts. These acts, while more abbreviated, contain the same general types of provisions as zoning, subdivision control, and building code enabling statutes.

Some local sensitive area regulations are adopted pursuant to constitutional or statutory home rule provisions.[11] However, general or special statutory enabling powers usually suffice without resort to home rule powers.

A brief look at the principal local regulatory techniques follows:

[8]State regulations is authorized only where local units fail to adopt and administer satisfactory controls. Florida, Nevada, Oregon, and Minnesota authorize quite broad state regulation in these circumstances. Maine and Colorado authorize very limited state regulation. Wyoming, North Carolina, Virginia, and Maryland do not authorize state regulation.

[9]*See* E. Strauss and J. Kusler, *Statutory Land Use Control Enabling Authority in the Fifty States,* U.S. Department of Housing and Urban Development, Federal Insurance Administration (1976).

[10]*Id.*

[11]Thirty-four states authorize municipal or county exercise of home rule powers. *See* table 4 in E. Strauss and J. Kusler, *Statutory Land Use Control Enabling Authority in the Fifty States,* U.S. Department of Housing and Urban Development, Federal Insurance Administration (1976), for a listing of relevant statutory and constitutional provisions.

A. Zoning

Zoning is the most widespread sensitive area implementation technique at the local level. Traditional zoning, as opposed to sensitive area zoning, has been adopted by most larger cities in the country and by many towns and counties. Zoning divides communities into districts on a zoning map and applies varying use standards to the districts through a written text. Zoning often contains a wide variety of provisions specifying permitted and prohibited uses within particular areas and minimum standards governing lot sizes, building heights, and setback from roads.

Sensitive area zoning follows the general steps outlined in figure 2. Zones are mapped either as primary zones or as "overlay" districts. Sensitive area zoning restrictions include:

A. Restrictions upon the *types of uses* permitted in critical zones and subzones such as prohibition of fills in wetlands.

B. Bulk restrictions establishing *minimum size, location, and density specifications for uses* including building setbacks, building heights, side yard requirements, and lot sizes.

C. *Performance standards* defining the maximum permissible impact of specific uses on resources such as removal or disturbance of vegetation, alteration of flood flows, alteration of drainage, and so forth.[12] Performance standards are usually applied through special permit requirements. New uses require special permits. To obtain a permit, the applicant must demonstrate that use impacts will not exceed permissible levels.

While local zoning is a broad sensitive area management tool, it is also subject to many limitations including limited data base, lack of administrative expertise, inadequate geographical perspective, and failure to take into account the unique features of each site. Other limitations include statutory exemptions for agricultural uses, nonconforming uses, and public utilities. In addition, courts have generally held that zoning is not applicable to public uses.[13]

B. Subdivision Regulations

Subdivision regulations are also adopted at the local level to meet broad land-use control objectives. They are less common and less effective for sensitive area protection since they do not control the type of land use or subsequent development. Subdividers are required to prepare detailed maps (called plats) prior to sale of lots or prior to building. Plats must be reviewed and approved by the planning commission. The commission determines whether lands are suitable for their intended purposes and whether the plats are in compliance with zoning and other regulations. Typically, subdividers are required to install roads, sewers, water, and sometimes park areas to meet the needs of subdivision residents.

[12]Performance standards relate to protection from natural hazards (100-year floods) and the use impact upon natural systems. In other words, emphasis is upon the end result, rather than use type or design. *See* C. Thurow, W. Toner, and D. Erley, *Performance Controls for Sensitive Lands,* American Society of Planning Officials, Report Nos. 307, 308 (1975), for an excellent description of local programs and examples of ordinance provisions.

[13]*See, e.g.,* Ann Arbor Twp. v. United States, 93 F. Supp. 341 (D.C. Mich., 1950) (federal uses exempted); Town of Bloomfield v. New Jersey Authority, 18 N.J. Highway Authority, 18 N.J. 237, 113 A. 2d 658 (1955) (state use exempted); Town of Oronoco v. City of Rochester, 293 Minn. 468, 197 N.W. 2d 426 (1972) (local governmental uses generally exempted).

Figure 2

Local sensitive area regulation: a step by step approach. (Source: Maine Shoreland Zoning Project, University of Maine, 1972.)

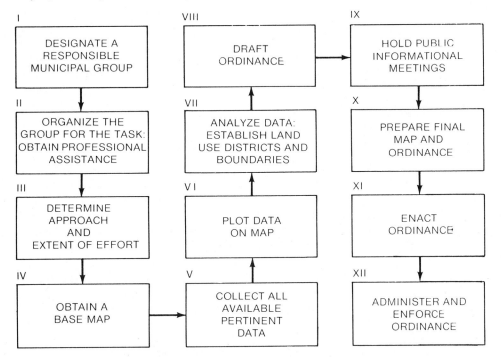

While subdivision regulations affect limited aspects of land use, they have been well received by the courts and do have several useful features in minimizing development impact upon sensitive areas. First, they require case-by-case consideration of each proposed development to permit an evaluation of project impact and the attachment of conditions to minimize impact. Communities usually have considerable bargaining power in this process. Second, subdividers may be in a better position to undertake detailed fact-finding than private landowners. They employ surveyors and other specialists in preparation of the plat and may be able to pass costs on to subsequent purchasers.

C.   Building Codes

Building codes are a more limited tool for sensitive area protection than subdivision regulations. They do not determine the types or locations of uses allowed in particular areas. However, they may impose either inflexible design standards or more generalized performance standards for flood, seismic disturbance, or other natural hazards protection. In some instances they also influence the location of buildings. For example, a code requiring very expensive flood proofing in a flood hazard area may practically preclude development in the area. Special types of building codes such as architectural controls and historic building preservation codes are sometimes used to preserve scenic beauty and protect historic sites.

D. Special Codes

In addition to conventional regulations, a variety of special codes are adopted to reduce the impact of particular uses. These include air, water, and noise pollution controls, sanitary codes, regulations for junkyards and other nuisance uses, sign regulations, strip-mining controls, regulation of filling and grading, dune protection regulations, beach setbacks, encroachment lines, and tree-cutting regulations. Special codes generally require that developers seek permits which conform to the ordinance standards.

4. COMMON DENOMINATORS IN IMPLEMENTING PROGRAMS

State and local regulatory programs for sensitive areas reveal striking similarities in basic issues and implementation approaches. In part, these similarities are due to the technical and scientific problems of determining the impact of various uses upon natural resources and establishing standards to minimize these impacts. They are also due to budgetary, legal, political, and administrative constraints common to all programs. There are eight major areas of agreement:

A. With few exceptions, regulatory efforts balance preservation and development needs through the establishment of *performance standards* rather than prohibition of all uses. The approach reflects a genuine effort to promote multiple land uses and minimize the impact of development upon important resources.

B. Programs are generally shaped by similar *constitutional, political,* and *financial restraints.* All programs have been faced with state and federal constitutional guarantees of due process, including prohibitions against discrimination and the taking of private property without just compensation. This has favored the use of performance standards and special permit approaches. Programs have been required to cope with traditional home rule and strong concepts of private property, favoring local involvement in most state programs. Other problems have included limited budgets and staff for definition of areas, standard-setting, and administration. Limited budgets and staffs have resulted in the phased, area-by-area approaches and the application of money-saving techniques as discussed below.

C. The adequacy of the data base is a principal issue in all programs. The mapping of areas and evaluation of individual permits is complicated by (1) *the diversity in resource values and hazards* typically found in a single critical area as in flood plains where varying soils, slopes, and vegetation affect the severity of height of flooding; (2) *the varying impact of the design, construction, and operation of any single new use* on site-specific resource values and hazards; and (3) *the cumulative effect* of the proposed use, ancillary and adjacent uses, and future uses on the specific site and on the resource area as a whole. Often minor variations in the location or design of a proposed use substantially affect impact.

Due to these technical problems and the lack of detailed data, state and local programs *make widespread use of "special permit" procedures* whereby a board of experts (1) evaluates the impact of each proposed use at a particular site through case-by-case data gathering; (2) determines acceptable levels of impact through application of statutory, administrative rule, or ordinance quantified standards, or more often, through application of generalized guidelines and policies as applied to that site; and (3) denies, permits, or conditionally permits the proposed use. This approach tailors project restrictions to the natural resource values found at particular sites but requires expertise in evaluation of the cumulative impact of future development.

E. Limited budgets have resulted in *a wide range of money-saving techniques.* (1) Developers are required to prepare environmental impact statements or supply other types of data. (2) Data gathering and regulation of areas under development pressure are carried out on a priority basis for areas with special values and hazards. (3) Nomination procedures,[14] workshops, public hearings, and other public involvement techniques are used to solicit information from local units of government, other agencies, and interested citizens. They are used to locate potential critical areas with special values or hazards, such as habitats of rare and endangered species. (4) Permit issuance is partially or wholly delegated to local units of government who must carry out necessary data gathering and conduct public hearings. The latter requirement reduces state program costs where necessary data is available at the local level or can be gathered inexpensively by experts living near the sites.

F. *Successful programs* often combine several characteristics: (1) strong local involvement in program administration and enforcement; (2) strong state technical assistance and data gathering; (3) clear and specific minimum state standards for local controls; (4) flexibility and options built into standards for local regulatory efforts; (5) an enabling statute which expresses clear program goals and contains specific definition criteria; (6) adequate program funding; (7) a cost-conscious approach to all phases of program implementation so that limited funds are not all allocated to one program phase such as sensitive area mapping; (8) dynamic program leadership; (9) expert and imaginative agency staff; (10) strong public involvement and education through workshops, hearings, guidebooks, and newspaper releases; (11) a genuine attempt to balance public and private interests and a willingness to negotiate where nonessential values and hazards are involved; (12) careful monitoring and enforcement efforts; and (13) a fact-conscious approach to the evaluation of individual development permits. The latter should emphasize relatively accurate maps and air photos at reasonable scales— 1:24,000 or larger—combined with case-by-case data gathering to resolve boundary disputes and evaluate individual permits.

G. Major *impediments* to successful efforts include: (1) inadequate funding or a defeatist attitude held by the program staff; (2) inadequate leadership; (3) failure to involve local units of government; (4) inexperienced and unimaginative program staff; (5) uncooperative and inflexible attitudes in state program administration such as "let landowners and local governments be damned;" (6) poor public education and public involvement; (7) enabling statutes with weak definition criteria and vague outlines of agency or local government responsibilities; (8) expenditures of scarce funds on small scale maps or other data of little use in program implementation; (9) inability or unwillingness to carefully evaluate development permits; (10) failure to promulgate rules and guidelines for the processing of individual development permits; and (11) political pressures which result in policies or development permits inconsistent with natural resource values and hazards.

---

[14]Individuals, organizations, or local governments are asked to "nominate" or suggest areas with special resource values or hazards needing protection or management.

Table 3

Resource management objectives.

Area	Objectives	Principal Regulatory and Non-Regulatory Implementation Techniques
A. Promote Resource Use		
Agricultural Lands	Prevent subdivision, intensive residential, commercial or industrial development, fill, grading, or other activities which disturb the soil or preempt agricultural uses. Control adjacent uses which would conflict with agriculture. Some development is possible.	State or local agricultural zoning; application of open space tax incentives; acquisition of areas (rare).
Forest Lands	Prevent land subdivision, intensive development, fill, grading, or other activities which either destroy the soil or withdraw lands from long-term forestry. Some development is possible.	Local forest conservation or forest recreation zoning; local tree cutting regulations. Some state forest protection acts require permits for tree cutting. Application of open space tax incentives and special "forest crop" tax laws.
Mining Areas	Prevent subdivision and intensive development. Prevent adjacent uses which will interfere with mining. Some development is possible. Override local regulations which prevent mineral extraction, in some instances. Require land reclamation.	State or local mineral resource zoning; special permits for mining with reclamation requirements.
B. Minimize Losses from Natural Hazards		
Flood Plains Areas	Prevent development in flood way areas and coastal high hazard areas. Require that development in outer flood hazard areas be elevated on fill or flood-proofed. Adequately protected development may occur in outer areas.	State permits; local floodway and flood plain zoning; subdivision controls and building codes; easement or fee acquisition in some instances.
Erosion Areas, Particularly Coastal	Prevent development in seriously threatened areas; require protection of development in other areas and adoption of erosion control measures. Development may occur in some areas.	State permits; local hazard area zoning, regulatory setbacks and special regulations for fill and grading; dune and beach protection regulations; easement or acquisition in some instances.
Landslide, Mudslide and Avalanche Areas	Prevent development in severely threatened areas. Adequately protected development is possible in some areas.	State permits; local hazard area zoning; open space acquisition.
Earthquake Zones	Prevent development along fault lines, require protection in other areas. Development is possible in most areas if designed to withstand earthquakes.	State permits; local hazard area zoning; open space acquisition.
Areas Unsuitable for On-Site Waste Disposal	Prevent on-site waste disposal unless soil limitations are overcome. Development is possible if adequately sewered.	State or local sanitary codes, plumbing codes, subdivision regulations, and flood plain regulations (in flood hazard areas).

Table 3 (continued)

Area	Objectives	Principal Regulatory and Non-Regulatory Implementation Techniques

C. Control Uses to Serve Multiple Objectives

Area	Objectives	Principal Regulatory and Non-Regulatory Implementation Techniques
Land Adjacent to Parks	Require that structures be set back from park boundaries; require that uses be designed to minimize impact upon parks; and in some instances, promote private recreation development consistent with park needs. Some development is appropriate.	Buffer area zoning; residential and recreational zoning; regulations requiring open space; state or local air, water and noise pollution controls; sign board regulations.
Coastal Areas, Shoreland Areas	Require that structures be set back from the water; prevent water pollution; reduce damages from flooding, erosion and other hazards; maximize public recreation; promote use of shore for water-related activities such as marinas, ports, loading areas. Reduce conflicts between uses. Some development is acceptable.	State permits; local zoning, subdivision, and building codes; tax incentives; easement or fee acquisition for some areas.
Scenic Areas Recreation Rivers	Protect recreation and scenic values; reduce damages from natural hazards; regulate signboards; control dams and other water resources projects; in some instances allow limited residential and recreational development as well as development related to resource use; reduce conflicts between uses.	State and local permits; conservation and recreational-residential zoning; tax incentives; easement or fee acquisition for some areas.

D. Preserve Lands in An Undeveloped Condition to Protect Natural Values

Area	Objectives	Principal Regulatory and Non-Regulatory Implementation Techniques
Wetlands	Prevent subdivision, fill, dredging, vegetation removal; protect water quality and quantity; no development desirable in most areas.	State permits and protection orders; local conservancy zoning and subdivision controls; open space tax incentives and conservation easement or fee acquisition (in some instances).
Areas of Special Scientific Interest	Prevent development and all land alteration (some areas).	Open and conservancy zoning; state hunting regulations; tax incentives, easement or fee acquisition.
Wild Rivers, Wilderness Areas	Preserve lands in an open condition; protect vegetation; prevent mining and other land alterations; control dams, filling, dredging.	Open space or forestry zoning; tax incentives; easement or fee acquisition.

H. Even programs functioning with fair success concede the *need for improvements* such as: (1) increased funding for all phases of program development and implementation; (2) improved land suitability and land capability methodologies to provide systematic documentation of natural values and hazards at particular sites; (3) improved project impact evaluation methodologies; (4) studies to indicate threshold disturbance levels for natural systems; (5) statutory amendments, in some cases, to clarify authority and definition criteria; (6) formulation of sensitive area policies within a broader context of population growth limits and resource utilization policies; (7) improved public education; (8) improved monitoring and enforcement of regulations; and (9) improved techniques for dealing with the cumulative impact of uses.

5. PROGRAMS FOR PARTICULAR TYPES OF AREAS

Considerable similarity exists in the definition criteria, data, and development standards applied to each type of area at state and local levels and from state to state. The following discussion highlights these similarities.[15]

A. Flood Plains

At least twenty-four states either directly regulate floodways or floodway and flood fringe areas or establish standards for local regulation.[16] More than 17,000 local units of government have adopted or indicated an intent to adopt flood plain zoning, subdivision controls, building codes, or special codes in order to qualify for federal flood insurance. As such, flood plain regulations are the most extensive and the oldest of the sensitive area controls.

The 100-year flood (flood of the magnitude likely to occur once each 100 years) serves as the basis for mapping and regulation in most programs. This standard has been adopted for the National Flood Insurance Program and by federal agencies.

Flood plain areas are primarily mapped by the federal government through the National Flood Insurance Program, the flood control efforts of the U.S. Army Corps of Engineers, and the natural resource data gathering efforts of the U.S. Geological Survey and Soil Conservation Service. A flood profile—a graph showing flood elevations along a stretch of stream—and flood boundary maps based upon engineering calculations are usually prepared. Sometimes soil maps, historic flood records, air photos of flooding, and even "eye-balling" techniques are included on a preliminary basis. Where more detailed federal data is available, many flood plain regulatory programs distinguish inner flood conveyance areas adjacent to a stream, called floodways, from outer areas subject to lower flood depths and velocities called flood fringe areas (See figure 3). Floodways are usually mapped through engineering calculations designed to prevent damaging retardation of flood flows.

---

[15]This discussion addresses major types of sensitive area programs. For example, flood hazard programs are examined, but not seismic area programs.

[16]*See* Appendix B. *See* also J. Kusler, *A Perspective on Flood Plain Regulations for Flood Plain Management,* Chapter 6, Department of the Army, Office of the Chief of Engineers, Washington, D.C. (1976).

Figure 3

Flood hazard areas. (Source: Minnesota Department of Natural Resources, Flood Insurance, St. Paul, Minn., 1972.)

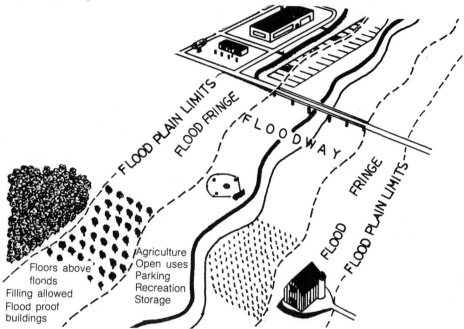

Usually, state and local flood plain programs prohibit permanent buildings and fills in floodway areas but permit a wide range of structural uses in flood fringe areas if elevated or structurally flood-proofed to a flood protection elevation. (See tables 4 and 5).

Special permit approaches are often applied to all structures and fills where floodway and flood fringe areas are not mapped in advance of regulation. Case-by-case data gathering is carried out for each special permit to determine whether the proposed use is located within the floodway or flood fringe portion of the hazard area and establish flood protection elevations. Such an approach requires considerable technical expertise and data gathering capability.

Due to widespread adoption, flood plain regulations have been the most extensively litigated of the sensitive area controls. Courts have strongly endorsed the objective of flood loss reduction,[17] but sometimes have found deficiencies in specific regulations as applied to particular property. Several cases have invalidated restrictions as unreasonable;[18] one case found regulations discriminatory;[19] and a fair number of cases have invalidated tight regulations for a broad flood plain area as a taking when all economic use of the land was prevented.[20]

[17]*See, e.g.,* Turner v. County of Del Norte, 24 C.A. 3d 311, 101 Cal. Rptr. 93 (1972); Vartelas v. Water Resources Comm'n, 146 Conn. 650, 153 A.2d 822 (1959); Iowa Natural Resources Council v. Van Zee, 261 Iowa 1287, 158 N.W. 2d 111 (1968); Turnpike Realty Co. v. Town of Dedham, 284 N.E. 2d 891 (Mass., 1972).

[18]*See, e.g.,* Kesselring v. Wakefield Realty Co., Inc. 306 Ky. 725, 209 S.W. 2d 63 (1948); Sturdy Homes, Inc. v. Township of Redford, 30 Mich. App. 53, 186 N.W. 2d 43 (1971).

[19]City of Welch v. Mitchell, 95 W. Va. 377, 121 S.E. 165 (1924).

[20]*See, e.g.,* Dooley v. Town Plan and Zoning Comm'n, 151 Conn. 304, 197 A. 2d 770 (1964); Baker v. Planning Board, 353 Mass. 141, 228 N.E. 2d 831 (1967); Morris County Land Twp. Co, v. Parsippany-Troy Hills Tp., 40 N.J. 539, 193 A.2d 232 (1963).

Table 4
Principal flood plain regulatory goals.

Goal	Regulatory Tool	Comment
1. Prevent land uses which will increase flood heights and velocities with resulting flood damage to other lands.	1. Special permits for dams and levees to prevent floodway blockages, catastrophic flood losses.	Dam permit statutes have, in most instances, been adopted at state level.
	2. Zoning, subdivision and encroachment regulations to preserve floodway areas and prevent obstruction of stream channels.	Floodway restrictions have been adopted at both state and local levels. Strong common law precedent.
	3. Zoning to preserve flood storage areas.	Not common at the state level but some storage regulations adopted at local level. Some adverse court cases where a prohibitory approach has been used.
	4. Subdivision or drainage regulations controlling drainage design.	Many local subdivision regulations contain drainage requirements to prevent blockages of flows or increased discharge to downstream properties.
	5. Soil conservation regulations requiring land treatment (soil and water conservation practices).	Regulations requiring land treatment are practically nonexistent, although several local soil conservation districts have adopted regulatory standards for soil conservation practices.
2. Prevent land uses which will cause nuisances other than increased flood heights or velocities.	1. Regulation of dams to insure their structural safety.	Most dam permit laws are exercised at the state level.
	2. Zoning, building codes, or other regulations for hazardous uses in the flood plain such as chemical treatment plants, oil and gas storage facilities, nuclear power plants, etc. which may cause fires or other hazards during floods.	Special hazardous use regulations have been adopted at state and local levels and at federal levels in some instances (*e.g.,* the Atomic Energy Commission regulations for nuclear power plants).
	3. Zoning and other regulations applying to storage of materials, placement of mobile homes in the flood plain, construction of wooden residences or other uses which may be carried by flood waters onto other lands thereby increasing the force of flood waters and causing litter problems.	Adopted at both state and local levels. In many instances, land owners fail to consider the nuisance effects which private flood fringe structures may cause to other lands if they float off of their foundations. State and local flood fringe restrictions are designed to minimize these problems.
	4. Regulation of uses with water pollution potential such as sewerage treatment plants, chemical plants, and solid-waste disposal sites.	Most pollution controls are exercised at the state level.
3. Prevent victimization and fraud.	1. Interstate land sales acts requiring the filing of an accurate descriptive statement on land with regulatory agency and prospective buyers.	A federal Interstate Land Sales Act has been adopted and is administered by H.U.D., which requires disclosure of flood hazards. More than a dozen states have adopted individual state acts with a few specifically addressing the flood problem.
	2. Subdivision review acts requiring that subdivided lands be suitable for intended uses.	Subdivision regulations have been primarily adopted at the local level. Many ordinances specifically address the flood problem.
4. Reduce community costs due to flooding.	1. Regulations prohibiting the extension of sewer, water, roads or other public facilities into flood areas.	Adopted by some local communities.
	2. Zoning regulations requiring that all facilities provided to private structures be elevated or otherwise protected to the flood protection elevation.	Adopted by some states and many local units of government. These provisions also reduce pressure for construction of flood control works.
	3. Subdivision regulations requiring that developers install flood-proofed facilities in new subdivisions.	Commonly adopted at the local level.
5. Promote most suitable use of land throughout a community, region, state.	Community-wide zoning based upon land suitability.	Adopted at the local level, except for Hawaii, where statewide zoning has been adopted.

Table 5

A comparison of flood plain regulatory tools.

Tool	Distinguishing Features	Application to New Uses	Application to Existing Uses	Who Administers	Extraterritorial Application
Zoning	1. Map and text. Regulates type of use and provides minimum specifications for uses in each zone. 2. Can protect floodway. 3. Can establish protection elevations. 4. A tool of comprehensive planning. 5. Does not regulate land division or provide detailed standards for building design or materials.	1. Wide potential in regulating construction, land alteration, tree cutting, many other aspects of land use.	1. Some potential for eliminating nuisance floodway or flood fringe uses. 2. Often requires that existing uses be brought into conformity if abandoned, destroyed, or substantially repaired.	1. Zoning administrator issues most permits. 2. Board of Adjustment issues variances and special exceptions.	1. Authorized in 40 percent of states.
Subdivision	1. Text only. Applies to sale and division of land. Approval of "plat" required. 2. Does not in itself regulate type of land use. Regulations apply uniformly.	1. Wide potential in requiring disclosure of flood hazards, insuring that lands are suitable for intended purposes, and requiring installation of public facilities by subdivider.	None.	1. Planning Commission.	1. Authorized in 60 percent of states. Particularly useful tool for urbanizing areas.
Building Code	1. Text only. Applies to building design and materials. Building permit required. 2. Does not regulate type of use of land or division of land.	1. Wide potential in establishing detailed construction standards including structural floodproofing measures.	Usually none; however, housing codes (a variety of building code) applies to existing as well as new uses.	1. Building Inspector.	1. Authorized in only 4 states.

Figure 4

Use standards for two-district flood plain zoning ordinance. (Source: see table 5.)

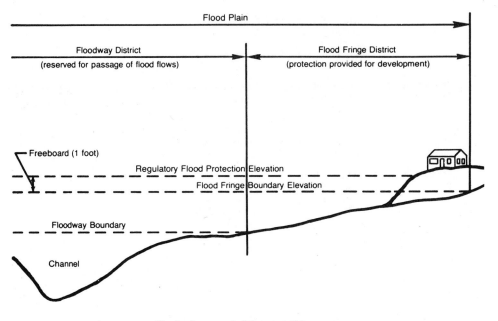

B. Lake and Stream Shores

Six states have adopted special legislation for the protection of inland shoreland areas: Maine, Vermont, Washington, Wisconsin, Minnesota, and Michigan.[21] In addition, California and Nevada have created a joint Lake Tahoe Agency. The acts of Maine and Washington apply both to inland and ocean shorelines and the acts of Wisconsin and Minnesota apply to the Great Lakes as well as inland lake and stream areas.

All six states define shorelands in relationship to the high water mark: areas within 1,000 feet in Michigan and Vermont; 250 feet in Maine; and 200 feet in Washington. Wisconsin and Minnesota regulate river as well as lake shorelands for up to 300 feet from the high water mark or to the landward side of the flood plain. (See figure 5). Maine controls a 250-foot river shoreland area. Washington regulates a 200-foot strip. These shoreland definition criteria reflect political and administrative considerations rather than precise resource characteristics.

In general, shoreland programs do not actually map definition boundaries. They rely upon field surveys to determine whether a use is within the resource area. However, programs often map more discrete subzones such as wetlands, flood plains, erosion areas, wildlife habitats, and recreational development zones.

Two approaches have been used to classify shoreland areas more specifically. The first approach, applied in Wisconsin, identifies individual subzones such as wetland areas around individual lakes. A second approach, used in Minnesota, classifies lakes in their entirety for "natural environment, recreational development," and

---

[21]*See* Appendix B. For a more detailed description of state shoreland programs, *see* B. Berger, J. Kusler, and S. Klinginer, *Lake-Shoreland Management Programs: Selected Papers,* Univ. of Mass. Water Resources Research Center, Publ. No. 69, Technical Report, Amherst, Mass. (1976).

Figure 5

Wisconsin shoreland delineation. (Source: Southeastern Wisconsin Regional Planning Commission, *Floodland and Shoreland Development Guide.* **Planning Guide No. 5, Waukesha, Wisconsin, 1968.)**

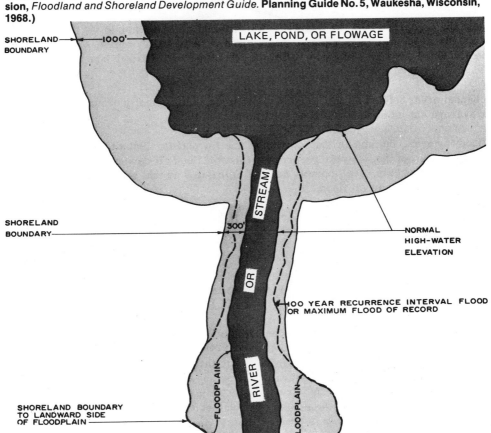

other uses (See figure 7). Varying shoreland use standards apply to lot size, water frontage, building setbacks, and other matters in each class.

All shoreland regulatory programs apply state standard-setting for local adoption of zoning, subdivision controls, and, in some cases, sanitary codes. State minimum standards serve multiple goals which include pollution control, protection of wildlife, prevention of land use conflicts, protection of development from flood and erosion hazards, protection of wetlands, protection of scenic beauty, and protection and enhancement of recreation values. In general, standards permit low density residential and recreational uses in shoreland areas. However, they place tight restrictions on wetland areas and floodways.

The shoreland zoning programs of all states make extensive use of special permit procedures. Generally, a special permit is required for any use with a substantial potential impact upon adjacent uses, water quality, or scenic beauty. Case-by-case evaluations are carried out by the zoning boards of adjustment or planning commissions. Typical special permit uses include marinas, apartments, restaurants, filling in wetlands, substantial tree-cutting, and heavy grading. The Minnesota, Maine, and Wisconsin model shoreland ordinances establish detailed but unquantified standards for evaluation of special permit uses.

Figure 6
Interrelationship of water and shoreland uses.

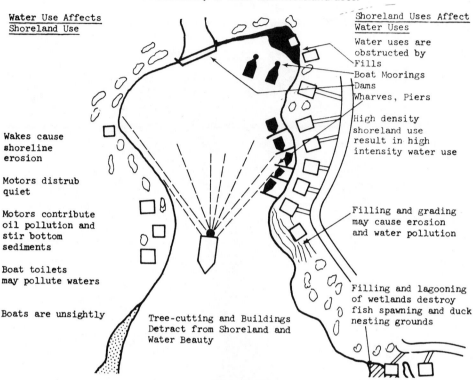

Water Use Affects
Shoreland Use

Wakes cause
shoreline
erosion

Motors distrub
quiet

Motors contribute
oil pollution and
stir bottom
sediments

Boat toilets
may pollute waters

Boats are unsightly

Tree-cutting and Buildings
Detract from Shoreland and
Water Beauty

Shoreland Uses Affect
Water Uses

Water uses are
obstructed by
Fills
Boat Moorings
Dams
Wharves, Piers

High density
shoreland use
result in high
intensity water use

Filling and grading
may cause erosion
and water pollution

Filling and lagooning
of wetlands destroy
fish spawning and duck
nesting grounds

Figure 7
Classification scheme for public waters. (Source: Minnesota Department of Natural Resources, Division of Waters, Soils and Minerals, *Shoreland Management, Classification Scheme for Public Waters,* **Supplementary Report No. I, St. Paul, Minn., 1971.)**

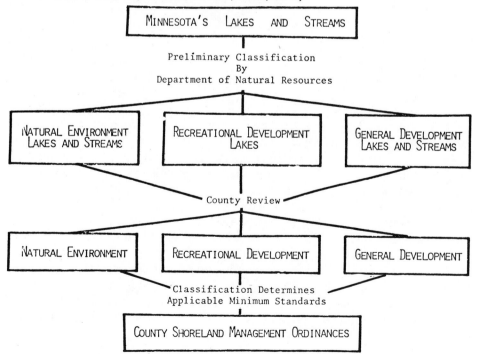

MINNESOTA'S LAKES AND STREAMS

Preliminary Classification
By
Department of Natural Resources

NATURAL ENVIRONMENT LAKES AND STREAMS

RECREATIONAL DEVELOPMENT LAKES

GENERAL DEVELOPMENT LAKES AND STREAMS

County Review

NATURAL ENVIRONMENT

RECREATIONAL DEVELOPMENT

GENERAL DEVELOPMENT

Classification Determines
Applicable Minimum Standards

COUNTY SHORELAND MANAGEMENT ORDINANCES

Figure 8

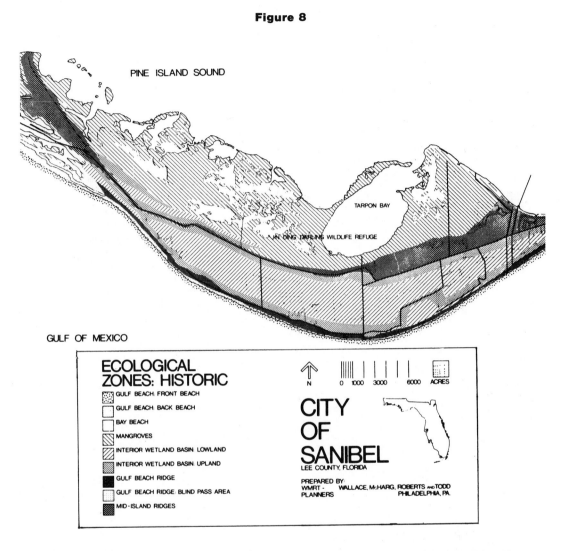

Only a few court cases have considered the validity of traditional zoning for shoreland areas or special shoreland area regulations. A landmark Wisconsin case, *Just v. Marinette County*,[22] strongly endorsed cooperative state/local shoreland zoning. This case upheld very tight wetland protection controls and stated that a landowner has no inherent right to destroy the natural suitability of the land.

C. Coastal Zone Programs

All coastal and Great Lake states exercise some control over coastal zone uses. (See Appendix B). Regulations range from minimal beach setbacks, as in Florida and Hawaii, and wetland regulations in 15 states to comprehensive coastal zone acts, as in North Carolina and California where uses are regulated within a broad coastal

[22]56 Wis. 2d 7, 201 N.W. 2d 761 (1972).

Figure 9

Illustration of an estuarine resources classification system. (Source: Oregon Land Conservation and Development Commission, Draft 3, *Coastal Planning Goals and Guidelines*, Salem, Ore., 1976.)

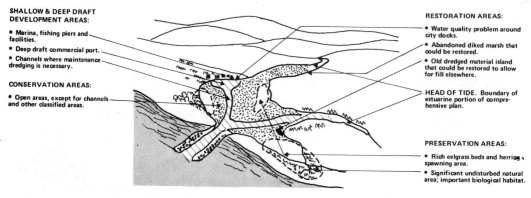

SHALLOW & DEEP DRAFT DEVELOPMENT AREAS:

• Marina, fishing piers and facilities.
• Deep draft commercial port.
• Channels where maintenance dredging is necessary.

CONSERVATION AREAS:

• Open areas, except for channels and other classified areas.

RESTORATION AREAS:

• Water quality problem around city docks.
• Abandoned diked marsh that could be restored.
• Old dredged material island that could be restored to allow for fill elsewhere.

HEAD OF TIDE. Boundary of estuarine portion of comprehensive plan.

PRESERVATION AREAS:

• Rich eelgrass beds and herring spawning area.
• Significant undisturbed natural area; important biological habitat.

Figure 10

Illustration of a shorelands classification system. (Source: see figure 9.)

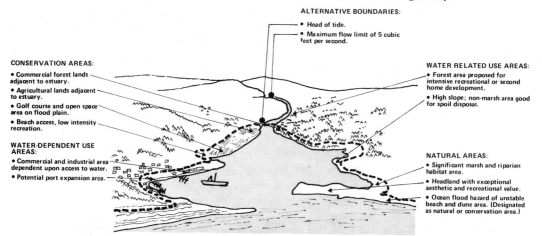

ALTERNATIVE BOUNDARIES:

• Head of tide.
• Maximum flow limit of 5 cubic feet per second.

CONSERVATION AREAS:

• Commercial forest lands adjacent to estuary.
• Agricultural lands adjacent to estuary.
• Golf course and open space area on flood plain.
• Beach access, low intensity recreation.

WATER-DEPENDENT USE AREAS:

• Commercial and industrial area dependent upon access to water.
• Potential port expansion area.

WATER RELATED USE AREAS:

• Forest area proposed for intensive recreational or second home development.
• High slope; non-marsh area good for spoil disposal.

NATURAL AREAS:

• Significant marsh and riparian habitat area.
• Headland with exceptional aesthetic and recreational value.
• Ocean flood hazard of unstable beach and dune area. (Designated as natural or conservation area.)

zone. Many wetland and some broader programs involve direct state control.[23] However, the Washington, North Carolina, California, Maine, Wisconsin, and Minnesota programs rely primarily upon local control within a framework of state standards. State and local coastal zone regulatory programs have been stimulated by the National Coastal Zone Program although many state programs predate the national legislation.

Regulatory acts generally define the coastal zone to include lands within a specified distance of the highwater mark. Coastal zone boundaries include a narrow shoreline area in Washington, 250 feet in Maine, 1,000 feet in Wisconsin, Minnesota, and Michigan, and 1,000 yards in California and coastal counties in North Carolina. The Delaware and New Jersey coastal zone acts, directed to industrial development, define coastal zone boundaries in relationship to particular roads. The distances selected have reflected political realities and the need to form mappable and measurable boundaries.

[23] *E.g.,* The coastal wetland programs of Georgia and Rhode Island; the broader coastal zone programs of Rhode Island (certain uses) and Delaware (industrial uses).

Figure 11

Distribution of wetlands of the United States according to their relative values for waterfowl within each state, 1955. (Source: Adapted from Circular 39, U.S. Fish and Wildlife Service, Department of Interior, *Wetlands of the United States,* **Washington, D.C.)**

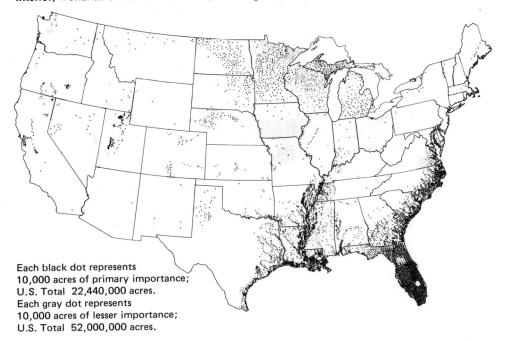

Each black dot represents
10,000 acres of primary importance;
U.S. Total 22,440,000 acres.
Each gray dot represents
10,000 acres of lesser importance;
U.S. Total 52,000,000 acres.

Implementation of broad coastal zone programs has required the definition of more discrete coastal subzones such as wetlands, erosion areas, flood areas, and recreation areas. (See figures 8, 9, 10.) The National Coastal Zone Management Act and the basic enabling acts of several states require the identification of such subzones of "particular concern." They may include virtually all other types of resource areas. Many of the standards applied to coastal zone mineral resource areas, flood plains, erosion areas, and wetlands resemble those for individual resource areas.

Courts have been receptive to coastal zone regulations, particularly where they relate to protection of public waters. For example, courts have approved minimum five-acre lot zoning for an area of special scenic beauty and historic interest along the Maryland shore,[24] control of fill in San Francisco Bay,[25] a statute affirming the public use of beaches in Oregon,[26] a statute prohibiting the removal of stones from beaches in Massachusetts,[27] open space zoning for a beach area in California,[28] flood hazard regulation in New Jersey,[29] an oil refinery siting act in Maine,[30] and coastal wetland regulations in many states.[31]

[24]County Commissioners v. Miles, 246 Md. 355, 228 A. 2d 450 (1967).

[25]Candlestick Properties, Inc. v. San Francisco Bay Conservation Development Commission, 11 Cal. App. 3d 557, 89 Cal. Rptr. 897 (1970).

[26]Thorton v. Hay, 462 P. 2d 671 (Oreg., 1969).

[27]Commonwealth v. Tewsbury, 11 Met. 55 (Mass., 1946).

[28]McCarthy v. Manhattan Beach, 41 Cal. 2d 879, 264 P. 2d 932 (1953).

[29]Spiegel v. Beach Haven, 46 N.J. 479, 218 A. 2d 129 (1966).

[30]In the Matter of Maine Clean Fuels, Inc. 310 A. 2d 736 (Me., 1973).

[31]*E.g.,* Potomac Sand and Gravel Co. v. Governor of Maryland *et al.,* 266 Md. 358, 293 A.2d 241 (Md.

Figure 12

Comparison of the levels of organic matter production in different types of ecosystems. (After Teal and Teal, 1969.) Coastal wetlands, with annual production rates of 5-10 tons per acre, are the most productive areas on earth. (Source: R. Darnell *et al., Impacts of Construction Activities in Wetlands of the United States,* U.S. Environmental Protection Agency, Office of Research and Development, Corvallis Environmental Research Laboratory, Corvallis, Ore., 1976.)

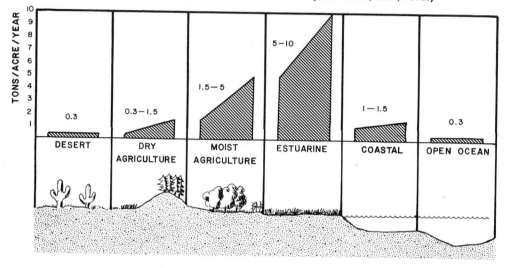

D. Wetlands

At least fifteen states regulate or establish standards for local regulation of coastal wetlands. Six states exercise some control over inland wetlands.[32] More than 1,000 local communities have adopted wetland protection regulations pursuant to these acts or other standards contained in broader shoreland or coastal zone acts.[33] For example, 49 Wisconsin counties apply conservancy zoning to wetland areas as part of shoreland zoning. The expanded jurisdiction of the U.S. Army Corps of Engineers under the "404" permit law requires Corps' permission for fills in waters of the U.S. and adjacent wetlands, and is a stimulus for state and local programs. Federal permits will not be issued where a state or local permit is denied.

Coastal wetlands are usually defined in reference to vegetation and high-water marks. Air photos, high-water records, and field surveys are used to prepare maps.

The definition of inland wetlands has been more difficult. The wide variation in vegetation types, fluctuating water levels, and the importance of particular wetland types for flood storage, wildlife, and other purposes have caused disagreement. Inland wetlands are usually defined in reference to specific vegetation, flooding, and,

---

Ct. of Appeals 1972), *cert. denied,* 409 U.S. 1040; Sibson v. State, 336 A.2d 239 (N.H. 1975). *See* cases cited in Appendix D.

[32]*See* Apendix B. In most instances, statutes are primarily designed to protect wetlands. In some instances, wetland protection is a component of broader coastal regulation (*e.g.,* Washington, California. For a more detailed analysis of state wetland statutes and programs *see* J. Kusler, Draft, *Strengthening State Wetland Regulation,* Environmental Law Institute, produced for the Office of Biological Services, U.S. Fish and Wildlife Service, Washington, D.C. (1978).

[33]*See* J. Kusler, C. Harwood, and R. Newton, Draft, *Our National Wetland Heritage, A Protection Handbook,* Environmental Law Institute, produced for the Office of Biological Services, U.S. Fish and Wildlife Service, Washington, D.C., (1977) for analysis of local programs.

Figure 13

Wetland values and hazards. (Source: J. Kusler and C. Harwood, Draft, *Wetland Protection: A Guidebook for Local Government,* **Environmental Law Institute, Washington, D.C., 1977.)**

VALUES

Isolated Wetlands
(Permanently high ground water levels due to discharge and drainage)

1. Waterfowl feeding and nesting habitat
2. Habitat for both upland and wetland species of wildlife
3. Flood water retention area
4. Sediment and nutrient retention area
5. Area of special scenic beauty

Lake Margin Wetlands

1. See values for "isolated wetlands" above
2. Removal of sediment and nutrients from inflowing waters
3. Fish spawning area

Riverine Wetlands

1. See values for "isolated wetland" above
2. Sediment control, stabilization of river banks
3. Flood conveyance area

Estuarine and
Coastal Wetlands

1. See values for "isolated wetland" above
2. Fish and shellfish habitat and spawning areas
3. Nutrient source for marine fisheries
4. Protection from erosion and storm surges

Barrier Island

1. Habitat for dune-associated plant and animal species
2. Scenic beauty

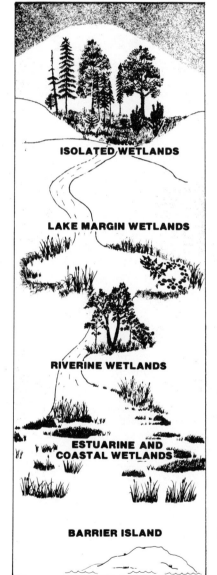

ISOLATED WETLANDS

LAKE MARGIN WETLANDS

RIVERINE WETLANDS

ESTUARINE AND
COASTAL WETLANDS

BARRIER ISLAND

HAZARDS

Isolated Wetlands

1. Flooding and drainage problems for roads and buildings due, in some instances, to widely fluctuating surface and ground water elevations
2. Serious limitations for on-site waste disposal
3. Limited structural bearing capacity of soils for roads and buildings due to high content of organic materials

Lake Margin Wetlands

1. See hazards for isolated wetland above

Riverine Wetlands

1. See hazards for "isolated wetland" above
2. Flood conveyance areas subject to deep inundation and high velocity flows
3. Sometimes erosion areas

Estuarine and
Coastal Wetlands

1. See hazards for "wetlands associated with rivers" above
2. Often severe flood hazard due to tidal action, riverine flooding, storm surges, and wave action
3. Sometimes severe erosion area in major flood due to wave action

Barrier Island

1. Often high energy wind and wave zone
2. Often severe erosion area
3. Protect backlying lands from high energy waves

Figure 14

Wetland types.

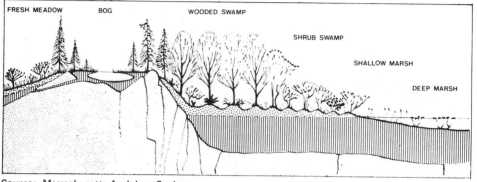

Source: Massachusetts Audubon Society.

in the case of Connecticut, soil type. Air photos, soil maps, and field surveys are used for mapping.

Wetland regulatory objectives vary depending upon the program. They include protection of fish spawning and duck nesting areas, flood storage, pollution control functions, hunting areas, aquifer recharge areas, rare plants and animals, scientific study areas, scenic beauty, and the function of wetlands as nutrient and sediment traps for the protection of lakes, streams, and ponds. Development may be regulated to reduce flood damages, prevent water pollution from onsite waste disposal, and prevent threats to safety from construction on peaty soils with inadequate support.

State and local regulatory efforts often tightly control all fill, excavation, and structural development in wetlands. Open space uses such as wildlife preserves, harvesting of marsh hay, and outdoor recreation are permitted. State programs rely primarily on a permit approach, sometimes combined[34] with protective orders for particular wetland areas. Local programs make less use of special permit approaches and often prohibit fill and development.

Supreme court decisions in Wisconsin,[35] Maryland,[36] New Hampshire,[37] and other states[38] support tight wetland controls. Nevertheless, courts in New Jersey,[39] Massachusetts,[40] and Maine[41] have held or warned that wetland regulations which prevent all economic uses are unconstitutional.

While adverse decisions suggest caution in wetland control, the Wisconsin *Just v. Marinette County*[42] case took an interesting approach to the taking issue which may

[34]Protective orders are authorized by the coastal wetlands statutes of Maine, Massachusetts, North Carolina, and Rhode Island and the inland wetland statute for Massachusetts. Protective orders establish detailed written standards for particular wetlands and include both a text and map.

[35]Just v. Marinette Co., 56 Wis. 2d 7, 201 N.W. 2d 761 (1972).

[36]Potomac Sand and Gravel Co. v. Governor of Maryland *et al.,* 266 Md. 358, 293 A. 2d 241 (1972).

[37]Sibson v. State, 336 A. 2d 239 (N.H. 1975).

[38]*See* Appendix E.

[39]Morris County Land Improvement Co. v. Parsippany-Troy Hills, 40 N.H. 539, 193 A. 2d 232 (1963).

[40]Commissioner of Natural Resources v. S. Volpe and Co., 349 Mass. 104, 206 N.E. 2d 666 (1965) (Court remanded decision for further findings); MacGibbon v. Board of Appeals of Duxbury, 356 Mass. 635, 255 N.E. 2d 347 (1970).

[41]State v. Johnson, 264 A. 2d 711 (Me. 1970).

[42]56 Wis. 2d 7, 201 N.W. 2d 761 (1972). *See* note 58 in Part 8, *infra.*

Table 6

Summary of state wild and scenic rivers programs. (Source: Bureau of Outdoor Recreation, Wild and Scenic Rivers, Outdoor Recreation Action, No. 43, U.S. Department of Interior, Bureau of Outdoor Recreation, Washington, D.C., Spring 1977.)

State	System or Program	How Established (date) Legislative	Admin.	Number of Rivers
Alabama	System	—	1969	1
Alaska	None	—	—	—
Arizona	None	—	—	—
Arkansas	None	—	—	—
California	System	1972	—	9
Colorado	None	—	—	—
Connecticut	None	—	—	—
Delaware	None	—	—	—
District of Columbia	None	—	—	—
Florida	Program	—	1972	0
Georgia	System	1969	—	0
Hawaii	None	—	—	—
Idaho	None	—	—	—
Illinois	None	—	—	—
Indiana	System	1973	—	2
Iowa	System	1970	—	1
Kansas	None	—	—	—
Kentucky	System	1972	—	8
Louisiana	System	1970	—	43
Maine	System	1966	—	1
Maryland	System	1971	—	9
Massachusetts	Program	1971	—	0
Michigan	System	1970	—	6
Minnesota	System	1973	—	4
Mississippi	None	—	—	—
Missouri	None	—	—	—
Montana	None	—	—	—
Nebraska	None	—	—	—
Nevada	None	—	—	—
New Hampshire	None	—	—	—
New Jersey	None	—	—	—
New Mexico	None	—	—	—
New York	System	1973	—	61
North Carolina	System	1971	—	2
North Dakota	System	1975	—	1
Ohio	System	1968	—	8
Oklahoma	System	1970	—	5
Oregon	System	1971	—	8
Pennsylvania	Program	1972	—	0
Puerto Rico	None	—	—	—
Rhode Island	None	—	—	—
South Carolina	System	1974	—	0
South Dakota	Program	1972	—	0
Tennessee	System	1968	—	11
Texas	None	—	—	—
Utah	None	—	—	—
Vermont	None	—	—	—
Virginia	System	1970	—	2
Washington	None	—	—	—
West Virginia	System	1969	—	5
Wisconsin	System	1965	—	3
Wyoming	None	—	—	—
Total		24	2	190

be followed by many states. It held that a landowner has no inherent right and cannot claim a taking for uses which threaten public waters or destroy the natural suitability of the land.

E. Scenic and Wild Rivers

Twenty four states have adopted legislation for the protection of wild, scenic, or recreation rivers.[43] (See table 6.) State programs have been stimulated by the National Scenic and Wild River program, which now applies to 19 rivers. State designated rivers may be included in the national program, subject to the approval of the Secretary of the Interior. Inclusion in the national program protects the rivers from federal water resources projects.

States such as Oklahoma, California, Virginia, and Maryland impose particularly tight controls on dams or other structures in designated rivers but do not regulate shoreland areas. In contrast, Oregon directly regulates a quarter mile corridor along scenic and wild rivers. Minnesota and Michigan authorize state standard-setting for local regulation in corridors of up to 1,320 feet and 400 feet, respectively. Maryland authorizes direct state regulation for the Youghiogheny River and Wisconsin authorizes state standard-setting for local regulation along the lower St. Croix.

Scenic and wild river acts generally define several classes of rivers, although the Wisconsin act refers only to "wild rivers." The Maryland act addresses "scenic" and "wild" rivers. The Minnesota act addresses "wild," "scenic," and "recreation" rivers. Michigan has developed administrative guidelines for designating "wilderness," "wild scenic," and "country scenic" rivers. In general, acts provide that wild, scenic, and recreation rivers are to be distinguished from other waters based upon their "extraordinary," "unusual," or particular "water conservation, scenic, recreational, or wildlife values."

Most enabling statutes directly designate certain rivers or stretches of rivers for regulatory control. However, the administering agency is usually authorized to study and designate other rivers. Detailed advance data gathering rarely precedes statutory designation of rivers. However, data gathering often precedes adoption of regulatory guidelines. Maryland, Virginia, and Ohio, which have largely nonregulatory programs, have also carried out detailed inventory efforts.

Principal regulatory objectives include preserving water quality and free-flowing river conditions and protecting natural scenic beauty, vegetation, wildlife, and recreation values. Secondary objectives include minimizing conflicts between uses, controlling access to areas, protecting health and safety, and reducing possible flood losses.

Programs generally prohibit all new dams, fills, or obstructions in waters and other major sources of water pollution. Land use regulations include: (a) use restrictions with most areas limited to conservancy and light residential uses; (b) controls on fills and grading, tree-cutting, and mineral extraction; and (c) specifications for permitted uses such as minimum lot sizes and building setbacks from the water. General guidelines have usually been prepared and then tailored to specific rivers.

---

[43]*See* Bureau of Outdoor Recreation, "Outdoor Recreation," Spring 1977, Report No. 43, Washington, D.C., for a complete listing. The entire report is devoted to description and analysis of scenic and wild rivers.

Figure 15

Stream protection buffer.

Fixed stream buffer

Floating stream buffer

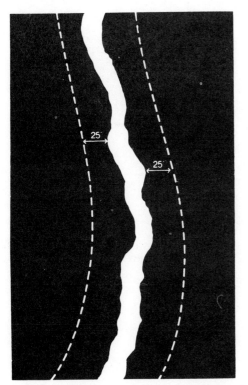 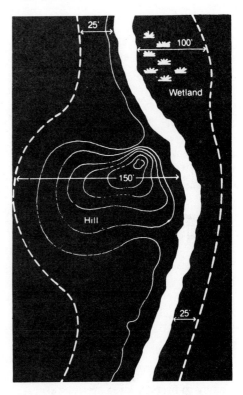

Source: see Figure 19.

All programs regulating dams and other waterway obstructions require state special permits. Oregon has administered a state permit system for shoreland areas for seven rivers involving 520 river miles since 1971. Most permits involve residential uses. Only about one-quarter of the permits requested have been refused. Other programs also make widespread use of special permit techniques for land uses.

Several federal and state court cases have sustained regulations prohibiting dams in rivers with special scenic and recreation values.[44] The Oregon Supreme Court sustained shoreland regulations for a one-fourth mile wide corridor along the Rogue River.[45]

F. Areas of Scientific Interest

Land acquisition, rather than regulation, has been used to protect or preserve areas of unique scientific interest (except wetlands) in most instances. However, Maine has adopted a special "Register of Critical Areas" Act which authorizes an

[44]*See* Namekagon Hydro Co. v. Federal Power Comm'n, 216 F. 2d 509 (1954) in which the court upheld an order of the Federal Power Commission denying a license for the construction of a dam and hydroelectric project on the Namekagon River in northern Wisconsin. *See also* note 45 *infra*. Application of Hemco, Inc., 283 A. 2d 246 (1971) in which the Maine Supreme court upheld state denial of a dam permit to protect "sport fishing, undamaged stream bed and white water canoeing."

[45]Scott v. State *ex rel.* State Highway Comm'n., 23 Oreg. App. 99, 541 P. 2d 516 (1975).

Figure 16

Common threats to parks from adjacent lands. (Source: J. Kusler *et al., Data Needs and Data Gathering for Areas of Critical Environmental Concern,* **Part I: Summary Report, University of Wisconsin, Institute for Environmental Studies, Report 53, Madison, Wis., 1975.)**

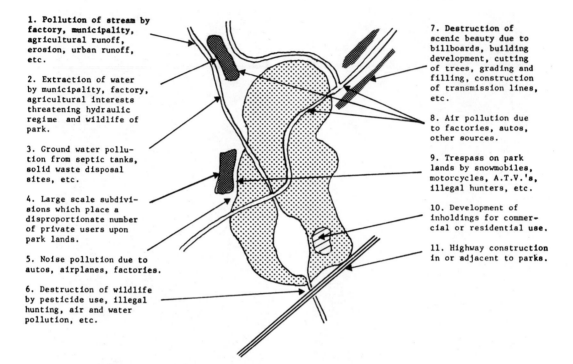

1. Pollution of stream by factory, municipality, agricultural runoff, erosion, urban runoff, etc.

2. Extraction of water by municipality, factory, agricultural interests threatening hydraulic regime and wildlife of park.

3. Ground water pollution from septic tanks, solid waste disposal sites, etc.

4. Large scale subdivisions which place a disproportionate number of private users upon park lands.

5. Noise pollution due to autos, airplanes, factories.

6. Destruction of wildlife by pesticide use, illegal hunting, air and water pollution, etc.

7. Destruction of scenic beauty due to billboards, building development, cutting of trees, grading and filling, construction of transmission lines, etc.

8. Air pollution due to factories, autos, other sources.

9. Trespass on park lands by snowmobiles, motorcycles, A.T.V.'s, illegal hunters, etc.

10. Development of inholdings for commercial or residential use.

11. Highway construction in or adjacent to parks.

agency to prepare a register of natural areas and exercise interim regulatory controls. Local conservancy zoning has been applied in some states to protect areas of special flora, fauna, and geologic or ecologic interest.

Despite the limited present use of regulations in the U.S., experience in the British Isles suggests that regulations can effectively protect areas of scientific interest, if combined with public education, tax incentives, and, in some instances, easement acquisition.[46] In the British Isles, the Nature Conservancy, a statutory body, is responsible for identifying and preserving areas of special scientific interest, including sites of special flora, fauna, and geologic interest. Preservation is achieved in part through the creation of natural reserves, land acquisition, or voluntary agreements with landowners. Nevertheless, local government controls provide the major protection for scientific areas.

To begin, the Nature Conservancy maps areas. Local land use control agencies must consult with the Conservancy before granting permission for development impacting the mapped sites. The Conservancy may appear on its own or as an expert at public hearings on proposed development. The approach has worked with considerable success.

Like the English approach, regulations adopted to date in this country (Maine, Florida) make extensive use of special permits. Landowner education and the use of

[46]*See* Part 4, J. Kusler, *Public/Private Parks and Management of Private Lands for Park Protection,* University of Wisconsin, Institute for Environmental Studies, Madison (1974).

incentives to gain landowner cooperation is essential. The landowner has the power to destroy the values at the site despite the existence of controls. Further, without education and incentives, landowners may raise constitutional challenges to the plans and regulations.

As one might expect, regulations designed to preserve areas of special scientific interest have not been widely litigated in the U.S., although many courts have sanctioned land use regulations designed to protect wildlife.[47] In contrast, some cases have struck down special hunting restrictions imposed on lands adjacent to game preserves[48] and highly restrictive wetland regulations.[49]

G. Areas Adjacent to Parks

Areas adjacent to local, state, and federal parks are of environmental concern for two reasons.[50] Many of these areas are, in their own right, of special scenic beauty or scientific interest. In addition, uses located within such areas may impact upon adjacent parks through water pollution, air pollution, increased traffic, noise, destruction of wildlife, or destruction of scenery.

Conflicting adjacent land uses are now a major problem for many state and federal parks. (See Tables 7 and 8.) The problem becomes more severe with increased park use. Conflicting uses often include motels, restaurants, campgrounds, grocery stores, camping suppliers, gasoline stations, drive-in theaters, souvenir shops, and other types of development along park boundaries, on private land within parks, and along park access roads.

To date, only a small number of state and local regulations have been adopted solely to protect park areas. One joint state/federal/local park protection plan was prepared for the Gettysburg National Military Park. State and local planning efforts are underway for Voyageurs National Lakeshore in Minnesota and a special Adirondack Park Commission has been created in New York. A model parkway protection ordinance was prepared for lands adjacent to the Blue Ridge Parkway.

Precedent for park protection regulations is also found in the experiences of Cape Cod and other national recreation areas applying the "Cape Cod formula." This approach involves the adoption of federal standards for private lands within park boundaries. The federal government suspends its condemnation powers for those lands as long as the local governments regulate in accordance with federal standards.

Finally, the English have had extensive experience with park protection controls. The English national park system consists almost entirely of private land subject to tight development control.[51]

---

[47]*See* the wetland cases cited above. *See also* Geer v. Connecticut, 161 U.S. 519 (1895) in which the U.S. Supreme Court sustained regulations on the taking of wildlife.

[48]*E.g.,* State v. Becker, 215 Wis. 564, 255 N.W. 144 (1943).

[49]*E.g.,* Morris County Land Improvement Co. v. Parsippany-Troy Hills Tp., 40 N.J. 539, 193 A. 2d 232 (1963).

[50]*See* J. Kusler, *Public/Private Parks and Management of Private Lands for Park Protection,* University of Wisconsin, Institute for Environmental Studies, Report 16 (1974), for a discussion of threats to parks and techniques for reducing threats.

[51]*Id.,* Part 4.

Table 7

Threats to federal parks, historic sites, recreation areas, and parkways from uses on adjacent lands.' **(Source: J. Kusler,** *Public/Private Parks and Management of Private Lands for Park Protection,* **University of Wisconsin, Institute for Environmental Studies, Madison, 1972.)**

Threat	Number of Areas Reporting Threat (out of a total) of 88 areas)
A. Incompatible development	
(1) Residential	
a. Single family	30
b. Multi-family	13
c. Other	9
(2) Industrial	18
(3) Commercial	
a. Campgrounds	5
b. Motels	6
c. Hotels	4
d. Other	11
(4) Roads	20
(5) Signboards	12
B. Other types of threats	
(1) Trespass from adjacent lands	
a. Pedestrian	9
b. Off-the-road vehicles	32
(2) Litter	42
(3) Destruction of scenic beauty	37
(4) Air pollution	29
(5) Water pollution	34
(6) Noise problems	31
a. Autos	12
b. Industries	5
c. Other	23
(7) Special problems	24

The regulation of lands adjacent to parks may have multiple and somewhat contradictory objectives: (1) protecting park values and amenities; (2) providing basic accommodations and services to meet the needs of park visitors; and (3) accomplishing local community goals for growth and increased tax base. Other specific objectives may include preventing air and water pollution, controlling water extraction that interferes with water supply within the park, protecting wetland and wildlife areas related to the park area, protecting scenic beauty, controlling vegetation removal and tree-cutting, controlling uses that disrupt the flow of traffic, and separating incompatible uses.

Courts have sustained a number of regulations that protect parks including control of signboards along parkways[52] and access controls for parks and

---

[52]*See, e.g.,* General Outdoor Adv. Co. v. City of Indianapolis, 202 Ind. 85, 172 N.E. 309, 72 A.L.R. 453 (1930) (Court upheld regulation of signs within 500 feet of park); People v. Sterling, 267 App. Div. 9, 45 N.Y.S. 2d 39 (1943) *reh.* and *app. den.* 267 App. Div. 852, 47 N.Y.S. 2d 285 (Court upheld park commission's ban of signs in Adirondack area.)

Table 8

Threats to state parks from uses on adjacent lands. (Source: see table 7.)

Threat	Number of States Reporting Threat (out of 39 states)
A. Incompatible development	31
(1) Residential	
a. Single family	22
b. Multi-family	11
c. Other	13
(2) Industrial	18
(3) Commercial	
a. Campgrounds	9
b. Motels	12
c. Hotels	7
d. Other	14
(4) Roads	15
(5) Signboards	17
B. Other types of threats	
(1) Trespass from adjacent lands	
a. Pedestrian	15
b. Off-the-road vehicles	29
(2) Litter	21
(3) Destruction of scenic beauty	25
(4) Air pollution	18
(5) Water pollution	28
(6) Noise pollution	24
a. Autos	17
b. Industries	8
c. Other	11

boulevards.[53] Courts have held that diminution in land value caused by regulations is not a "taking" where part of the value was created by adjacent public uses.[54] However, attempts to prohibit all private development may encounter arguments similar to those used to defeat coastal wetland regulations. Private landowners may contend they are prevented from all private economic uses in order to bestow an uncompensated benefit upon the public.

---

[53]*See* Annot.,: "Power of Park Commission to Directly Regulate or Prohibit Abutter's Access to Street or Highway." 73 A.L.R. 2d 671 (1960); Burke v. Metropolitan District Commission, 262 Mass. 70, 159 N.W. 739 (1928) (Court upheld park commission's restrictions of abutter's access to one driveway along a park); State v. City of Toledo, 75 Ohio App. 378, 31 Ohio Ops. 144, 62 N.E. 2d 256 (1944) (Court held that municipality can limit the ingress and egress of an owner of land abutting a park or boulevard.)

[54]*See, e.g.,* Kelbro v. Myrick, 113 Vt. 64, 30 A. 2d 572 (1943), in which the Vermont Supreme Court upheld the regulation of signs in part on the theory that display of signs was a privilege, not a right, and that the value of the property for signboard use derived from the public thoroughfare from which signs could be seen. *See also* New York State Thruway A. v. Ashley Motor Court, 10 N.Y.S. 2d 640 (1961).

Table 9

Techniques to protect parks from incompatible uses. (Source: see table 7.)

Park Protection Objective	Technique	Use Restriction	Advantage of Technique	Limitation of Technique
Control junkyards and similar nuisance uses adjacent to parks and along access roads.	1. Open space or recreational zoning.	Prohibit junkyards in mapped zones.	Well accepted politically and legally.	Usually applies only prospectively.
	2. Special codes.	Prohibit junkyards within specified distances (100 feet, 500 feet, 1000 feet, etc.) of parks and access roads.	Controls upon nuisance uses often apply partially or wholly to existing as well as new uses.	Restrictions are less specifically tailored than with mapped zone approach.
Prevent flood problems upon parklands caused by use of adjacent lands.	1. Floodplain zoning.	Control development in upstream flood storage areas and downstream floodways.	May achieve either open space objectives.	Flood storage regulations have in some instances been held unconstitutional "takings" of property.
	2. Easement or fee acquisition of floodplain.	Purchase floodplain for open space use.	May permit public use and wildlife preservation of acquired lands.	Costly; reduction in local tax base.
	3. Construction of dams.		Control of flood waters.	Costly; environmental damage.
Preserve scenic beauty of park.	1. Setbacks or buffer zoning for areas immediately adjacent to park and access roads.	Prevent most development within 1000, 2000, 5000 feet of park.	Tight control of private development at low public cost.	May unconstitutionally "take" property if no economic uses are available for land; may be unfair to landowners.
	2. Residential—recreational zoning.	Prevention of all but recreational and low density residential use. Restrictions upon grading, tree-cutting, other types of activities.	Permit some private uses while achieving a considerable degree of park protection.	Limited residential use may, to some extent, disturb scenic beauty; enforcement problems and variances common.
	3. Tree-cutting regulations as part of zoning, special codes.	Prevent or control tree-cutting within designated areas.	Preservation of trees may permit low density residential and commercial development with minimum scenic impact.	Difficult to administer.
	4. Building codes.	Limitation upon building height, materials.	Relatively simple adoption procedures.	Apply only to new uses; achieve limited degree of protection.
	5. Billboard controls.	Restriction or prohibition of billboards.		Usually apply only to new uses.
	6. Architectural controls contained in zoning or special codes.	Control of building design, landscaping.	May permit considerable amount of development if development is designed to mesh with natural scene.	Requires architectural expertise; may stifle creativity.

Table 9 (continued)

Park Protection Objective	Technique	Use Restriction	Advantage of Technique	Limitation of Technique
	7. Scenic easements.	Prohibit all or most development, tree-cutting, grading, etc.	Permit long-term regulation of land without unconstitutionally "taking" property; permit continued private use of land; less costly than fee purchase.	Relatively costly; does not permit active public uses; enforcement problems in some instances.
	8. Fee purchase.	Prohibit all private development.	Control all private uses and permit public use of land.	Costly; removes land from local tax rolls.
	9. Tax incentives for open space uses.	Limit density of development; encourage clustering of buildings; require buffer zones; require dedication of park areas.	Minimize the impact of land development upon parks; gain additional parkland for public use.	May be difficult to administer; unfair, in some instances, to subdividers.
	10. Tax incentives for open space uses.	Indirect control only.	Encourage open space private land uses consistent with park needs.	Reduce local tax base; constitutional problems in some states with uniformity of taxation provisions; likely to be effective only if combined with regulations.
Control water pollution.	1. State-level pollution controls.	Prevention or control of "point" sources of pollution.	State-level regulation not so subject to bias by local property interests.	Regulations usually do not apply to urban runoff, agricultural pollution, erosion problems.
	2. Local sanitary codes.	Control of septic tanks and other on-site waste disposal.	Administered at local level; often apply to existing as well as new uses.	Enforcement often a problem; regulations, even if enforced may not prevent enrichment of groundwaters.
	3. Subdivision regulations.	Require installation of sewers and water supply, control grade and fill operations which will cause water quality problems.	Protect water quality and insure sanitary conditions at the expense of the subdivider.	May be difficult to require sewers in rural areas where there are no municipal sewage treatment plants.
Preserve wildlife.	1. Conservancy zoning.	Prohibition or tight control of all development in wetlands, areas of special ecological interest.	Protection of ecological relations which transcend park boundaries.	Tight regulations may be attacked on the ground that regulations "take" property without payment of compensation.

Table 9 (continued)

Park Protection Objective	Technique	Use Restriction	Advantage of Technique	Limitation of Technique
	2. Special hunting and fishing regulations.	Special control of hunting or fishing in areas adjacent to parks.	Protect wildlife which may travel some distance outside of parks.	Regulations have been held discriminatory in some states.
	3. Regulation of pesticide and herbicide application.	Control of chemical use on adjacent lands which may drift or flow into park areas or kill wildlife wandering onto adjacent lands.	Protect water quality as well as wildlife; prevent cumulative food chain problems.	Difficult to enforce in some instances.
Prevent noise pollution.	1. Zoning restrictions.	Prevent or establish noise performance standards for factories, gravel extractions, other noisy uses.	Administered in combination with other local regulations.	Difficult to enforce.
	2. State, federal or local special regulations for transportation uses.	Prevent autos, trucks, snowmobiles, airplanes in selected areas.	State or federal regulations can apply to interstate uses not ordinarily subject to effective local control.	Difficult to administer, enforce.
Prevent trespass on park lands by unauthorized vehicles, individuals.	1. Special codes.	Prevent entry into park except at official entry points by snowmobiles, motorcycles, A.T.V.s.	Low cost.	Difficult to enforce.
	2. Conservation easements.	Preservation of wetlands, wildlife areas from development, most other private uses.	Protect wildlife, permit limited public access to streams, lakes, and other fishing areas on a permanent basis.	Quite costly; enforcement problems in some instances; do not prevent all private uses which may disturb ecologically sensitive communities.
	2. Fee acquisition.	Preserve wetlands, ecological areas by preventing all private uses.	Preserve areas in perpetuity; protect sensitive areas from private uses.	Costly; removes land from tax base.
Prevent air pollution.	1. Air pollution controls in zoning or special codes.	Prevent or establish performance standards for factories, stubble and leaf burning, other air pollution sources.	Administered in combination with other local regulations.	May be difficult to administer, enforce.
	2. Highway regulations.	Restriction on use of autos in certain areas.	May also reduce noise, traffic congestion, visitor overuse.	Difficult to administer; expertise required.

H. Forestry Areas

Many states, such as Wisconsin, Minnesota, and Oregon, encourage and assist private tree farms and sustained yield timber operations through tax incentives and fire prevention efforts.[55] A smaller number regulate private forestry practices to achieve these objectives.[56] Washington, Maryland, Minnesota, and other states have adopted state tree-cutting regulations. State shoreland zoning regulations in Wisconsin and Maine also incorporate tree-cutting regulations. Hawaii has mapped and tightly regulated special forest protection zones.

Local tree-cutting restrictions are more common.[57] Zoning enabling acts specifically authorize forest protection in Wisconsin, Minnesota, and a number of other states. Many cities, towns, and counties have adopted tree-cutting regulations using either this broad zoning enabling authority or special enabling acts. Regulations typically require a permit for the cutting of trees in residential, conservancy, wetland, or other districts.

Tree-cutting regulations serve one or two principal objectives: (1) protecting sustaining yield forest base and (2) preserving amenities such as scenic beauty or wild-life. Ancillary objectives include protecting watershed areas, controlling erosion, and preventing forest fires.

Generally, regulations do not prohibit all tree-cutting. They control harvesting practices and, in some instances, require replanting. Most tree-cutting regulations operate entirely on a special permit basis with general performance standards related to tree-planting, erosion, and scenic beauty. Forest recreation zones adopted by Wisconsin counties in the 1920's and 30's prevent most structural uses in forest districts.

Judicial reaction has been favorable to tree-cutting regulations although their validity has not been extensively litigated. In *State v. Dexter*,[58] the U.S. Supreme Court upheld a Washington statute requiring permits for tree-cutting and landowner participation in a state reforestation program. In *Perely v. North Carolina*,[59] the Court upheld North Carolina's tree-cutting and slash disposal regulations for watershed areas.

Whether or not courts will uphold restrictive forest district regulations, especially those preventing all structural uses not associated with forest operations, remains to be seen. Favorable judicial reaction is likely where forestry is an economically viable use, land values are low, land is presently in large lot forest uses, and tax incentives are available.

Despite the limited adoption of forest protection regulations, more programs are likely as conversion of forestry land to second homes, agriculture, and active recreation land produces shortages in wood and wood products.

[55]*See* E. Solberg, *New Laws for New Forests,* University of Wisconsin Press, Madison, Wis. (1961) for a description of the Wisconsin effort.

[56]*E.g.,* Idaho, Washington, Massachusetts.

[57]*See* C. Bingham, *Trees in the City,* American Society of Planning Officials, Planning Report No. 236 (1968).

[58]32 Wash. 2d 51, 202 P.2d 906, *aff'd.* 338 U.S. 863 (1949).

[59]249 U.S. 510 (1919).

I. Prime Agricultural Land

Only Hawaii has adopted state zoning for prime agricultural lands.[60] The 1955 statewide zoning law created agricultural districts and placed all lands in one of four zones: (1) conservancy, (2) agricultural, (3) rural, and (4) urban. The agricultural districts were designed to preserve the pineapple and sugar cane industries. District maps were based upon soils, existing use of land, acreage, and other factors. Vermont also provides limited regulatory protection for prime agricultural lands through provisions in its large-scale development site review act.

Despite the limited regulation of agricultural lands at state level, many counties and towns have adopted exclusive agricultural districts or, more commonly, agricultural-residential districts permitting low density uses. Some local agricultural zone regulations and state controls in Hawaii prohibit virtually all nonagricultural uses or activities. However, many local regulations permit low density uses on five to 100 acre lots. The latter approach is more acceptable politically but opens a wedge for nonagricultural development.

Agricultural regulations are adopted to preserve existing production areas and prime agricultural soils of sufficient size for economical agricultural operations. Secondary objectives include preventing incompatible uses, preserving open space, protecting flood plains, minimizing public service costs, and protecting the local tax and economic base.

Despite the widespread adoption of local agricultural zones, few courts have considered their validity. A 1968 Utah decision sustained a grazing district classification that limited the market value of certain road frontage land to $20-30 per acre where the free market value was $10,000 per acre.[61] The court held that the landowner had purchased the land with full knowledge of restrictions and could not claim hardship. Some indirect support for agricultural zoning may also be found in the rationale of the Wisconsin wetland case cited above[62] which held that a landowner has no absolute right to destroy the natural suitability of his land. On the other hand, a Wisconsin case held an agricultural zoning classification invalid when it was applied to lands clearly unsuitable for agriculture.[63]

Although state-level agricultural protection laws have been adopted in only a few states, at least 45 states provide property tax incentives for agricultural and open-space uses.[64] The laws generally authorize a "roll back" tax which requires landowners to pay all or a substantial portion of the unassessed tax if the land is subsequently developed. The California effort, the Williamson Act, required several changes in the California constitution and numerous statutory modifications. Nevertheless, the program has been only partially successful. Farmers have failed to utilize the program fully while subdividers gain speculative benefits.

---

[60]*See* R. Poirier, *State Zoning: A Case Study of the Concept Administration, and Possible Application of the State of Hawaii Land Use Law,* M.A. Thesis, Urban and Regional Planning, University of Wisconsin, Madison (1967).

[61]Chevron Oil Co. v. Beaver Co., 22 Utah 2d 143, 449 P. 2d 989 (1969).

[62]Just v. Marinette Co., 56 Wis. 2d 7, 201 N.W. 2d 761 (1972).

[63]Kimee v. Town of Spider Lake, 60 Wis. 2d 640, 211 N.W. 2d. 471 (1973).

[64]*See* J. Keene *et al., Untaxing Open Space,* Prepared by the Council on Environmental Quality, U.S. Government Printing Office, Washington, D.C. (1976).

Figure 17

Concept of integrated mining, reclamation, and land-use planning.

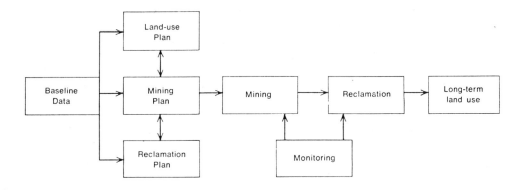

J. Mineral and Energy Resource Lands

The environmental and energy crises have focused attention on energy resource areas containing coal, oil, gas, and oil shale; metal deposits such as iron, zinc, lead, copper, aluminum, manganese, and rare metals; and deposits of aggregates such as sand, gravel, clay, and granite. Apparently, only Colorado[65] has mapped mineral deposits expressly for regulatory purposes. However, many state geological surveys and the United States Geologic Survey have surveyed mineral deposits. In addition, 37 states have adopted mine reclamation laws to meet a wide range of objectives.[66] Many communities have also adopted regulations controlling or preventing gravel extraction, mining, and oil and gas extraction in residential and commercial areas.[67] Some communities have adopted special resource protection districts for sand and gravel deposits.

Regulatory objectives include: (1) protecting mineral and energy resource areas from encroachment by incompatible uses; (2) preventing waste; (3) preventing nuisances from mineral operations; and (4) reclaiming mined areas.

The degree of restrictiveness required depends on the type of area, mode of anticipated extraction, specific objectives, and other factors. Very tight control of subdivision and adjacent uses is needed to protect surface deposits mined through open pit methods. In contrast, residential, commercial, and industrial developments may be permitted closer to areas where deep shaft mining is used to extract metal ores.

---

[65]*See* S.D. Schochow, R.R. Shroba, and P.C. Wicklein, *Sand, Gravel, and Quarry Aggregate Resources, Colorado Front Range Counties,* Colorado Geological Survey, Department of Natural Resources, Denver, Colorado (1974).

[66]*See* E. Imhoff, T. Friz, and J. LaFevers, *A Guide to State Programs for the Reclamation of Surface Mined Areas,* U.S. Geological Survey Circular 731, Washington, D.C., (1976) for a listing, description and analysis of these laws.

[67]*See* "Annot.: Prohibiting or Regulating Removal or Exploitation of Oil and Gas, Minerals, Soil, or Other Natural Products Within Municipal Limits," 10 A.L.R. 3d 1226 (1966) for a discussion of cases contesting these restrictions.

Table 10

Uses of non-metallic minerals. Non-metallic mineral resources are most widespread. Because of their low bulk value they are also more threatened by incompatible development than metallic deposits (iron, copper, lead, *etc.*) and oil and gas.

A. Unconsolidated
   1. Sand - Uses
      a. Fine Aggregate
      b. Fill
      c. Molding (Foundry Sand)
   2. Gravel - Uses
      a. Concrete and Bituminous Aggregate
      b. Roadstone (Various Types and Grades)
      c. Fill and Riprap
      d. Railroad Ballast
   3. Clay - Uses
      a. Brick and Tile
      b. Specialty Ceramics
   4. Peat
B. Consolidated
   1. Crushed Stone - Dolomite - Uses
      a. Concrete and Bituminous Aggregate
      b. Roadstone (Various Types and Grades)
      c. Fill and Riprap
      d. Railroad Ballast
      e. Agricultural Limestone
      f. Lime
      g. Flux
   2. Crushed Stone - Quartzite - Uses
      a. Abrasives
      b. Railroad Ballast
   3. Crushed Stone - Rhyolite, Greenstone, Weathered Granite - Uses
      a. Roofing Granules
      b. Roadstone
   4. Dimension Stone - Granite, Gabbro, Dolomite, Sandstone - Uses
      a. Building Stone (Several Types)
      b. Flagging
      c. Veneer
      d. Monumental
   5. Sand - Uses
      a. Molding (Foundry Sand)
      b. Abrasives and Blasting Sand
      c. Filtration
      d. Glass and Chemical Uses
   6. Shale - Uses
      a. Brick and Tile
      b. Specialty Ceramics

Both state and local regulations typically require special permits for all mineral, oil, and gas extraction. Each proposal is evaluated on its merits for compatibility with adjacent uses, adequacy of the reclamation plan, impact upon roads, and other factors. Development conditions are often attached, and require particular methods of operation, fencing and screening, and reclamation.

Local zoning regulations which prevent or tightly control extraction of early products in residential districts have been widely litigated.[68] Courts usually uphold these controls despite severe economic impact because of threatened nuisances.

[68] *Id.*

Table 11

National assessment of shore erosion. (Source: Department of Army, Corps of Engineers, *Report on the National Shoreline Study*, **Washington, D.C., 1971.**)

Region	Total Shoreline (miles)	Significant Erosion (miles)	Critical Erosion (miles)	Non-Critical Erosion (miles)	Non-Eroding (miles)
North Atlantic	8,620	7,460	1,090	6,370	1,160
South Atlantic-Gulf	14,620	2,820	980	1,840	11,800
Lower Mississippi	1,940	1,580	30	1,550	360
Texas Gulf	2,500	360	100	260	2,140
Great Lakes	3,680	1,260	220	1,040	2,420
California	1,810	1,550	80	1,470	260
North Pacific	2,840	260	70	190	2,580
Alaska	47,300	5,100	100	5,000	42,200
Hawaii	930	110	30	80	820
Total For Nation	84,240	20,500	2,700	17,800	63,740

The U.S. Supreme Court and state courts have upheld state regulation of oil and gas operations to prevent waste.[69] These cases provide conceptual precedent for mineral resource protection districts to achieve the same objectives. In addition, the Colorado supreme court specifically upheld a local mineral protection district.[70]

The fixed supply of mineral resources provides a strong incentive for future regulatory programs despite the variety of difficult issues raised. Assuming that minerals should be preserved for future use, what consumption rates are acceptable? What assumptions should be made concerning technological advances in mining or energy production? Or what of the development of substitutes for metals and other materials? To what extent should the state overrule local zoning that prohibits mineral extraction?

K. Erosion Areas

Coastal erosion is a major concern in Florida, California, Hawaii, Michigan, and other states.[71] Hawaii and Florida establish 50-foot coastal setbacks to minimize

[69]*See, e.g.,* Bandini Petroleum Co. v. Superior Court, 284 U.S. 8 (1931); Lindsley v. Natural Carbonic Gas Co., 220 U.S. 61 (1911); Champlin Refining Co. v. Corp. Comm. of Oklahoma, 286 U.S. 210 (1932).

[70]*See* Famularo v. Board of County Commissioners, 505 P. 2d 958 (1973).

[71]For a discussion of erosion problems in coastal areas, *see* Department of the Army Corps of Engineers, *Report on the National Shoreline Study,* U.S. Army Corps of Engineers, Washington, D.C. (1971). For a discussion of techniques to calculate recession rates, *see* Great Lakes Basin Commission, *Proceedings of the Recession Rate Workshop* (Dec. 5-6, 1974), Great Lakes Basin Comm'n, Ann Arbor, Mich. (1975).

Figure 18

Coastal flood and erosion hazards. (Source: J. Kusler *et al.,* **Vol. 2,** *Regulation of Flood Hazard Areas to Reduce Flood Losses,* **U.S. Government Printing Office, Washington, D.C., 1971.)**

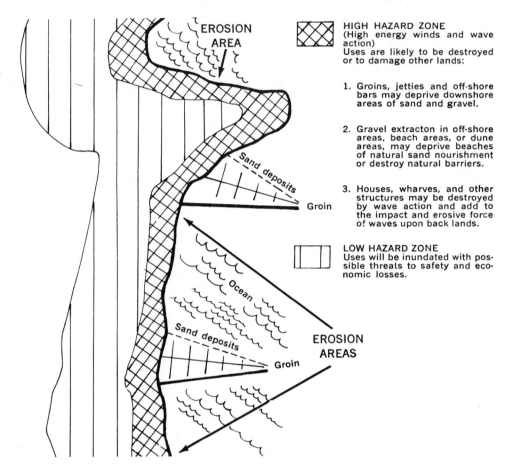

erosion and flood damages and serve resource protection goals. The Michigan shoreland program has defined and regulated erosion areas along Lake Michigan based on air photos and site surveys. Time sequence photos define setback lines representing a 30-year protection period.

Broader soil and water conservation surveys have been carried out to identify inland erosion areas in many states. Regulations have been adopted in some instances to control subdividing and building on highly erosive soils.

Courts have sustained a variety of state and local regulations for beach erosion areas.[72] A Colorado court sustained local soil conservation regulations to reduce wind erosion.[73]

---

[72]*See, e.g.,* Commonwealth v. Tewksbury, 11 Met. 55 (Mass 1846) in which the court upheld a statute prohibiting removal of sand and gravel from beaches to protect natural storm and erosion protective barriers; Spiegle v. Beach Haven, 46 N.J. 479, 218 A. 2d 129 (1966) in which the court upheld building setback and fence ordinances for coastal flood and erosion area.

[73]Oberst v. Mays, 148 Colo. 285, 365 P. 2d 902 (1961).

Figure 19

Erosion and weathering. (Source: C. Thurow, W. Toner, and D. Erley, *Performance Controls for Sensitive Lands,* **American Society of Planning Officials, Planning Advisory Service, Report Nos. 307, 308, Chicago, Ill., 1975.)**

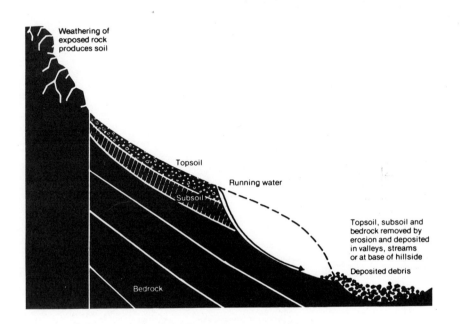

Figure 20

Slope-density restrictions which state the degree of development density acceptable on a particular slope are becoming a primary mean of hillside protection. (Source: see figure 19.)

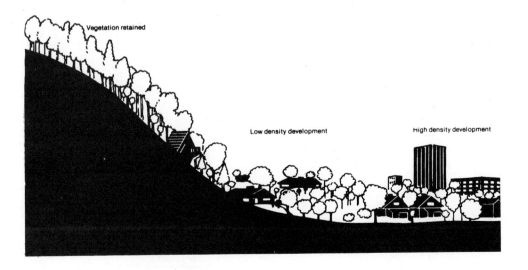

Figure 21

Area of critical state concern designation and implementation procedure, Ch. 380 Florida Statutes. (Source: E. Tin, "The Florida Critical Area Program: Ideas for Barrier Island Protection," *in Barrier Islands and Beaches,* **Technical Proceedings of the 1976 Barrier Islands Workshop, Annapolis, Maryland, May 17-18, 1976, The Conservation Foundation, Washington, D.C., 1977.)**

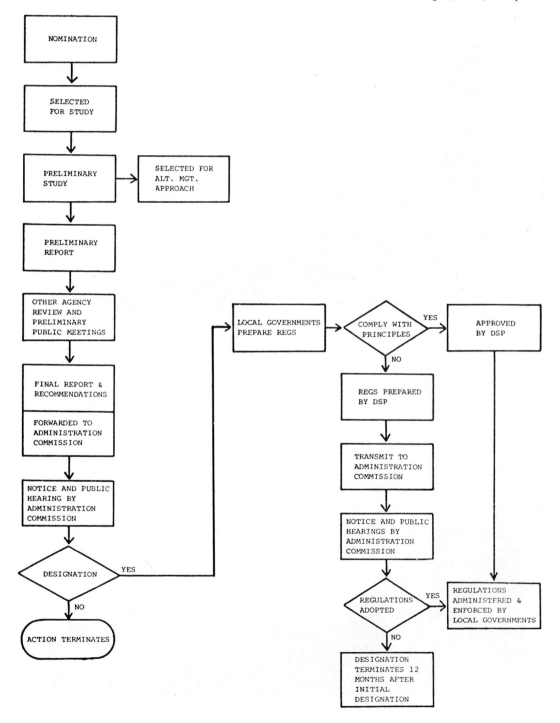

L. Scenic Areas

Vermont bases special control over large-scale development for areas above 2,500 feet primarily on scenic values. Wild and scenic rivers are defined, to a considerable extent, by the natural beauty of adjacent shorelands. Maine strongly considers aesthetic factors in its review of large-scale development. However, fixed criteria are not used for evaluating scenery in each of these programs. Air photos and field surveys have been used to identify areas with special topographic and vegetative qualities. Many courts have afforded increased weight to protection of aesthetics,[74] although this was not traditionally considered a valid sole police power objective.[75]

M. Comprehensive Sensitive Area Acts

In addition to the regulatory programs for individual areas, comprehensive sensitive area regulatory programs authorize the regulation of many types of areas by a single state agency. They have been adopted in Florida and Minnesota, and partial elements have appeared in Oregon and Colorado. All programs are in early stages of implementation. All involve state standard-setting for local regulation of areas and direct state regulation only in the event of local inaction.

These comprehensive sensitive-area programs depend primarily on "nomination and screening" procedures for initial identification of areas. In the nomination process, local units of government, other agencies, and interest groups suggest areas in need of special protection. Using this approach, the Florida program has designated three areas: Big Cypress, Green Swamp, and the Florida Keys. Other areas are under consideration. The Minnesota program has designated the St. Croix wild riverway.

To date, comprehensive critical area efforts have focused on water-oriented natural areas. Regulatory standards have been performance-oriented. Apparently no state supreme court has considered the validity of these regulations.

Other efforts to define sensitive areas comprehensively are underway in Maine, North Carolina, Maryland, Colorado, Nevada, Virginia, California, and Wyoming. In addition, Missouri and Wisconsin have developed criteria for defining areas, although both states lack implementing legislation.

[74]*See, e.g.,* People v. Stover, 12 N.Y.S. 2d 462, 191 N.E. 2d 272 (1963), *appeal dism.*, 375 U.S. 42 (1963).
[75]*See, e.g.,* Barney and Casey Co. v. Milton, 324 Mass. 440, 87 N.E. 2d 9 (1949) and cases cited therein.

Part **2**

RESOURCE
CONSERVATION GOALS

Eight principal resource conservation and land management goals underlie sensitive area programs discussed above. They supplement more traditional land planning goals such as separation of incompatible uses. They may be restated as goals or recommendations for future efforts.[1]

2-1 *Private and public decision-makers should consider the short-term and long-term impacts of development upon sensitive areas, the reversibility of impacts, and alternatives to development.*

Sensitive area programs often require that public and private developers evaluate development impact and consider development and preservation alternatives.[2] This serves a primary regulatory objective—to encourage informed decision-making. Informed decision-making is also facilitated by sensitive area mapping and public education efforts. Informed decision-making does not, of course, insure protection of regional or national interests if the benefits but not the costs of development accrue to landowners.

---

[1]As common denominator recommendations they must be tailored to reflect factual and political situations.

[2]Many programs require environmental impact statements for larger projects. Impact information is needed to apply regulatory criteria.

2-2 *Uses incompatible with sensitive area values or hazards and not requiring a sensitive area location should be shifted to other sites.*

Public and private development should be shifted from sensitive areas to alternate sites if the total societal benefits of development at the sites equals or exceeds those within critical areas. Programs often require that developers demonstrate why proposed activities require sensitive area locations and why alternate sites cannot be used.[3] Development is often confined to the margins of sensitive areas where alternate locations are not feasible.

2-3 *Uses which cause nuisances, threaten public safety, or violate pollution standards should be prohibited.*

The primary objective of floodway and erosion area programs is the prevention of uses with serious "offsite effects," blocking flood flows, accelerating erosion, increasing storm damage, or causing water pollution. Regulations designed to serve these objectives have strong legislative and judicial support.[4]

2-4 *Resource areas should be protected from incompatible uses.*

The encroachment of development into renewable and nonrenewable resource areas physically preempts resource use. Nuisance suits and tight regulation of resource industries may also result where smells, dust, run-off, noise, and incidents of timber harvesting, mining, and oil and gas operations interfere with development. To protect resource areas from incompatible residential and second home development, Hawaii and many local communities have adopted exclusive agricultural and forestry districts. A few areas have adopted exclusive mineral resource districts.

2-5 *Essential water resource and related ecological systems should be protected.*

The majority of sensitive area programs have been adopted to protect the quantity and quality of inland and coastal waters and associated rich plant and animal life. Water is, of course, essential to all land uses and broader ecological systems. Ecological systems such as wetlands are important because of their commercial, aesthetic, educational, cultural, and scientific values. (See figure 22.)

Protection of water resources and ecological systems requires a multijurisdictional perspective and consideration of both individual impacts and the cumulative impact of existing and anticipated uses. (See table 12 for general performance standards.)

2-6 *Uses in hazard areas should be reasonably protected against hazard.*

Regulations adopted for flood, erosion, seismic, and other hazard areas are designed to protect adjacent lands, the public, and uses within areas from increased hazards. Flood plain regulations typically require that residences and other structures be elevated above the 100-year flood level or structurally flood-proofed to that level. This has sometimes been questioned as "protecting a man against himself." Nevertheless, damage to individual uses may burden public coffers and damage individuals other than the occupant. Flash flooding or storm waves threaten not only the owner of a house in a floodway or coastal high hazard area but also his family and guests. Unaware purchasers may be victimized. The public may be saddled with the costs of flood relief, flood control works, flood insurance, or other

---

[3]For example, the Vermont state site review act applying to larger developments denies permits where there is evidence that development or subdivision will endanger necessary wildlife habitat or endangered species and that "a reasonably acceptable alternative site is owned or controlled by the applicant which would allow the development or subdivision to fulfill its intended purpose."

[4]*See* note 21, Part 9, *infra.*

Figure 22

The tidal marsh land and sea interrelationships. (Source: J. Kusler, C. Harwood and R. Newton, *Our National Wetland Heritage, A Protection Guidebook,* **Environmental Law Institute, Washington, D.C., 1978.)**

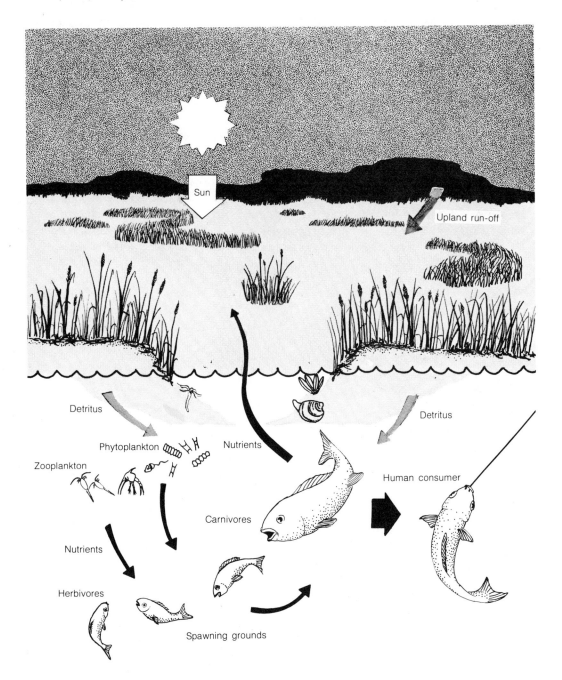

remedial measures. The community tax base and economic status suffer when factories, commercial establishments, or private homes are destroyed or seriously damaged.

2-7 *The impact of permitted uses should be minimized by controlling density, design, precise location, construction materials, methods of construction and operation, tree-cutting, dredging, and other features.*

As noted earlier, sensitive area programs emphasize careful control of uses to minimize development impact through performance standards and conditions attached to permits rather than outright prohibition of uses. This approach reduces waste and conserves resources but may result in the gradual destruction of an area unless cumulative impact is considered and the overall density of uses limited.

2-8 *Sensitive area programs should serve broad local, state, and national economic, social, and environmental goals.*

Sensitive area programs are often designed to serve broader land and water use management goals in several ways. Regulations require that proposed uses comply with applicable rules and regulations at all levels of government, including local zoning, subdivision, building, and other codes, state dredge and fill regulations, plumbing codes, housing codes, mining regulations, regional development impact regulations, federal subdivision regulations, and federal rules for fills in navigable water. Programs also require that proposed uses be consistent with public service policies governing roads, sewers, waters, and broader land and water plans.

In some instances, broader social and economic concerns justify intensive development of sensitive areas. However, all costs and benefits should be considered and the case for development clear. Developers should bear the burden of proof. All reasonable measures should be taken to minimize developmental impact.

Table 12

Land use standards for protecting water resources. This table outlines land use standards for protecting lake, stream, estuary, coastal, wetland, and ground water resources. The left hand column states general performance standards for protecting storage and conveyance of flood waters, fish and wildlife habitat, water supply, and transportation values. Standards applicable in a particular circumstance depend upon the characteristics of the water body and shoreland area and management objectives. Nevertheless, the simultaneous application of standards is often desirable for high quality lakes, streams, wetlands, estuaries, and coastal areas with a wide range of recreation, wildlife, and other values.

Standard	Common Uses Requiring Control	Impact of Uncontrolled Uses	Application of Standard
Prevent filling of water bodies by sand, gravel, solid wastes, structures, etc.	1. Land fill operations 2. Dredge and spoil disposal 3. Construction of roads, dikes, dams, reservoirs 4. Activities on adjacent lands or in the watershed causing sedimentation such as agricultural operations, timber cutting, road building, urban runoff, mining operation, channelization	*Irreversible* without great expense 1. Destruction of flood storage and flood conveyance capability 2. Accelerated runoff 3. Destruction of wildlife and vegetative values 4. Reduced ground water infiltration 5. Destruction of scenic, recreation, education, pollution control values 6. Interference with navigation	1. Control fills and activities which require fills such as dwellings, factories, roads 2. Establish buffer areas to reduce sedimentation from upland sources 3. Establish performance standards for upland uses
Protect shoreland and wetland vegetation from cutting, trampling, grading, etc.	1. Forestry (some instances) 2. Cranberry cultivation 3. Agriculture 4. Pollution from urban runoff, solid waste disposal, liquid waste 5. Off-the-road vehicles 6. Filling, grading 7. Soil removal 8. Construction of utility lines	*Reversible* unless a species is destroyed or the basic substrate is no longer suitable for revegetation 1. Accelerated runoff 2. Increased erosion 3. Damage to wildlife habitat 4. Destruction of scenic beauty 5. Destruction of natural storm barriers (*e.g.,* mangroves) 6. Reduced recreational, educational values (in some instances)	1. Adopt tree cutting and other regulations pertaining to vegetation removal 2. Restrict the use of off-the-road vehicles 3. Regulate grading, filling, soil removal, building construction, pollution sources
Protect aquatic wildlife (fish, birds, reptiles, mammals)	1. Habitat destruction (all types) 2. Hunting 3. Collecting 4. Filling, grading, dredging 5. Highway construction and vehicular traffic through wetlands 6. Off-the-road vehicles	*Reversible* (sometimes) 1. Destruction of endangered species (sometimes) 2. Reduced commercial fishing, harvesting of fur and game species 3. Reduced hunting and fishing opportunies 4. Reduced recreation, scenic, education, scientific study opportunities	1. Protect wildlife food supply and habitat 2. Regulate hunting 3. Protect buffer areas 4. Control use of off-the-road vehicles 5. Control pollution 6. Adopt tree cutting and wetland regulations

Table 12 (continued)

Standard	Common Uses Requiring Control	Impact of Uncontrolled Uses	Application of Standard
Protect source of light energy for aquatic plants by controlling water turbidity	1. Agricultural runoff 2. Dredging operations 3. Timber harvests 4. Mining 5. Urban runoff 6. Road building 7. Filling and grading for site preparation	*Reversible* 1. Destruction of vegetation 2. Destruction of aquatic life 3. Disturbance of wildlife habitat 4. Decreased recreation, educational, scientific study functions	1. Establish performance standards for wetland uses and uses in upland areas contributing sediment and other materials 2. Provide buffer areas
Control extraction of wetland soils	1. Grading 2. Muck farming 3. Mining (sand and gravel placer deposits) 4. Dredging, channelization 5. Topsoil removal 6. Construction of reservoirs	*Irreversible* (depends) 1. Disturbance or destruction of vegetation and wildlife habitat 2. Turbidity in waters 3. Decreased recreation, education, wildlife values	1. Control of mining, dredging, lagooning and other soil removal
Protect supply of water (quantity)	1. Agricultural drainage 2. Channelization of streams 3. Pumping of streams, lakes, ground water supplies 4. Establishment of dikes, levees, sea walls blocking exchange of tidal flows, flood waters 5. Drainage for mosquito control projects 6. Upstream reservoirs	*Reversible* (depends) 1. Destruction or deterioration of aquatic and wetland vegetation 2. Reduced acquifer recharge 3. Disturbance or destruction of species which depend upon wetlands for breeding, feeding, nutrients 4. Increased salinity (in some instances) due to decreased dilution resulting in damage to wildlife, vegetation, recreation opportunities	1. Control agricultural drainage, stream channelization, dams, water extractions 2. Manage reservoirs, flood gates, etc. to maintain water supply
Maintain free circulation of waters	1. Dikes, dams, levees, seawalls, roads 2. Irrigation projects 3. Fills, grades, buildings	*Reversible* (depends) 1. Deprive wetland plants and animals of nutrients from flood flows, other sources 2. Prevent the feeding and breeding of aquatic species in wetland areas 3. Build-up of salinity (in some instances)	1. Require that bridges and roads be constructed with minimum impedence to natural drainage 2. Design floodgates and seawalls to maintain tidal action 3. Control construction of dams, dikes, levees 4. Require that wetland structures be elevated in water bodies on pilings
Protect natural nutrient sources (principally phosphorus and nitrogen)	1. Upstream reservoirs 2. Dikes, levees, seawalls which prevent periodic flooding of wetland and deposition of nutrient rich sediments	*Reversible* 1. Reduced wetland wildlife, vegetation 2. Reduced scenic, educational, scientific values	1. Regulate dikes, dams, levees, seawalls

Table 12 (continued)

Standard	Common Uses Requiring Control	Impact of Uncontrolled Uses	Application of Standard
Prevent damaging influx of nutrients	1. Agricultural runoff throughout watershed 2. Urban runoff throughout watershed 3. Grading and fill operations 4. Sewage disposal discharges 5. Use of septic tanks	*Reversible* (depends) 1. Accelerated filling of lakes and wetlands with no outlet 2. Anaerobic bottom conditions, fish kills possible 3. Accelerated growth of aquatic plants (undesirable in some circumstances) 4. Tendency, in some instances, toward a monoculture 5. Altered plant and animal species 6. Fly and odor nuisances (possible)	1. Water pollution controls 2. Sanitary codes prohibiting septic tanks in wetlands and buffer areas 3. Regulations for agricultural activities to minimize nutrient inflows 4. Fill and grading regulations
Prevent influx of toxic chemicals	1. Application of pesticides, algicides to water bodies and to wetlands directly for mosquito control, weed control, algae control 2. Application of pesticides to agricultural, forestry uses throughout the watershed 3. Urban runoff from sheet flow and stream sewers 4. Municipal and industrial sewage disposal	*Reversible* (depends) 1. Destruction of aquatic and wetland plant and animal species including rare and endangered species 2. Destruction of vegetation (in some instances) 3. Threats to the public safety from swimming, eating fish and shellfish; waterfowl exposed to toxic chemicals	1. Tight control of toxic chemicals throughout watershed areas 2. Tight point source pollution controls 3. Maintenance of shoreland buffers
Prevent damaging thermal changes	1. Reservoirs 2. Utility plants (serious offender) 3. Industrial uses 4. Sediment loading from road building, agriculture, etc.	*Reversible* (sometimes) 1. Destruction of wetland wildlife, alteration in species composition 2. Decrease in recreation, scientific study, educational activities	1. Thermal pollution standards for point source discharges 2. Control of agriculture and road building to reduce water turbidity, sedimentation.

Part **3**

GENERAL CONSIDERATIONS IN PROGRAM DESIGN AND IMPLEMENTATION

Program implementation requires program design consistent with technical, political, legal, and budgetary constraints. Many of the goals discussed here are considered later at greater length.

3-1 *Sensitive area programs should build upon existing land use and resource management programs.*

Local sensitive area programs are typically adopted pursuant to zoning and subdivision control enabling acts. The regulations overlay more traditional land use regulations and are administered and enforced through existing land use control mechanisms such as planning commissions, zoning boards, and zoning administrators. This approach is cost-effective and integrates sensitive areas with broader land use control programs. Nevertheless, local land use control efforts often lack the necessary data and expertise to administer sensitive area controls effectively. Additional data and technical assistance are needed.

At the state level, sensitive area programs must be authorized by an explicit flood plain, wetland, shoreland, or other enabling act. State agencies are not ordinarily authorized to exercise land use control functions. Nevertheless, some state coastal programs depend on the "networking"[1] of existing planning, land use planning, and

[1] With such an approach (*e.g.*, the Massachusetts coastal zone program), a program is implemented through a combination of existing wetland, floodplain, pollution control, and other statutes.

regulatory functions rather than a new statute. Even where a new statute is adopted, state programs often utilize the manpower and expertise of existing agencies and depend on existing legislation such as pollution, fills and dredging, and park controls.

3-2 *Programs should consider local, state, and national interests.*

Most programs discover that a strong local role is politically required in sensitive area regulation. Those most directly affected by decisions desire strong involvement in policy formation. However, a state or federal role in standard-setting is also desirable to reflect broader interests.

The need to reflect local, state, and national interests has often resulted in a hierarchy of policies. These include, first, general federal guidelines (such as the National Coastal Zone, Flood Insurance, and Scenic and Wild Rivers acts), then more specific state statutes and administrative regulations, and finally, even more specific local ordinances.

3-3 *Programs should balance public interests and private expectations and options.*

Balancing short- and long-term public resource management needs with land-owner rights and expectations has proven necessary. The issue is not just legal sufficiency. Sensitive area programs are legislative acts and depend upon electoral support. The balancing of public and private interests may be reflected in many program aspects including lists for permitted and prohibited uses and performance standards for permitted uses.

3-4 *Programs should insure fair treatment of landowners, procedural due process, and expeditious review of permits.*

Opposition to sensitive area regulations is commonly based on fears that the regulations will ignore landowner interests, be arbitrarily administered, or require lengthy and costly permit reviews. Developers are often willing to accept tight regulations if they believe competitors will be similarly regulated and if review procedures are certain and swift. Carefully stated statutory or ordinance standards encourage impartial review of permits. A sound data base, agency expertise, and genuine consideration of landowner needs are also important. Procedural due process is encouraged through public hearings, careful permit review procedures, and court or judicial appeals. Combined permit processing procedures can expedite permit review.[2]

3-5 *Programs must comply with statutory and constitutional requirements.*

Programs must comply with statutory and administrative procedures to avoid court suits and gain political acceptability. Common procedural requirements include notice and hearing prior to adoption of regulations and preparation of environmental impact statements for major agency activities. Regulations must also meet broader state and federal constitutional tests pertaining to due process and protection of private property. (See Part 8 below.)

3-6 *Programs must balance the interests of competing political groups to achieve political acceptability.*

Sensitive area programs depend on legislative and public support for adoption and funding. Political acceptability depends on many factors including the balancing of competing interests (*e.g.,* farmers interested in draining wetlands and hunters interested in their preservation), and simultaneous consideration of public, private,

[2]*See* Bosselman, F., *The Permit Explosion,* The Urban Land Institute, Wash., D.C. (1976).

state, and local interests. It depends in part on reasonable program cost, public awareness, public involvement in policy formation and program design, and the availability of data to demonstrate the importance of areas to states and localities. Accommodation of competing political interests is often best achieved through involvement of competing groups in the design of enabling and implementing efforts.

3-7 *Programs must be technically sound and based on adequate data.*

Standards for individual uses and the evaluation of permits must in many circumstances be based on scientific and engineering determinations. Mapping flood plains, wetlands, mineral resource, and other districts requires technical surveys and analysis. Zone boundaries must coincide with soil, wildlife, flood, and other resource parameters even where they cross roads, property lines, and other features. The rationality and fairness of critical area regulations depend, in large measure, on this technical base. Rationality and fairness, in turn, determine political and legal acceptability.

3-8 *Programs must be capable of administration.*

Regulations are of little value if they cannot be administered or enforced due to unrealistic definition of criteria, inadequate map scales, or complicated project evaluation criteria. Administrative needs must be reflected in program design, such as the use of air photos as base maps to facilitate location of sensitive area boundaries.

3-9 *Programs must be cost-effective.*

Limited budgets are a major constraint on data gathering, data analysis, standard-setting, administration, and enforcement. Consequently, programs must incorporate cost-saving techniques. They should maximize use of existing data, utilize air photos, define and regulate on an area-by-area or case-by-case basis, share program responsibilities with several levels of government, involve interest groups and private citizens in data gathering and permit evaluation, and shift a portion of the data gathering burden and program costs to developers.

3-10 *Programs must involve and educate the public.*

Public support is essential for program enforcement. Public involvement in program design and implementation can help develop this support. Direct public involvement may take several forms: (1) referenda[3]; (2) public hearings and workshops on proposed plans and policies; (3) public hearings on permit proposals; (4) citizen involvement on special committees; and (5) citizen and interest group involvement in data gathering, permit, and environmental impact statement evaluation and monitoring efforts.

Although public involvement is desirable, public hearings are sometimes overdone. In addition, public inputs may be of limited value on such highly technical issues as tolerance limits for rare and endangered species.

Public education is also necessary to gain support and enforce regulations. Public education concerning hydrological, biological, and other technical issues may take the form of workshops, public hearings, manuals, films, slide shows, lectures, and personal consultations.

3-11 *Programs must develop priorities for allocation of funds and manpower.*

Sensitive area programs invariably discover that it is impossible to deal with all issues or areas at once. Priorities must be developed in mapping, administration, and

---

[3]*E.g.,* the California coastal zone program was originally created by referendum.

enforcement efforts. For example, mapping is often carried out first for threatened areas. Programs often place primary emphasis upon case-by-case evaluation of individual development permits.

3-12 *Programs must develop tangible, incremental approaches to land use decision-making while dealing with the cumulative impact of development.*

While piecemeal implementation on a priority basis is required by scarce funds and manpower, the cumulative impact of development must also be considered. This can be achieved through carefully prepared overall policies for environmental quality; performance standards for individual uses which take into account overall policies; the assessment of cumulative impact in evaluating individual permits; and limitations on ultimate use density.[4]

3-13 *Programs must insure the necessary level of expertise for program administration and enforcement.*

Local sensitive area programs are often handicapped by a lack of biological, botanical, engineering, and other types of expertise needed for data gathering and analysis and permit evaluation. The lack of professional staff may be compensated for by utilizing expert citizen groups and local science teachers, technical advisory committees, and consultants. Regulations may require that developers hire consultants and undertake necessary technical evaluations. Technical assistance is also often available from state and federal agencies and nearby universities and colleges.

3-14 *Programs should insure certainty for future land uses through written rules while at the same time providing flexibility in the consideration of individual uses and areas.*

Regulatory agencies often favor flexibility in evaluating individual areas and uses through adoption of general, unquantified use standards. Landowners favor detailed written rules which provide certainty in the use of land. To balance the need for both, programs make widespread use of special permit procedures combined with quantified and non-quantified performance standards. Such an approach can take into account the highly diverse factual circumstances encountered within individual sensitive areas and the varying impacts of specific uses. Often several types of standards are combined:[5] (1) clear statement of regulatory goals and findings of fact; (2) minimal quantified standards governing such engineering topics as flood protection elevations and pollution discharges; (3) general guidelines concerning the compatibility of uses with environmental values and adjacent uses; and (4) a more general listing of factors and considerations pertaining to public welfare to be taken into account in processing individual permits.

3-15 *Programs must emphasize monitoring and enforcement to insure implementation of policies.*

Monitoring and enforcement are often the weakest phases of sensitive area programs. Monitoring is particularly troublesome for state programs with limited field enforcement personnel and offices tens or hundreds of miles from regulated areas. State and local monitoring and enforcement efforts can often be strengthened by periodic air photos or aerial surveillance, field inspections on a spot check basis, and involvement of interest groups, such as hunting clubs and bird watches, to help monitor areas and report violations.

[4]*See* discussion in section 5-5 below.
[5]*See* discussion in section 5-10 below.

3-16 *Programs should be coordinated with tax policies and public works construction.*

Sensitive area regulations are often undermined by inconsistent tax policies. Sensitive areas are often taxed at potential development value despite tight state or conjunctive state/local controls. The failure to integrate tax and regulatory and taxation functions is due to separation of governmental functions (*e.g.*, regulation by a state regulatory agency, taxation by a local unit of government) and the belief that regulations may at some point in time be modified to permit development. Nevertheless, continued high taxes lead to landowner complaints and, in some instances, court decisions that regulations take property without compensation. To remedy this inconsistency, several critical area acts require reduced taxation consistent with development controls.[6]

Inconsistency between public works policies and regulation are another common problem. In general, the units of government adopting regulations are not forced to apply the regulations to their own public buildings, road building, construction of dikes, dams and levees, or other public works. In other words, a city may prohibit stuctures in private floodway areas and then construct schools, bridges, libraries, or other public uses on similarly endangered public lands. Such blatant contradictions in policy are more common than one would suppose and are due in part to the separation of regulatory and public works planning and construction functions in state and local government. Nevertheless, more subtle contradictions are also important such as the extension of sewer, water, and roads to critical areas where regulations prevent development.

To reduce contradictions, an executive order in Wisconsin requires that state public works comply with flood plain regulations. A New York flood plain statute requires flood protection measures for public works.[7] The Washington shoreland protection statute requires broad coordination of public and private policies.[8]

---

[6]For example, N.Y. Kenney's Consol. L. Ann., §25-0302 (Supp. 1977-78) provides:
   The placing of any tidal wetlands under a land-use regulation which restricts its use shall be deemed a limitation on the use of such wetlands for the purposes of property tax valuation, in the same manner as if an easement or right had been acquired under the same municipal law. Assessment shall be based on present use under the restricting regulation.
Similarly, the Washington shoreline protection act provides that the restrictions imposed by the statute "shall be considered by the county assessor in establishing the fair market value of the property." Wash. Rev. Stat. §90.58-290 (Supp. 1977).

[7]N.Y. Kenny's Consol. L. Ann., §36-0111 (Supp. 1977-78) provides:
   1. State agencies shall take affirmative action to minimize flood hazards and losses in connection with state-owned and state-financed buildings, roads and other facilities, the disposition of state lands and properties, the administration of state and state-assisted planning programs, and the preparation and administration of state building, sanitary and other pertinent codes. Such action shall include, but not be limited to, requirements for the evaluation and reduction of flood hazards in the siting, planning, construction and maintenance of such facilities and the administration of such programs; needed and economically feasible flood-proofing and other protective measures of existing state facilities; and appropriate flood hazard restrictions binding upon purchasers and persons acquiring state lands and properties, or interests therein, and their successors.

[8]Wash. Rev. Stat., §90.58.340 (Supp. 1977) provides:
   All state agencies, counties, and public and municipal corporations shall review administration and management policies, regulations, plans, and ordinances relative to lands under their respective jurisdictions adjacent to the shorelines of the state so as to achieve a use policy on said land consistent with the policy of this chapter, the guidelines, and the master programs for the shorelines of the state. The department may develop recommendations for land use control for such lands. Local governments shall, in developing regulations for such areas, take into

3-17 *Programs should, in some circumstances, combine regulatory and non-regulatory approaches.*

Regulations have advantages of low cost, continued private use of land, and sustained tax revenues. However, they are subject to limitations. (1) They do not, in most instances, apply to public uses (local, state, and federal). (2) They rarely apply to existing uses (except for major additions, rebuilding, abandonment). (3) They cannot, in most instances, prevent all private use of land without constitutionally taking private property. (4) They cannot allocate private lands to active public uses such as hiking and recreation without payment of compensation. Political opposition is another common limitation.

Some state and local programs authorize easement or fee acquistion as well as regulation to achieve broader objectives. For example, the Michigan natural rivers act authorizes both regulation and fee or easement acquisition.[9] The Connecticut floodway statute authorizes the regulatory agency to take land and structures within defined encroachment lines whenever the agency finds they "constitute a hazard to life and property in the event of flood."[10] The Massachusetts coastal wetland protection statute authorizes the administering agency to take a fee or easement interest in land if a court finds that regulations take property.[11]

Acquisition is selectively applied to areas requiring total prohibition of private uses or public access. However, acquisition is also subject to limitations including high costs, political opposition in some circumstances, and loss of tax base. Easements have been widely advocated as an alternative to fee acquisition but not widely applied due to high costs (up to 90% of development value) and enforcement problems.[12]

---

consideration any recommendations developed by the department as well as any other state agencies or units of local government.

[9]Mich. Comp. L.. §281.765 (Supp. 1977-78) provides:

Sec. 5 The commission may acquire lands or interests in lands adjacent to a designated natural river for the purpose of maintaining or improving the river and its environment in conformance with the purposes of the designation and the plan. Interests which may be acquired include, but are not limited to, easements designed to provide for preservation and to limit development, without providing public access and use. Lands or interests in lands shall be acquired under this act only with the consent of the owner.

[10]Conn. Gen. Stat. Ann., §25-4d (1975).

[11]Mass. Ann. L., CH. 131, Sec. 40A (1974 & Supp. 1977-78) provides:

Any person having an interest in land affected by any such order, may within ninety days after receiving notice thereof, petition the superior court in equity to determine whether such an order so restricts the use of his property as to deprive him of the practical uses thereof and is therefore an unreasonable exercise of the police power because the order constitutes the equivalent of a taking without compensation. If the court finds the order to be an unreasonable exercise of the police power, as aforesaid, the court shall enter a finding that such order shall not affect any other land than that of the petitioner.

[12]For a general discussion of easements *see* Cunningham, "Scenic Easements in the Highway Beautification Program," 45 *Denver L.J.* 168 (1968); Jordahl, "Conservation and Scenic Easements: An Experience Resume," 39 *Land Econ.* 343 (1963).

Part 4

DEFINITION OF
SENSITIVE AREAS

The tension between the ideal and the practical is particularly relevant to the definition of sensitive areas. Existing efforts to define areas usually employ simple and direct criteria. They emphasize political acceptability and administrative feasibility rather than scientific purity. Statewide resource analyses rarely occur prior to the adoption of enabling legislation, or even later during program administration. In addition, extensive study seldom precedes formulation of definitions, even for statutes quite specific in definition criteria such as the 100-year flood plain. Attempts to map sensitive areas are carried out on a case-by-case or area-by-area basis.

Despite the lack of rigor, existing sensitive area definition criteria appear quite successful. This is due partly to the application of special permit procedures and case-by-case data gathering to refine regulatory policies during the administration of programs. Special permit procedures identify site-specific natural resource values and hazards and apply development standards consistent with these characteristics.

Attempts to develop and apply highly systematic approaches could have killed or hindered many programs. Wrangling over definitions, political fear, and too much cerebral activity could occur at the expense of action. The ultimate test for definition criteria is usefulness. To meet this test, definitions must be politically acceptable, rational, legally and scientifically sound, and inexpensive to use.

Table 13

Types of land considered critical. This table outlines types of land considered "critical" or sensitive by statutes and planning reports. Note that some of these definitions address natural resource areas and historic and development sites.

Term Used	Statute or Report	Classes Designated	"Tests" for Criticalness Indicated or Implied
"Area of Critical State Concern"	Florida Environmental Land & Water Management Act of 1972	Section 380.05: (1) area containing or having a significant impact upon environmental, historical, natural, or archeological resources of regional or statewide importance. (2) area significantly affected by or having a significant effect upon an existing or proposed major public facility or other area of major public investment. (3) proposed area of major development potential which may include a proposed site of a new community designated in a state land development plan. (4) an area subject to periodic flooding.	"Regional or statewide importance:" See also Section 380.05 which provides that the state planning agency must, upon recommending critical areas, "state the reasons why the particular area proposed is of critical concern to the state or region, the dangers that would result from uncontrolled or inadequate development of the area, and the advantages that would be achieved from the development of the area in a coordinated manner . . ."
"Critical Areas"	Maine State Register of Critical Areas Act of 1974	Section 3312: "Areas containing or potentially containing plant and animal life or geological features worthy of preservation in their natural condition, or other natural features of significant scenic, scientific or historical value."	Section 3314: "A. The unique or exemplary qualities of the area or site; B. The intrinsic fragility of the area or site to alteration or destruction; C. The present or future threat of alteration or destruction; D. The economic implications of inclusion of a critical area in the register."
"Areas of Critical Concern"	Minn. Critical Areas Act of 1973	Section 116G.05: "An area significantly affected by, or having a significant effect upon an existing or proposed governmental development which is intended to serve substantial numbers of persons beyond the vicinity in which the development is located and which tends to generate substantial development or	Section 116G.02: "Areas that perform functions of greater than local significance," that development decreases "their value and utility for public purposes," or "unreasonably endanger life and property." Section 116G.06 requires the designated agency to "state the reasons why the particular area proposed is of

Table 13 (continued)

Term Used	Statute or Report	Classes Designated	"Tests" for Criticalness Indicated or Implied
		urbanization. (2) "An area containing or having significant impact upon historical, natural, scientific or cultural resources of regional or statewide importance."	critical concern to the state or region, the dangers that would result from uncontrolled or inappropriate development of the area and the advantages that would result from the development of the area in a coordinated manner . . ."
"Area of State Interest"	Colorado Land Use Act of 1974	Section 106-7-201: "1. Mineral resource areas; 2. Natural hazard areas; 3. Areas containing or having significant impact upon, historical, natural, or archaeological resources of statewide importance; and 4. Areas around key facilities in which development may have a material effect upon the facility or the surrounding community."	106-7-101, 106-7-102: (1) "Protection of the utility, value and future of all lands within the state." (2) State "significance" or "interest" (3) Hazard
"Areas of Critical or More Than Local Concern"	Wyoming State Land Use Planning Act of 1975	Section 9-850 "Areas defined and designated by the commission where uncontrolled or incompatible large scale development could result in damage to the environment, life or property, where the short or long term public interest is of more than local significance. Such areas are subject to definition by the commission as to their extent and shall include but are not limited to: —fragile or historical lands, —natural hazard lands, —renewable resource lands, —new town lands, and —such additional areas as the commission determines to be of more than local concern."	Section 9-850: (1) Damage to environment, life or property (2) Of more than local significance

Table 13 (continued)

Term Used	Statute or Report	Classes Designated	"Tests" for Criticalness Indicated or Implied
"Areas of Particular Concern"	Coastal Zone Management Act of 1972	Geographical areas of particular concern are not defined within the 1972 Act. Administrative guidelines promulgated by N.O.A.A. for coastal zone program development grants spell out the following "representative factors": (1) Areas of unique, scarce, fragile, or vulnerable natural habitat, physical feature, historical significance, cultural value, and scenic importance (2) Areas of high natural productivity or essential habitat for living resources including fish, wildlife, and various trophic levels in the food web critical to their well-being (3) Areas of substantial recreational value or opportunity (4) Areas where developments and facilities are dependent upon the utilization of, or access to, coastal waters (5) Areas of unique geologic or topographic significance to industrial or commercial development (6) Areas of urban concentration where shoreline utilization and water uses are highly competitive (7) Areas of significant hazard if developed, due to storms, slides, erosion, settlement, etc. (8) Areas needed to protect, maintain, or replenish coastal lands or resources, such as areas including coastal flood plains, aquifer recharge areas, sand, dunes, coral and other reefs, beaches, offshore sand deposits, and mangrove stands	Section 306(c)(9) of the 1972 Act requires that coastal zone management programs "make provisions for procedures whereby specific areas may be designated for the purpose of preserving or restoring them for their conservation, recreational, ecological, or aesthetic values." The guidelines for coastal zone management grants further clarify land to be considered of particular concern. They state that "It should be noted that geographical areas of particular concern are likely to encompass not only the more-often cited areas of significant natural value or importance, but also: (a) Transitional or intensely developed areas where reclamation, restoration, public access and other actions are especially needed (b) Those areas especially suited for intensive use or development. In addition, immediacy of need should be a major consideration in determining particular concern."

Table 13 (continued)

Term Used	Statute or Report	Classes Designated	"Tests" for Criticalness Indicated or Implied

Areas of "Statewide Critical Concern"	*Summary Report,* California Office of Planning and Research (1973)	—Park, reserve and wilderness areas
		—Recreation, access and connecting links
		—Historic, archeological and cultural resources
		—Wildlife habitats
		—Forest lands
		—Agricultural lands
		—Mineral areas
		—Water sources
		—Energy sources
		—Geologic hazard areas:
		  Earthquake shaking
		  Volcanic eruptions
		  Tsunami
		  Fault displacement
		  Landslides
		  Subsidence
		  Erosion activity
		  Expansive soil
		—Fire hazard areas
		—Flood-prone areas
		—Critical air areas
			(1) Scarcity
			(2) Hazard
			(3) Importance to society
			(4) Accessibility
			(5) Of greater than local significance

"Sensitive Areas"	Missouri Department of Community Affairs. Part II of *Missouri: Physical Characteristics and Constraints for Development,* Part III (Areas Sensitive to Development in Missouri) (1973)	"Any area(s) of land where uncontrolled growth and development has resulted in significant damage to important historic, cultural or aesthetic values, natural systems, processes, or resources which are of more than local significance or would unreasonably endanger the life and property as a result of natural hazards. Such areas may include —*areas with known or potential nonrenewable natural resources* including minerals and mineral fuels, the extraction and use of which will be required for continued maintenance and development of our economy, —*areas with high susceptibility for groundwater pollution,* —*areas with known or potential construction and*	(1) Hazard (2) Importance to society (3) Of greater than local significance and A. *Growth and Development Characteristics* of the area to include stabilized areas, potential growth areas, and rapid growth areas B. *Physiographic and/or geologic limitation* of the area to include: a) thin soil cover, severe slopes, solid waste disposal limitations, septic tank limitations b) karst topography and related features c) soil limitations d) erosion potential e) high water table f) serious flooding problems g) water supply limitations h) extensive mined out areas with collapse potential i) scenic areas C. *Provisions for land use controls* in the area from

Table 13 (continued)

Term Used	Statute or Report	Classes Designated	"Tests" for Criticalness Indicated or Implied
		land development problems related to soil, bedrock and/or topography including, but not limited to, unstable soils and slopes, thin soil cover, high water table and karst topography and associated features, —*areas subjected to periodic flooding,* including floodplains and areas subjected to backwater and flash flooding, —*areas with a history of earthquake activity* including those in which earthquakes have been accompanied by displacement along a fault as recent as the Pleistocene epoch of geologic time as well as those areas in which earthquakes have no known relationship to faults at the surface. —*lake and river shorelands development* of a significant nature, —*rare or valuable ecosystems,* —*significant developed or undeveloped agricultural lands,* —*scenic, archaeologic, or historic areas;* and —*forest lands."*	the standpoint of the existence or non-existence of county planning *and* zoning (not just planning) in the area and, generally, the extent to which it is enforced D. *Pollution problems experienced* to include air, surface water, groundwater, and sight pollution
"Critical Resource Area"	University of Wisconsin, *The Investigation of a Critical Resource Information Program (CRIP) for Wisconsin* (1974) prepared under contract with the Wisconsin Department of Administration	—Forest —Wetlands —Grasslands —Water resources (groundwater, surface water) —Agricultural land —Mineral deposits —Special geological features —Historical, architectural and archeological structures and sites —Scenic areas	"A 'significant' natural or cultural resource is or will be in short supply in a portion of the state, the entire state or the nation. In addition, a significant resource is valuable in terms of one or more of the following: economic value, recreational value, aesthetic value, research value, educational value, philosophical value or human health or safety." "The term critical applies to geographical defined

Table 13 (continued)

Term Used	Statute or Report	Classes Designated	"Tests" for Criticalness Indicated or Implied
			areas within which one or more significant resources are found." Relative critically of a resource depends upon —Resource quantity and size —Location —Cost of maintenance or preservation —Degree of present or future scarcity —Extent to which the resource may be an integral component of the life support system of man

"Critical Environmental Area"	Virginia Division of State Planning and Community Affairs, *Critical Environmental Areas* (1972)	"1. a) Groupings of historic buildings located with relatively undisturbed contiguous natural areas.
		b) Roads through undisturbed countryside containing scenery and buildings uniquely historic and representative of Virginia.
		c) Natural wildlife habitats supporting unique fish or wildlife populations, species whose range in the State is restricted or whose numbers are so limited as to warrant special consideration.
		d) Natural areas possessing unique physical characteristics as:
		  1) Beaches having unusually white sand, exceptional width, good water quality, or dune development.
		  2) Bluffs having unusual exposed geologic strata, or beautiful vistas.
		  3) Inland river banks having wild character, profuse blooming flora, unusual flora communities, unusual crystalline beauty, or excep-
			1. "Area which has unusual natural or man-made features which are worthy of protection by State or local government."

Table 13 (continued)

Term Used	Statute or Report	Classes Designated	"Tests" for Criticalness Indicated or Implied
		tional water quality. 4) Rivers with churning action, having visual interest, waterfalls or sinking streams. 5) High altitude lakes or elevated lakes in pocosins. 6) Unaltered mountain covers, significant peaks, natural arches, caves or tunnels. 7) Monadnocks, karst outcrops, and other unusual geologic formations. 8) Spectacular gorges. 9) Climax forest communities of mature individuals. 10) Forest communities at range limits such as balsam, fir, red spruce and arboritae. 11) Endangered forest species such as native chestnut and elm.	
		e/Areas possessing qualities suitable for future park development such as: 1) Being accessible from population centers and well travelled tourist routes. 2) Having good scenic qualities, yet relatively level terrain to permit the construction of any necessary facilities. 3) Possessing bodies of water or potential pond and lake sites. 4) Being a relatively large and undeveloped tract.	2) "Area" which is crucial to an ecological system and should be protected from inappropriate development. Such areas will not readily support intense development or may be hazardous to the public health and safety.
		"3) a) existing or potential urbanization whose rate or intensity of growth exceeds the capacity of an area to support it without itself being substantially despoiled. b) A major public or pri-	3. "Area includes certain natural, scenic, or historic areas which are presently endangered, or in obvious danger of destruction, alteration, or loss because of the activities of man."

Table 13 (continued)

Term Used	Statute or Report	Classes Designated	"Tests" for Criticalness Indicated or Implied
		vate facility or improvement which would significantly alter the natural or historic environment. c) Power generation and transmission facilities or any facility which might pollute the water or air, or despoil the natural, scenic, or historical qualities of an area." "4) a) Parks b) Historic preserves c) Game and fish management d) Trails e) Public forests f) Scenic areas g) Highways and parkways h) Water impoundment sites "2) a) Flood plain areas with special flood hazards and those which are located within the one hundred year flood level. b) Areas of severe topography where it is difficult to locate structures. Steep slopes with shallow soil profiles making it impractical to install subsurface sewage disposal facilities, to find adequate soil for cut and fill, and to find sufficient water of adequate quality for a domestic water supply. Areas where underlying rock formlations make it impossible for rock or earth slides to take place after heavy precipitation. c) Low wetlands which are regularly inundated at high tide. These areas are critical to the production of detritus, an important link in the food chain for nearly all marine life, and serve as spawning, breeding, or feeding	"Area appropriate for public use through future acquisition by State or local agencies. Many types of natural areas could qualify for public acquisition."

Table 13 (continued)

Term Used	Statute or Report	Classes Designated	"Tests" for Criticalness Indicated or Implied
		grounds for many marine species.	
		"5) a) Natural wildlife habitats of high productivity for uses by man. b) Primary agricultural production areas. c) Primary forest production areas d) Mineral resource areas to include ore deposits and major quarries."	"Area which can be considered to contain a primary state resource. Those can include wildlife, mineral, or agricultural pollution." Program also considers: —uniqueness —urban proximity factor —threat
"Districts of Critical State Concern"	American Law Institute Model Land Development Code, Art. 7-201	Section 7-201 "(a) an area significantly affected by, or having a significant effect upon, an existing or proposed major public facility or other area of major public investment; (b) an area containing or having a significant impact upon historical, natural or environmental resources of regional or statewide importance; or (c) a proposed site of a new community designated in a State Land Development Plan, together with a reasonable amount of surrounding land."	Section 7-201 —Regional or statewide importance —In designating areas of critical state concern the state land planning agency is to indicate the reasons why the area is designated, the dangers that might result from uncontrolled development, and the advantages of development in a coordinated manner.

Whatever approach is adopted, all energies and funds should not be directed to definition. The success of a program often depends more on the reasonableness of development standards than the precision of the original definitions.

4-1 *Efforts to define sensitive areas should, from their onset, consider how the definitions may be used to achieve practical goals through specific implementation techniques.*

Efforts to define areas without specific program goals or implementation techniques have proven of limited value. For example, communities with vague definitions of flood plain areas have usually found new definition efforts necessary prior to applying flood plain regulations.

4-2 *Definition criteria should be linked to specific development control policies.*

Sensitive area definitions usually serve two major objectives: (1) classification of the resource base and (2) identification of areas where particular development policies are appropriate. The two objectives are complimentary although some resource classifications may not be appropriate for specific development policies.[1] For example, floodways can be defined with many different perspectives—the 25-year, 50-year, 100-year, or 500-year floodway—with varying permissible backwater effects for each magnitude of flood. (See figure 23.) However, the 100-year floodway with one foot of less backwater effect is usually considered appropriate for performance standards requiring control of fills and structures. For application of such a standard, definition and mapping of the 10-year floodway would be of little use.

In general, definition criteria should anticipate one of two development control policies: (1) complete prohibition of all or particular types of development and uses or (2) application of specific performance standards.

4-3 *Definitions should be linked to features readily identifiable on the ground.*

Sensitive area definitions should include such natural resource features as topographic contours, soils, and vegetation. (See figure 24.) These can be identified by landowners, permit officers, and the enforcement agencies through air photos and field inspections. More or less arbitrary boundaries, such as a 1,000-foot coastal zone, may apply where a single overriding resource characteristic cannot be used. Where political and administrative considerations require arbitrary boundaries, subzones, such as coastal wetlands within broader coastal zones, should be identified.

---

[1]Recognition that designation of areas for regulatory purposes does not necessarily follow from classification of the resource base has led to various proposals that areas be first mapped descriptively, then analyzed, and finally remapped for regulatory purposes. This approach has an intuitive appeal but is expensive and time consuming. In addition, attempts to separate "descriptive mapping" from mapping for regulatory purposes often assume a false objectivity for descriptive mapping.

To be sure, slope areas of more than 10 percent can be mapped with objectivity since only a single, objective parameter—elevation—must be assessed. However, the descriptive mapping of a "wetland" must take into account a much larger number of variables (water levels, vegetation, etc.) with no universal agreement concerning the combination of variables which may be said to characterize a "wetland." The identification of a "coastal" or "shoreland" area is even more subjective since an enormous number of physical variables may be found within such areas and there is little agreement concerning the combination of characteristics which may be said to characterize "coastal" or "shoreland" areas other than proximity to water. In short, even objective description of critical areas requires subjective judgment and analysis of many factors. Any attempt, therefore, to characterize descriptive mapping of wetland, flood plain, *etc.*, as wholly objective is misleading unless definition critieria are first agreed upon.

Figure 23

What is a "regulatory floodway"?

THE REGULATORY FLOODWAY DEPENDS UPON THE SIZE OF FLOOD
CHOSEN AS A BASIS FOR REGULATION

For the purposes of this report, the regulatory floodway is defined as the calculated unobstructed
portion of a flood plain consisting of the stream channel and overbank areas necessary to convey
flood flows for a selected flood discharge without increasing flood levels more than a selected
increment above natural levels.

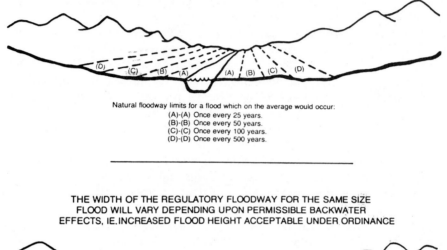

Natural floodway limits for a flood which on the average would occur:
(A)-(A) Once every 25 years.
(B)-(B) Once every 50 years.
(C)-(C) Once every 100 years.
(D)-(D) Once every 500 years.

THE WIDTH OF THE REGULATORY FLOODWAY FOR THE SAME SIZE
FLOOD WILL VARY DEPENDING UPON PERMISSIBLE BACKWATER
EFFECTS, IE. INCREASED FLOOD HEIGHT ACCEPTABLE UNDER ORDINANCE

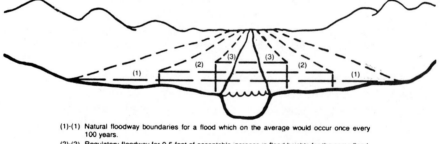

(1)-(1) Natural floodway boundaries for a flood which on the average would occur once every
100 years.
(2)-(2) Regulatory floodway for 0.5 foot of acceptable increase in flood heights for the same flood.
(3)-(3) Regulatory floodway for 1 foot acceptable increase in flood heights for the same flood.

4-4 *Sensitive area definition criteria and maps may be established through a
hierarchical process. General criteria in statutes should progress to more specific
criteria and maps developed by state agencies and local units of government.*

Efforts to define sensitive areas often involve a four-step process. (1) A legislature
adopts an enabling statute which defines the general classes of land subject to
regulation and authorizes an administrative agency to adopt more specific criteria
and to map areas. (2) The administrative agency adopts administrative regulations
which establish more specific definition criteria and procedures to supplement the
general criteria of the enabling structure. (3) The administrative agency, working in
conjunction with local units of government, conducts data gathering and actual
mapping of individual areas often on a case-by-case basis. (4) Local units of
government refine definition criteria and maps for local zoning and other types of
regulation.

4-5 *At an early stage in the definition process, agreement should be reached on such basic terms as "sensitive," "area," "critical," and "define," to facilitate understanding and to provide the basis for statute and ordinance drafting.*

Confusion in sensitive area programs results unless agreement is reached on these terms. There are no right or wrong definitions and there is no widely agreed upon meaning, but definitions are desirable. See the glossary of this report for examples.

4-6 *Priorities in sensitive area mapping should reflect geographical location and threat of development.*

Sensitive area programs invariably map resources on an area-by-area basis due to restraints on available funding and manpower. This will be discussed at greater length in the data gathering recommendations below.

4-7 *No single test adequately defines all types of sensitive areas. A variety of tests should be applied.*

A variety of legislative criteria or tests have been incorporated in enabling statutes and ordinances, including: (1) ability or inability of lands to meet particular needs of society; (2) uniqueness or rarity of lands; (3) the degree to which lands remain in a natural condition; (4) the degree to which the lands are of greater than local concern; (5) the need to preserve resources for future as well as present generations; (6) hazards or threats to society; (7) the sensitivity of areas; (8) the threat of irreversible harm; and (9) the adequacy of existing controls. (See table 14.) Three functional categories of critical or sensitive lands are suggested by these tests. Lands may be "critically scarce," meeting particular needs of society and in diminishing supply; "critically hazardous," demonstrating hazards or threats to society ; and "critically threatened," with some special value or hazard and under immediate threat of development.

4-8 *In some circumstances, enabling acts, administrative regulations, and ordinances should distinguish between "important" and "critical" lands within a type of area and identify subzones.*

Definition problems arise more often in formulating precise criteria for mapping and application of standards, such as the the 100-year plain versus and the 50-year flood plain, than with the selection of general definition criteria such as flooding.[2] Selective criteria reduce the total area subject to regulatory control, permit the application of tight development restrictions to limited special areas, promote multiple uses of lands, assist in planning and standard-setting efforts, and aid in the processing of proposals for development.

For some areas it has been necessary to identify subzones such as wetland and flood prone areas within broader coastal zones. Subzone identification helps apply specific resource protection standards. (See figures 8, 9, 10, 25.)

---

[2]The general identification of an area as a sand and gravel deposit, wetland, or agricultural land does little to indicate its specific potential or suggest development standards. More specific documentation of values and hazards is essential for detailed policy-making, and regulation.

For example, the identification of an area with soils suitable for agriculture does little to resolve conflicts as to highest and best use between agriculture, forestry, and wildlife or land subdivision without further information pertaining to slope, available water, existing uses, land ownership, and other factors. Similarly, flood maps indicating land "subject to flooding" suggest little. Flood damage reduction measures may be unneccesary if the area is subject to inundation once every 500 years, while tight regulation may be justified if the area is flooded monthly.

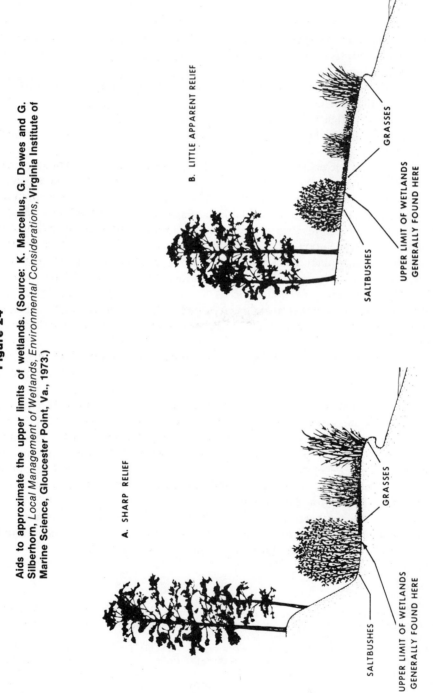

Figure 24

Aids to approximate the upper limits of wetlands. (Source: K. Marcellus, G. Dawes and G. Silberhorn, *Local Management of Wetlands, Environmental Considerations,* **Virginia Institute of Marine Science, Gloucester Point, Va., 1973.)**

Table 14

Criteria for classifying Minnesota lakes.

Criteria	Natural Environment		Recreational Development		General Development	
	1	**2**	**3**	**4**	**5**	**6**
Development Density	under three dwellings per mile	under three dwellings per	between 3 and 25 dwellings per mile of shoreline	under three dwelling per mile of shoreline.	over 25 dwellings per mile of shoreline	between 3 and 25 dwellings per mile of shoreline
Crowding Potential	less than 60 acres of water area per mile			between 60 and 225 acres of water per mile		greater than 225 acres of water per mile
Ecological Classification		winterkill-roughfish or bullhead-panfish		NOT winter-kill-roughfish or bullhead-panfish		NOT winter-kill-roughfish or bullhead-panfish
Lake Depth		under 15 feet deep		over 15 feet deep		over 15 feet deep
Shore Soil & Vegetation		few trees shrub vegetation, clay or wet soil, flat slopes		sand or loam soil, deciduous or coniferous veg., moderate to steep slopes		sand or loam soil, deciduous or coniferous veg., moderate to steep slopes
Others	a. small lakes (under 150 acres) b. Trout Streams and Wild Rivers				a. partially within an incorporated area b. Rivers and Streams	

Some statutes mandate the identification of subzones such as a Nebraska floodway regulation statute which requires that rules and regulations "reflect gradations in flood hazard based on flood frequency and other criteria."[3] A similar requirement is contained in the Montana floodway statute. A New Jersey statute applying to both floodway and flood fringe areas requires that "delineations shall identify the various subportions of the flood hazard area for reasonable and proper use according to relative risk."[4] Relative risk is defined as "the varying degrees of hazard to life and property in a flood hazard area which are occasioned by differences in depth and velocity of flood waters covering and flowing over it."

Some programs identify not only subzones but gradations in areas. For example, the Minnesota shoreland program places lakes into three major categories for regulatory purposes—natural environment, recreational development, and general development—based on six criteria listed in table 14.

There are practical limits to identifying gradations and subzones in advance of regulations, just as there are limits to map scale. Practicality depends upon a variety of factors such as the size of the area, variability in resource characteristics, land

[3]Neb. Rev. Stat., §2.1506.03 (1974).

[4]N.J. Stat. Ann., §58:16A-52 (1966).

values, and the regulatory approach. Gradations and subzones make little sense for a twenty-foot-wide ravine but may be important for the twenty-mile-wide lower Mississippi flood plain.

The extent to which definition and map gradations and subzones are desirable depends on the size of the area, development to be permitted, diversity of natural resources, existing uses, and the extent to which special permit procedures are to be used in the program. Efforts to define gradations and subzones must balance the ideal of rigorous definition criteria and extensive data gathering with the reality of low budgets, lack of experts, and political wrangling about precise definitional criteria. Although sophisticated definitions facilitate standard-setting and program implementation, interim definitions, based on subjective analysis, often prove initially sufficient.

4-9 *A variety of approaches may distinguish "important" from "critical" areas and identify gradations and subzones in areas.*

Eight tests have been used to distinguish areas requiring special regulation. (1) Size is often used to identify critical lakes, streams, wetlands, agricultural lands, and other types of areas.[5] Larger areas are less common and offer greater use potential and resource diversity than smaller counterparts. They also offer more complete protection for ecosystems and wildlife. For example, large areas are needed to protect certain rare and endangered species. The size of the management unit is also important in the conduct of profitable agriculture, forestry, and mineral operations. (2) Public perceptions play an important role in some definition efforts. Critical area programs in Florida and Minnesota use nomination procedures for suggesting potential sites and assigning priorities. In this process, local units of government, regional planning agencies, and interested individuals are asked to nominate particular areas for designation. The state screen nominations to narrow candidate areas. To date, the designated areas have reflected a variety of criteria but strongly emphasize visibility, public perceptions and preferences, and political acceptability. Public perceptions and preferences also aid in the formulation of development standards. Public hearings are usually held for proposed designations and standards. Other techniques that gain public participation include opinion polls, workshops, direct involvement or review by legislative bodies, and referendum techniques. (3) Quantified evaluations are used in the definition of flood plains and, to some extent, other critical hazard areas such as seismic areas. (4) The seriousness of threat to resources is a primary criterion in establishing data gathering and definition priorities. (5) Ranking approaches determine which areas have the optimum characteristics for the particular needs of society. They have been applied in some wetland and natural area acquisition programs, but rarely in regulatory efforts. (6) Multijurisdictional importance has been used by states in selecting areas for direct regulation. (7) Supply and demand analysis has been applied to some renewable and non-renewable resource areas, including agricultural lands and sand and gravel deposits, but rarely on a systematic

[5]Size is not, in itself, conclusive in determining the value or importance of a resource, but is often used in determining which areas should be regulated. Programs have often focused upon the larger areas. For example, the Vermont shoreland zoning act applies only to lakes of more than 20 acres. The Washington shoreline act defines shorelines of state significance to include specified coastal areas and shorelines of lakes of more than 1,000 acres. Stream shores are included where stream flow is 20 feet per second or more. As a matter of administrative policy, Wisconsin and Minnesota shoreland zoning programs have emphasized control of shorelands for lakes greater than 100 acreas.

basis. (8) Scarcity and uniqueness play an important indirect role in the definition of some wetlands and scientific areas.

In the long run, a scarcity analysis involving both supply and demand assessment may be the most satisfactory approach for determining the relative importance of nonhazard critical areas. It can provide an objective, quantified evaluation of their importance to society. Still, such an approach requires a considerable amount of data and many value judgments and assumptions. On the other hand, it offers hope for linking resource inventories and broader environmental, social, and economic planning.

State critical area programs often combine these eight tests to determine critical or very sensitive lands. They emphasize hazards, threats, scarcity, and public perceptions. An area is often selected for state regulation if three characteristics are found in combination. (1) The special natural resource values or hazards present affect citizens of more than one local jurisdiction or the state as a whole. (2) The area is subject to threats from development or existing uses. (3) Protection by local units of government is inadequate.

Shoreland and coastal programs also use a combination of tests for defining overall boundaries and identifying more specific gradations and subzones.

4-10 *To aid state and local definition efforts, enabling statutes establishing state or cooperative state and local programs should: (1) specify the general types of land to be regulated; (2) list criteria for selection of particular lands within a type; (3) establish general mapping or other designation procedures; (4) list goals for more specific definition and regulation; and (5) describe the harm or problems to be avoided.*

Efforts to draft sensitive area enabling statutes should balance the desirability of detailed development standards that clearly establish legislative intent with the need for flexibility and simplicity to meet varying conditions, provide for later refinement of definition criteria, and provide options to local government. These factors should be reflected in several elements of sensitive area enabling statutes.

(1) Definition criteria: Programs with specific definition criteria have, in general, encountered fewer problems during implementation than those with nebulous criteria. Arguments may be made for and against detailed statutory definitions as opposed to more generalized specification of areas, goals, and procedures. Considerable specificity in the enabling statute can help define the intent of the legislature and overcome agency hesitation to undertake regulation. It can also result in poor, unworkable definitions unless anchored in previous study. A very detailed definition may preclude the necessary regional and local inputs. As a rule of thumb, it is advisable to include rigid and exclusive definition criteria only where resource conditions and management needs do not vary appreciably throughout a state. Enabling statutes should at least list the types of land subject to regulation and general criteria for selecting particular lands.

(2) Mapping requirements: Experience with specific statutory mapping criteria varies. Inflexible large scale map requirements, such as coastal wetland maps at a scale of one inch to 200 feet,[6] have hindered programs where conditions vary throughout a state. General performance guidelines appear more satisfactory and require technical studies or use of soil maps.

---

[6]This scale of mapping is required by the Connecticut wetland regulation statute.

Experience also suggests that statutes should not require written notice to landowners before area mapping. This is much too time-consuming and expensive. Nevertheless, local public notice by publication and hearing should accompany the definition of most areas.

Statutes should not require legislative confirmation of sensitive area maps unless essential politically. This confirmation is time-consuming and of dubious technical value.

(3) Statement of regulatory goals and findings of fact: detailed statements of regulatory goals including suggested uses (*e.g.*, recreation, food, and fiber) and findings of fact concerning the problems leading to the legislation (*e.g.*, flood damages or water pollution) guide later agency efforts and justify regulations to landowners.

4-11 *The administering agency should adopt adminstrative regulations or guidelines where specific critical area definition, goals, criteria, and identification procedures have not been included in the basic enabling statute.*

Most state sensitive area programs have adopted administrative regulations to refine and supplement standards contained in the enabling act. Programs lacking specific criteria and procedures have the advantage of flexibility but are often inefficient and fail to provide agency staff with consistent procedures and local units of government and interested individuals with guidance.

In general, administrative criteria and guidelines include a more specific listing of the types of areas subject to control, tests and procedures for distinguishing "important" versus "critical" lands, requirements for identifying gradations and subzones, data gathering requirements, and formal procedures for designation. Often definition criteria and procedures are applied uniformly to all lands of a particular class (*e.g.*, designation of the 100-year flood plain as the regulatory flood plain throughout a state). However, criteria and procedures may also define subclasses of areas and may apply not only to state action but to local definition of areas as well.

Many of these statutory definition principles apply also to administrative regulations. However, data gathering by the implementing agency can justify the adoption of more specific criteria and standards than may be possible or politically acceptable in the enabling statute.

4-12 *States should encourage local units of government to participate in definition efforts and refine sensitive area definitions and maps.*

Strong local involvement has been a key to successful implementation and enforcement in most sensitive area programs, although the state has often played a major role in data gathering and standard-setting. Local input may be provided to state definition efforts through public hearings, nomination procedures, workshops, use of local base maps, and cooperative data gathering. To maximize local involvement and support, enabling statutes should provide options to local government in definition criteria and development standards. Local agencies may be asked to refine critical area maps through larger scale versions, alter boundaries to reflect field conditions, and identify subzones. The degree to which local agencies should be involved may differ depending on the type of area, local expertise, and local willingness to participate.

Table 15

Application of factors or tests to define sensitive areas.

Factor or Parameter	Some Relevant Data	Application to Particular Areas	Other Factors	Comments
Undisturbed or natural conditions	Existing use of the area	Areas of special interest (geological, floral, faunal)	Use potential to society	Few areas are in a totally undisturbed condition. Therefore, degree of disturbance is usually the issue.
	Plant and animal species present, whether they are indigenous, degree to which they represent the full range of species present prior to man, degree to which predator-prey relationships have been preserved, etc.	Wetlands	Scarcity	
		Wild and scenic rivers	Sensitivity	
			Degree of threat	
			Path of development	
	Physical alterations to area from forestry, road building, and grading		Adequacy of existing controls	
	Threats from air, water, and noise pollution, recreation uses, and hunting			
Threat of harm including path of development	Sensitivity of particular area	All types of areas including hazard areas where the intensity of existing and anticipated development is related to total economic and social losses which are likely to result from development	All other tests (depending upon the type of area)	Threat of harm is considered in some but not all efforts. It is of particular importance in establishing data gathering and regulatory priorities.
	Presence of buffer zones		Special attention to sensitivity and adequacy of existing controls	
	Type, rate, and intensity of present and anticipated development			

Table 15 (continued)

Factor or Parameter	Some Relevant Data	Application to Particular Areas	Other Factors	Comments
Uniqueness Rarity Scarcity	Total supply of a resource of area in a state, region, The present and future demand for the areas or areas' product.	Areas of special scientific interest Wetlands Historic and archeological sites Areas of special scenic beauty Areas of special recreational importance Prime agricultural lands Prime forest lands Mineral and energy lands	Undisturbed or natural condition (for areas listed above) Use potential in meeting particular needs of society (for virtually all areas) Whether area is of greater than local significance Need to preserve resources for future as well as present generations Sensitivity Degree of threat Path of development Adequacy of controls	A scarcity test may apply to all nonhazard critical areas (along with use potential in meeting the needs of society). Time frame and geographical scope are relevant to a determination of scarcity.
Use potential in meeting particular needs of society	Quantity of area Quality of area Accessibility Land ownership, existing uses, adjacent uses, and other factors related to the actual availability of the resource for particular uses	All areas	All other tests (depending upon class of area)	Use potential is relevant to definition of all critical areas.

Table 15 (continued)

Factor or Parameter	Some Relevant Data	Application to Particular Areas	Other Factors	Comments
Hazards or threats to society	Severity of threat Degree to which threat will endanger health or safety or only cause economic losses Degree to which threat on land will affect adjacent lands (third party effects) Costs of overcoming the threat.	Floodplains Seismic areas Avalance and mudslide areas Coastal erosion areas Slope areas with soil conditions unfit for building purposes Areas where soil conditions, geology, or hydrologic regime is such that water pollution will result from onsite waste disposal or other land practices Other hazard areas	Whether of greater than local significance (multi-jurisdictional impacts) Path of development Adequacy of existing controls	In many instances, hazard areas such as floodplains also possess special recreational or wildlife values. The areas should also be analyzed and identified as areas of special scientific interest or recreational importance through application of other tests. The application of hazard and non-hazard tests should be kept separate and not confused.
Matters of greater than local significance	Physical boundaries of critical area (whether area lies within a single local unit, state) Ecosystem or hydraulic system boundaries (whether predator-prey relationships, water resources systems, etc., transcend boundaries of single locality, state, etc.) Statewide or regional demand for particular type of area (see scarcity test) Statewide or regional impact (social, economic, health and safety) with use or non-use of area	All types of areas	All other tests (depending upon type of area)	The geographical scope is not an independent test but defines the perspective for application of other tests. A local critical areas program may be interested in areas of local significance. A state effort would be interested in areas of greater than local significance. And a national effort may be interested in areas of greater that statewide significance.

Table 15 (continued)

Factor or Parameter	Some Relevant Data	Application to Particular Areas	Other Factors	Comments
Need to preserve resources for future as well as present generations	Long-term foreseeable demand for a resource Sensitivity of a resource to irreparable harm or destruction Threats	All types of areas except hazard areas where the hazard is the sole consideration Particularly applicable to mining and similar non-renewable resource areas where the use by present generations must be balanced with those by future generations Areas of special scientific interest including habitat of rare and endangered species which may be driven to extinction unless protected Renewable resource lands (agriculture, forestry) where destruction of the topsoil will destroy long-term productive capabilities Historic and archeological sites	All other tests may be applied may be applied simultaneously except hazard Special attention to: Scarcity Use Potential Sensitivity Path of development Adequacy of existing controls	Time frame is, like geographical scope, an independent test in itself but emphasizes the long-term demands and preservation needs.

Table 15 (continued)

Factor or Parameter	Some Relevant Data	Application to Particular Areas	Other Factors	Comments
Sensitivity of areas	Number of types of species present or other values Long-term and short-term sensitivity of species Topography, vegetative cover, or other factors which to relate to vulnerability of area Presence of buffer zone	All types of areas except hazard areas where hazard is the prime consideration Sensitivity may also apply to some hazard areas such as coastal erosion areas and groundwater recharge areas with varying degrees of tolerance to development. Particularly applicable to areas of special scientific interest, with sensitive flora or fauna, wilderness areas and areas of special scenic beauty.	All other tests except hazard Special attention to: Undisturbed conditions Need to preserve for future as well as existing generations Path of development Adequacy of existing controls	Determination of sensitivity is of prime concern for the purpose of environmental impact analysis and in establishing data gathering and regulatory priorities
Adequacy of existing controls	Sensitivity of areas Presence of buffer areas Existing land uses Land ownership (generally private ownership poses graver threats) Whether state or local land use controls apply to land and the nature of these controls Whether principal benefits or burdens of an area accrue outside of the jurisdiction of the local units of government entrusted with regulatory responsibility	All areas. For mining and agricultural areas the issue may be unduly restrictive controls on landownership (zoning, preventing mining and agriculture) rather than too little control	All other tests (depending upon class of area) Special attention to undisturbed condition, scarcity, and path of development	Adequacy of controls is of importance in establishing data gathering and regulatory priorities

Part **5**

REGULATORY STANDARD-SETTING

Most development standards in sensitive area programs are performance-oriented. (See Appendix D.) They are designed to maintain the performance of the natural system, preserve resource values, and protect the public from hazards. At the local level, these performance standards are often coupled with traditional zoning approaches. Together they achieve a wide range of planning objectives. For example, performance standards designed to protect natural resource values and reduce hazards can easily join performance standards for controlling traffic or providing adequate public services for new uses.

The following recommendations primarily address performance standards for resource protection and hazard reduction. More traditional standards are addressed in other reports.[1]

5-1 *Sensitive area use standards should not be prohibitory for most areas and uses. The overall degree of restrictiveness in a given circumstance should be no greater than necessary to achieve management objectives.*

Principal sensitive area regulatory objectives differ from program to program.

---

[1]*See*, particularly, the hundreds of planning advisory service reports developed by the American Society of Planning Officials. *E.g.*, T. McFall, *Housing Planning: How to Meet H.U.D.'s 701 Requirements*, American Society of Planning Officials, Chicago, Ill. (1977).

(See tables 3, 16.) Nevertheless, similarities are found in the goals and general standards applied to coastal areas, lakeshores, wild and scenic rivers, flood plains, and wetlands where regulations are adopted to serve similar broad environmental and welfare goals:

1) *Minimize water pollution.* Standards to minimize water pollution may: (a) control direct discharge of pollutants by industries and waste treatment plants; (b) regulate grading and construction on slope areas to reduce erosion; (c) control filling and dredging of watercourses (d) mandate setback requirements and other requirements for septic tank systems; (e) establish specifications for solid waste disposal; (f) regulate tree-cutting and vegetation removal along the immediate shore of water to reduce erosion; (g) regulate wetland alteration to protect their function as sediment filters; (h) require building and road sites to be mulched to minimize erosion: and (i) regulate removal of topsoil, sand and gravel operations, and mining.

2) *Protect scenic beauty.* Standards to protect scenic beauty may: (a) control water pollution sources (see discussion above); (b) prohibit heavy industries and similar visually disruptive uses; (c) establish maximum building heights; (d) regulate tree-cutting and vegetation removal; (e) control dams, dikes, and levees; (f) regulate architectural design (adopted in some programs); (g) require minimum lot size and width requirements to reduce density; (h) require building setbacks from road and water; (i) control or prohibit signboards; (j) regulate construction of buildings on slopes and valley crests; (k) regulate open burning and other air pollution; (l) control mining; and (m) require underground siting requirements for power and telephone facilities (some instances).

3) *Protect wildlife.* Standards to protect wildlife may: (a) control wetland alterations; (b) regulate tree-cutting and vegetation removal; (c) control dams, dikes, levees, and channel straightening; (d) control pesticide use; (e) require that structures be designed and located to reduce impact of uses on wildlife; (f) regulate fill, grading, and mining operations; and (g) regulate hunting.

4) *Minimize flood damages.* Standards to minimize flood damages may: (a) prevent encroachment in floodway areas to preserve flood flow capacity; (b) tightly control uses in coastal wave action and wave-induced erosion areas; (c) require that uses in outer flood fringe areas be elevated or flood-proofed to a regulatory flood protection elevation (often the 100-year flood); (d) protect flood storage areas (some programs); and (e) regulate dikes, dams, and levees to insure safely designed and constructed structures.

Restrictive standards are sometimes required to achieve objectives.[2] For example, all structural uses may be prohibited in severe earthquake hazard areas. (See figure 25.) All structural uses may also be prohibited in floodways, wetlands, and prime agricultural lands to minimize hazards, preserve natural values, or protect the productive capability of the land. More often, use standards prohibit selected structural uses with high conflict potential and permit a wide range of additional uses conditionally. These are examined on a case-by-case basis.

Extensive conditions are typically attached to development permits. Such an approach is dictated in part by constitutional considerations, including a desire to avoid a taking of property. Equally important, it promotes multiple uses of land,

---

[2]A popular misconception equates all sensitive area regulation with the prohibition of development. This view is contrary to the regulatory policies now being applied or suggested for most areas across the country and engenders unwarranted opposition to efforts.

Figure 25

Building setbacks from fault lines. (Source: D. Nichols and J. Buchanan-Banks, *Seismic Hazards and Land-Use Planning,* **U.S. Geological Survey Circular 690, Reston, Va., 1974.)**

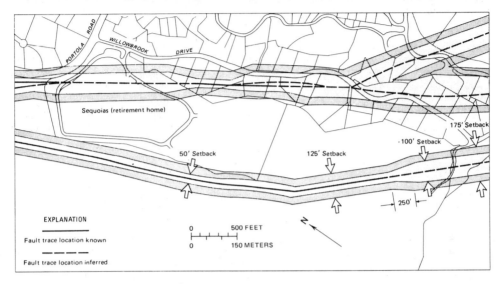

provides options in uses, and imposes only the degree of restriction required to achieve resource protection.

5-2 *Standard-setting for a particular area must consider three major factors:[3]* (1) *the special values and hazards found within the area;* (2) *the probable impact of particular types, designs, and densities of uses; and* (3) *acceptable levels of impact reflecting the sensitivity of the area of particular types of development, resource management, preservation goals, and legal and political considerations.*

Diversity of natural resource hazards and values encountered within particular areas often complicate sensitive area standard-setting. Variations in topography, vegetation, fauna, hydrology, soils, and geology must be reflected in reasonable regulations.

The impact of particular uses upon a sensitive area also depends on: (1) the precise location of the use; (2) its design; (3) the manner in which the use is constructed and carried out; (4) the impact of conjunctive uses such as roads, sewers, and water; and (5) the cumulative impact of similar uses. Case-by-case evaluation of uses is desirable in many instances to consider these variables.

Determination of acceptable impact is a policy question. In rare instances, technology may be used to determine acceptable impact such as protection requirements for a rare or endangered species. More often, acceptable impact is a question of preference and must be based on political and legal as well as technical considerations. More or less arbitrary levels may result. A variety of approaches may be used to gain legislative and public feedback to determine acceptable impacts including public hearings, workshops, opinion polls, direct legislative involvement in standard-setting, and referenda. Public hearings are used extensively in existing efforts.

[3]*See* tables 15 and 16 for a more complete listing of factors.

Table 16

Factors in standard-setting. Several factors are often explicitly or implicitly considered when formulating standards for an area. The list is not exhaustive, and other factors may be relevant in a given effort. All factors are highly interdependent. The complicated nature of standard-setting can be appreciated from this partial list.

Factor	Comment
1. Short term and long term land and water use goals (*e.g.,* protection of sensitive area values, reduction in hazards, prevention of water pollution, separation of incompatible uses, minimization of the cost of public services)	Enabling statutes set forth sensitive area management goals. In large measure, goals determine the scope and content of regulatory standards.
2. Natural resources within the area (soils, geology, vegetation, etc.)	Resources determine the suitability of the area for particular uses and the sensitivity of the area to particular uses. A diversified area such as a coastal flood plain may require not only flood standards but supplementary standards for subzones such as wetlands and beaches.
3. Anticipated uses	Standards are formulated for anticipated uses such as fills in wetlands and residential development in lakeshore areas.
4. Judgements concerning acceptable impact	Impact depends not only upon the types of uses but also on their design, specific location, the manner in which they will be carried out, and associated uses. Acceptable impact is not solely a scientific issue but also involves value judgements and political and legal considerations. Public preferences are also important.
5. Available data including its scale, accuracy, format, manipulative capability, etc.	Available data often determine the content and form of standards. Accurate and detailed data facilitate precise standards. Where inaccurate or generalized data are available at adoption of a program, generalized performance standards are often adopted which can be refined on a case-by-case basis as development permits are submitted. Lack of detailed initial data encourages adoption of interim regulations until more detailed data gathering can be completed.
6. Available funds and expertise	Local government units often apply rigid, prohibitory approaches to critical wetlands, flood plains, etc., where funds or staff expertise are insufficient to permit detailed data gathering or evaluation of permits. Special permit approaches which shift all or a portion of the data gathering and impact analysis burden to developers are also used in such circumstances.
7. Constitutional considerations	Standards must (1) serve acceptable police power goals, (2) not discriminate between similarly situated properties, or (3) take property without just compensation. In addition, the standards (the means) must have some tendency to accomplish regulatory goals (the ends).
8. Political acceptability	As legislative acts, land use regulations require majority approval by a legislative body. Even if adopted, politically tenuous regulations often fail to be adequately administered and enforced. Political acceptability depends upon many factors such as perceived public need for standards, public awareness of area values and hazards, the stringency of standards, the soundness of the regulatory scheme, length of standards, and exemptions.

Table 16 (continued)

Factor	Comment
9. Local, regional, or statewide land and water plans	Performance standards to protect critical areas and minimize development impact are often adopted prior to comprehensive planning. Although a sound approach, the integration of critical area standard-setting with broader planning can help achieve broad public welfare goals by evaluating alternative sites for development, the economic and social importance of uses, and the regional hydrologic, ecological, and cultural relationships of areas.
10. The amenability of the subject matter to quantified standard-setting	Some subjects, such as flooding, readily lend themselves to quantified standards while others, such as minimization of impact upon scenery, do not. Most regulations rely heavily upon discretionary, non-quantified standards due to problems with quantified analysis or lack of funds or staff for such analysis.
11. The state of the art in standard-setting	Increasingly sophisticated standards are needed as techniques for evaluating land suitability, impacts, and methods for minimizing impact are improved. Periodic upgrading is desirable.
12. The cumulative impact of uses	Sensitive areas may be gradually destroyed by development permitted on a case-by-case basis unless overall limits for impact are assigned and the cumulative impact of existing and future uses are considered.

5-3 *The necessary restrictiveness to achieve particular goals may often be achieved through:* (1) *prohibiting a small number of uses with serious and unacceptable impact;* (2) *permitting a substantial number of open space uses with minimal impact; and* (3) *requiring special permits for a variety of uses which may not have acceptable impact.*

An acceptable degree of regulatory control may combine prohibited, permitted,[4] and special permit uses.[5] A high degree of restriction is achieved when most or all uses are prohibited. A varying degree is achieved when many uses are special permit uses which may be permitted or denied. With the special permit approach, the regulatory agency has considerable discretion in fact-finding and applying general use standards to determine appropriate uses in specific circumstances.

---

[4]Uses permitted "as of right" are those nearly or completely compatible with critical area values (such as wildlife use for a wetland area). Permits are usually not required for such uses or, if required, are issued automatically. Common uses of right include hiking, picnicking, nature watching, camping, harvesting of natural crops, and other open space uses. Low intensity single family residences are permitted as of right in some areas. Permitted uses must, like special permit uses, conform to minimum regulation standards such as tree-cutting regulations, restrictions on filling or grading, or minimum lot sizes (for structural uses).

[5]Regulations typically require "special permits" for uses, which may or may not have adverse impact upon the resources and adjacent uses depending upon their design, precise location, the natural values and hazards at the site, adjacent uses, and other factors. Special permit uses may be termed "special exceptions," "variances," "conditional uses," or simply special permit use (the broad term used in the present reports). Special permits must be evaluated on a case-by-case basis by a regulatory board such as a state agency, a zoning plan commission, a city council, or a city plan commission prior to issuance.

5-4 Special permit requirements combined with performance standards should be applied to most areas and uses.

Special permit approaches combined with performance standards are often appropriate for sensitive areas with diversity in natural resources. Here the impact of individual uses varies. Case-by-case evaluation identifies values and hazards at sites and determines the impact of individual uses. Where special permit approaches are broadly applied *(e.g.,* a coastal zone) tight supplementary restrictions may be appropriate or narrow subzones requiring special treatment: dunes, wildlife areas, scenic areas, and high hazard areas where flooding, erosion, or seismic activity threaten health and safety.

5-5 Sensitive area standards should anticipate the cumulative impact of uses.

The major shortcomings of a special permit approach is its failure to consider cumulative impact. One technique for considering impact is to assume the worst and prevent all development with the theory that one permit will open a "wedge" for others. This approach has a simple logic but is generally unacceptable. Another technique projects future uses in evaluating permits. For example, a Minnesota model flood plain zoning ordinance requires that in evaluating flood heights caused by a proposed encroachment in a floodway area the height increase be calculated "based upon the reasonable assumption that there will be an equal degree of encroachment on both sides of the stream."[6]

[6]Minnesota Department of Natural Resources, *Sample Flood Plain Zoning Ordinance for Local Units of Government (Using Available Flood Information in the Absence of Detailed Engineering Studies),* Minnesota Department of Natural Resources, Division of Waters, Soils and Minerals, St. Paul, Minnesota (1970).

Cases have upheld regulations that consider the cumulative impact of fills or other uses upon navigable waters. For example, in Hixon v. Public Service Comm'n, 32 Wis. 2d 608, 146 N.W. 2d 232, 577 (1966), the Supreme Court of Wisconsin affirmed a denial of a permit to maintain a breakwater on the grounds that the breakwater was an unnecessary obstruction to navigation, did not allow for free flow of water, and was detrimental to the public interest. The court observed, (*Id.,* 146 N.W.2d at 589):

There are over 9,000 navigable lakes in Wisconsin covering an area of over 54,000 square miles. A little fill here and there may seem to be nothing to become excited about. But one fill, though comparatively inconsequential, may lead to another, and another, and before long a great body of water may be eaten away until it may no longer exist. Our navigable waters are a precious natural heritage; once gone, they disappear forever.

Similarly the California Supreme Court sustained regulations controlling the filling within San Francisco Bay and a 100 foot corridor. Candlestick Properties, Inc. v. San Francisco Bay Conservation and Development Commission, 11 Cal. App. 3d 557, 89 Cal., Rptr. 897 (1970).

A federal district court in Corsa v. Tawes, 149 F. Supp. 771 (D. Md. 1957) *aff'd* 355 U.S. 37 (1957), sustained a Maryland law prohibiting the use of certain nets for fishing in tidal waters. While not a wetland case, the analysis of the court is interesting in terms of future impacts (*Id.* at 74):

We think . . . that the protective hand of the State may be extended before danger is unmistakably imminent. Conditions may go unnoticed so long that when the threat is demonstrated it is too late to avert the harm. One witness for the plaintiffs testified that no matter how much a supply may be reduced by over-fishing, provided that the stock is not completely annihilated, it may in time replenish itself. We need not quarrel with this statement of scientific opinion, but in the practical management of its resources, the State may conclude that the time for action is long before the destruction has gone that far. The State is interested not merely in the preservation of specimens for museums but in conserving and perpetuating a constant supply.

On the other hand, a Pennsylvania court in National Land & Inv. Co. v. Kohn, 419 Pa. 504, 215 A.2d 597 (1965), held invalid a four acre minimum lot size classification despite arguments that since lots were not served by public sewer the cumulative effects of development within a period of years would cause water pollution problems. The court noted: "The township engineer's testimony on the subject of drainage and sewage was vague and unconvincing, consisting, as it did, of the bald statement that he felt there was a danger of pollution. In

Two approaches are available for dealing with future uses. Both require the definition of a maximum upper limit for present and future impact or define an overall environmental quality standard. Once this upper limit is defined, development standards can be promulgated which either (1) permit development on a "first come first serve" basis until the maximum acceptable impact limit is reached or (2) allow particular levels of impact for specific uses assuming that, over a period of time, a stated total number of uses may be permitted.

The first approach has been used for control of air, water, and noise pollution emission and the control of floodway encroachment, Air, water, noise, or flood standards are promulgated *(e.g.* water quality standards) which establish maximum tolerable levels of degradation or impact within a given area.

Uses are permitted until the maximum limit is reached. Then, new uses are prohibited unless emission levels of existing uses are cut back so that overall quality is maintained.

This approach has the advantage of simplicity, but it does not encourage minimization of impact by initial users. In addition, it results in differing treatment between permitted uses prior to reaching maximum quality levels and those subsequently proposed. Attempts to require existing uses to reduce pollution emissions or other impacts to permit new uses when maximum impact levels are reached have met with some success.

The second approach is more complicated but satisfactory in taking into account potential users. It has been embodied in some pollution control and floodway regulations, and involves three steps: (1) calculation of the maximum permissible impact or deterioration for an area (quality standards); (2) calculation of the total number of uses which now exist and may occur within an area; and (3) calculation of the total contribution acceptable for each potential use.

The key to such an approach is, of course, not only the determination of overall permissible impact but control over the total number of uses. One approach for calculating and limiting total uses is through acreage requirements *(e.g.,* each dwelling requires a five acre lot). A second approach has been employed in the Adirondack State Park which established "use indices" *(i.e.,* maximum permissible density levels) for various classes of land within the park.[7] Intensity indices range from unlimited intensity in urban areas to one dwelling unit for each forty-three-acre unit of land in conservation areas (about 65% of the park).

5-6 *Interim standards of a restrictive nature are justified to prevent irreparable harm to areas.*

The regulation of areas often requires time-consuming mapping and preparation of regulations. Restrictive interim protection standards, based on the best available

---

addition, this opinion was based upon the hypothetical case of the *entire* township being developed on the basis of one acre lots *maximum,* a situation very unlikely to occur in the near future and probably never." *Id.,* 215 A.2d at 609. *See also* Christine Bldg. Co. v. Troy, 367 Mich. 508, 116 N.W. 2d 816 (1962), where the court was unfavorable to arguments of long term anticipated development to justify present restrictions. The city argued that large minimum lot sizes would limit the density of population in proportion to anticipated sewer capacity. The court noted: "In the instant case, the population in the area involved presently amounts to 2,051. The city anticipates that by the year 2000 it will exceed 21,300. If we are going to speculate as to the future we might as well recognize the possibilities of technological advances with reference to sewage disposal. By the year 2000 the city might find itself able to handle and service a population much greater than the 21,300 limitation." *Id.,* 116 N.W. 2d at 820.

[7]N.Y. Exec. Code, §805 *et. seq.* (McKinney's Consolidated Laws, Annot., Supp. 1975).

information, are often justified during this period. Interim regulations are expressly authorized by some state sensitive area statutes[8] and local zoning and subdivision enabling acts. Statutory procedures must, of course, be carefully followed.

5-7 *Regulations should apply primarily to new uses. Extensive retroactive regulation is rarely acceptable politically and may result in successful court challenges.*

As a matter of political and legal necessity, regulations should be applied primarily to new uses or major alterations or extensions of existing uses. Retroactive regulation, while authorized by some statutes, has often proved unacceptable politically and difficult to enforce. However, regulations can be applied to new as old uses in areas where a considerable number of existing nonconforming uses exist. In addition, tight control of existing uses may be acceptable if they are nuisances or if they are abandoned, or substantially altered. Amortization of existing uses over a reasonable time period has been applied in some instances.[9]

5-8 *Nonstructural as well as structural uses should be controlled in highly sensitive areas.*

Traditional land use regulations and most sensitive area regulations focus on structural uses. However, nonstructural activities such as fill, removal of topsoil, mining, and tree-cutting may cause more complete damage to wetlands, dunes, areas of scientific interest, erosion areas, and agricultural lands. Nonstructural uses are regulated in some sensitive area programs.[10] Agricultural interests are particularly powerful and have often forced adopting of agricultural exemptions under local zoning enabling acts and state sensitive area statutes.

5-9 *Sensitive area standards should apply to government activities. Governmental uses are often a primary cause of resource gradation.*

Dams, roads, utility lines, and power generation plants are often major offenders in the destruction of sensitive resources. They should be subject to regulatory control. However, under most present statutes and case law, federal uses are not subject to state or local controls, state uses are not subject to local regulations, and local uses of a "governmental" nature are not subject to local regulations.[11] Congressional and state statutory amendments are needed to require governmental compliance with sensitive area standards.[12]

5-10 *Sensitive area standards should often combine: (1) quantified standards for amenable subjects; (2) nuisance standards to minimize impacts upon adjacent uses; (3) environmental standards to set limits for acceptable levels of environmental impact, and, in some instances; (4) broader public welfare standards to determine adequacy of public services, impact of a use upon tax base, and similar public welfare considerations.*

Adequacy of standards is a common legal and administrative issue where a legislative body such as Congress, a state legislature, or a city/county council

[8] *E.g.,* N.C. Gen Stat. §113A-114F. (Supp. 1974) (state interim regulations for coastal areas); N.Y. Envir. Res. Code §25-020 (McKinney's Consolidated Laws, Annot. Supp. 1975) (state interim regulations for wetlands); Wash. Rev. Code Ann. §36.70.790 (1964) (local interim zoning).

[9] *See generally,* Katarinic, "Elimination of Non-Conforming Uses, Buildings and Structures by Amortization—Concept Versus Law," *Duquesne U.L. Rev. 1* (1963); Annot., "Validity of Provisions of Amortization of Nonconforming Uses," 22 A.L.R.3d 1134 (1968) and cases cited therein.

[10] Fills are regulated in most weland and flood plain programs. Dredging is regulated in most wetland programs.

[11] *See* note 12 of Part 1, *supra.*

[12] *See* notes 7 and 8 of Part 3, *supra.*

delegates quasi-legislative or quasi-judicial functions to a regulatory agency or body. Rigid, quantified critical area standards are often not appropriate due to the diverse resource base and varying impact of different uses. Nevertheless, specific standards are desirable to: (1) provide landowners certainty in their use of land; (2) guide administrative boards in processing individual development permits; and (3) provide guidelines for judicial review of administrative action.

Often programs combine various types of standards to provide both specificity and flexibility:

(1) *Quantified standards*[13] establish minimum numeric use specifications: lot sizes and widths; building setbacks from water and roads; flood protection elevation requirements; earthquake protection requirements; maximum air, water, and noise pollution contributions; and park and open space dedication requirements.

(2) More general *nuisance standards* control the impact of uses upon adjacent lands:[14] blockages to flood flows; dust from sand and gravel operations; incompatibility of an industry in a residential neighborhood; and threats to public health or safety.

(3) *General environmental standards* control the impact of uses on wildlife, scenic beauty, mineral deposits, soils, geology, and vegatation.[15]

(4) *General welfare standards* control the impact of uses on public facilities and the tax base.

Courts have sanctioned delegation of power with quantitative and general nuisance standards. General environmental standards have not been widely litigated, but have also been sustained.[16] In determining the adequacy of standards, courts have examined the nature of the subject matter, whether it is subject to quantification, the expertise of the administering agency, procedures for issuance of permits, and review procedures.

Where little or no quantification is possible in standards, enabling statutes, administrative regulations, and ordinances should clearly state regulatory goals and specify special permit review factors and procedures.

5-11 *Sensitive area regulations must steer a middle course between complex, lengthy rules, which take into account the unique features of each use and each parcel of land, and general, simplistic rules applying to entire classes of uses in whole areas.*

[13]*See* Appendix D. For example, flood plain statutes often require protection of residences and other structures to the 100 year flood elevation.

[14]For example, N.C. Gen Stat., §143-215.57 (1974) requires that local units in regulating floodway areas consider the effects of floodway uses on other lands including potential damages caused:
　(1) By water which may be backed up or divered by such obstructions;
　(2) By the danger that the obstructions will be swept downstream to the injury of others; and
　(3) By the injury or damage at the site of the obstruction itself.

[15]Some statutes establish general guidelines for acceptance impact. For example, the North Carolina coastal zone act directs that permits for development in critical environmental areas are to be denied if (in the case of renewable resource areas) development "will result in loss or significant reduction of continued long-range productivity that would jeopardize one or more of the water, food, or fiber requirements of more than local concern" or (in the case of fragile or historic resources) "that development will result in major or irreversible damage to one or more historic, cultural, scientific, environmental, or scenic values or natural systems . . ." N.C. Gen Stat. §113A-120 (1975). Although these standards are not unquantified, the magnitude of acceptable impact is suggested by terms such as "substantial," "significant," and "major or irreversible damage." The regulatory agency may be aided in its determination of acceptable impact by a list of relevant factors and considerations.

[16]*See* notes 39 and 41 in Part 9, *infra.*

Variations in natural resources and impacts of particular uses should be reflected in sensitive area standards.[17] There are practical limits to the amount of prior data gathering which can be carried out, however, and to the length and detail of regulations. Often political acceptability is inversely proportional to the length and complexity of regulations.

5-12 *Standard setting procedures should provide inputs from those affected at the local and state levels.*

State sensitive area programs provide broad-based standards for areas affecting several jurisdictions or the state as a whole. However, it is often difficult to involve affected individuals at the state or regional levels. They lack organization and mechanisms for representation.

The need to consider several points of view has resulted in cooperative state/local programs where the state develops minimum standards for local controls. Often, local units of government and regional agencies participate in formulating these standards. Local units may then adopt their own more restrictive standards within the state framework.

An interesting approach to combine inputs from several levels was used in the Minnesota shoreland zoning program. The state agency responsible for adopting minimum regulatory standards first developed general guidelines for classifying lakes and shorelands according to use capability and classified all lakes in the state on a tentative basis. The guidelines and proposed lists were then submitted to local units of government for refinement based on local knowledge and preferences. Local units were supplied with air photos and other data. Based upon these materials and their own information the local units revised the tentative state classifications. Ultimate classification decisions were, therefore, local in nature—contributing greatly to their political acceptability. The state regulatory agency discovered, somewhat to its surprise, that local classifications were generally more restrictive than suggested state standards.

5-13 *State legislatures should not be involved in the complicated procedures of promulgating detailed use standards.*

Legislative involvement in sensitive area standard-setting is hindered by technical issues, complexity, and the need to tailor standards to particular facts. Legislative bodies in a few states must approve or disapprove standards drafted by state agencies,[18] but the practicality of the approach remains to be seen.

---

[17]The regulator is often faced with a dilemma. General rules facilitate regulatory administration and enforcement and minimize arbitrary issuance of permits. On the other hand, special rules tailored to differences in the factual base, varying impact of particular types of uses, and other complex factors are rationally and legally more acceptable. Where to draw the line?

There is, of course, no single answer. The drafter is often required to form general rules based on assumptions or determinations considered inappropriate by a scientist because they are too sweeping. For example, if a scientist was asked "how far should houses be set back from lakes to preserve scenic beauty, preserve wildlife, and prevent water pollution?", he would answer that the distance differs depending upon the design of the house, soils, topography, vegetation, wildlife, and other factors. Typically, he would recommend that standards be promulgated only after "more studies."

While this position has rational appeal, there are often compelling reasons to protect an area from imminent development. Delay of five to 10 years until more studies are completed is unacceptable. Detailed data gathering for every area is prohibitively expensive and time consuming.

[18]*E.g.,* critical area designations by the Minnesota State Planning Office must be confirmed within three years by the state legislature.

Table 17

Special permit evaluation procedures. The processing of special permits at state or local levels often involves these steps. Some programs omit or add steps.

The processing of special permits at state or local levels often involves the following steps. Some programs omit or add steps.

Step One: Preliminary discussion. The developer discusses the proposed project with the regulatory agency prior to submission of a formal project application. Preliminary discussion is particularly likely for large-scale development where the developer does not wish to invest in detailed plans until preliminary assurances of approval are given by the regulatory agency. Informal discussion provides an early screening of projects and negotiation as to project design before formal positions are taken by either the developer or regulatory agency.

Step Two: Submission of a formal application. The regulatory agency often supplies a special permit application form and guidelines concerning the submission of detailed project information. The agency may require an environmental impact statement or other fact-finding required to evaluate the impact of the proposed project.

Step Three: Review of the application by the regulatory agency. Review of an application often involves six substeps:

(1) **Circulation of the permit application to other interested agencies or regulatory bodies** to help develop relevant data and insure that the project meets other relevant regulatory specifications.

(2) **Conduct of necessary fact-finding to determine the compliance of the project with regulatory standards.** Often the developer is required to supply much of the needed data. However, the agency may also undertake original data gathering or hire outside consultants. Data gathering may concern not only environmental impact but effect of the project upon public services, public health, and the local or regional economy.

(3) **Conduct of a public hearing.** Virtually all special permit procedures require a public hearing to assist the agency in the gathering of facts, permit the developer to publicly introduce evidence in his behalf, provide other landowners and interested individuals with an opportunity to express support or disapproval, and generate a record for possible appeal of the regulatory decisions. Usually a hearing examiner conducts the hearing with little in the way of formal rules of evidence.

(4) **Application of use standards in light of all facts.** Following the public hearing the regulatory agency makes a decision on the permit in light of the regulatory standards and all of the facts brought to light. The cumulative effect of similar uses should and are (sometimes) considered.

(5) **Preparation of findings of fact and a proposed decision.** This usually takes the form of written recommendations with supportive materials assembled by the agency staff member in charge of the application.

(6) **Final approval or disapproval of the recommendations by the regulatory board, commission, or other body with decision-making responsibility.** Usually this is a "rubber stamp" operation for the staff agencies' recommendations except where substantial policy issues are involved. The final decision is, in some instances, issued as a formal order. Conditions are often attached to permit approvals.

Step Four: Monitoring of Development. Monitoring is needed to insure compliance with the approved permit application and any attached conditions. This may be done by agency staff or by law enforcement officers. It may also involve the filling of periodic reports by the developer.

Step Five: Appeal of the Permit (this would precede monitoring in the case of a permit refusal). In some instances statutes or ordinances provide for rehearing of permit applications by the administering agency. In others, an administrative appeal is provided to an appeal board. Court appeals is the most common procedure even where earlier administrative appeals are provided. Courts may review the permit *de novo* or on the record.

5-14 Varying analysis procedures and methods are needed to establish standards for individual types of areas.

Detailed technical studies rarely precede the adoption of use standards in state and local sensitive area programs. Nevertheless, general principles of analysis are applied and more specific use evaluations often carried out by the regulatory agency on a case-by-case basis as individual special permit applications are submitted. Analysis procedures for particular areas include:

(1) Quantitative evaluation of the frequency and severity of hazards and the adequacy of proposed protection measures are desirable in flood, seismic, erosion, and landslide areas. In some instances, quantified evaluation may be carried out for individual uses. For example, case-by-case analysis can evaluate the impact of floodway uses upon flood heights and flood velocities, including the threatened damage to adjacent, upstream and downstream uses.

(2) Informal supply and demand analysis is desirable in coastal and inland recreation areas and for renewable and nonrenewable forestry areas, prime agricultural lands, and mineral resource areas. Use potential is detemined by natural soil features, geology, slopes, availability of water, accessibility, and size.

(3) Land water interrelations should be analyzed prior to adoption or on a case-by-case basis for flood plain, shoreland, wetland, watershed, aquifer, and coastal areas and uses.[19] Impacts should be determined through analysis of soils, vegetation, ground water flow systems, and surface drainage.

(4) Uniqueness, fragility, sensitivity, and degrees of disturbance should be considered in standard-setting and permit processing for wetlands, scientific areas, wild and scenic rivers, wilderness areas, sites of rare and endangered species, and wildlife habitats. Development standards and buffer areas should reflect the sensitivity of areas and possible threats.

(5) Existing uses and public services should be considered for many types of areas and uses. The development permit process can evaluate the compatibility of proposed uses with existing uses, prevent nuisances and threats to public safety, and insure the adequacy of public services.

Case-by-case evaluations to assess environmental impact and compatibility with adjacent uses are often applied to special permit uses where prior planning efforts are not possible or practical. Few critical area acts specifically require prior comprehensive planning. However, the extent to which prior planning is desirable depends on the: (1) nature of the regulatory standards and scope of goals; (2) importance of natural resource factors in determining the suitability of lands; and (3) degree to which nuisances are involved. Prior planning is particularly desirable where: (1) regulations serve broad public welfare as well as resource protection goals; (2) natural resource factors do not play a dominant role in determining land suitability; and (3) adjacent uses may be incompatible.

5-15 Special permit approaches are particularly useful in areas with diverse resources, a limited data base, and broad management objectives.

The special permit approach is particularly appropriate for areas with highly diverse resources. Here the impact of individual uses differs greatly and inflexible uniform standards make little sense. Special permit approaches have several important advantages:

---

[19]*See* table 12.

(1) They may be adopted where little data exists or wide variations occur in the mapped sensitive area. Much of the necessary data gathering is carried out as development proposals are submitted. The cost of data gathering is reduced through environmental impact statement requirements and other techniques that shift a portion of the data gathering burden to the developer.

(2) They increase the number of uses possible within an area. They promote multiple land uses, reduce landowner complaints, and reduce possible judicial attack on the grounds that the regulations unconstitutionally take private property.

(3) They permit tailoring of use restrictions to the specifics of each proposed use and the natural resources found at a site. This reduces under- or over-regulation of uses which often accompanies inflexible traditional zoning.

(4) They permit more complete protection of natural resources by regulating many aspects of proposed uses through discretionary, nuisance, environmental, and public welfare standards.

(5) They may achieve broad regulatory objectives without lengthy and complicated regulations by establishing general goals and criteria.

(6) They permit weighing and balancing complex factors rather than rigid evaluation of single factors.

5-16 *Expertise and data gathering capability must be available during administration of special permit programs.*

Arbitrary issuance of special permits often results when case-by-case data gathering capability and expertise are not available. This is particularly serious for local programs in rural areas. Sources of technical data and analysis include special expert advisory boards such as conservation commissions, shifting of a portion of the data gathering and analysis burden to developers, employment of consultants, and use of technical assistance provided by state and federal agencies.

5-17 *Sensitive area standards should reflect the practical limitations of impact evaluation methodologies.*

Numerical standards more precise than can be measured through available evaluation techniques present administrative nightmares and may undermine the political and legal acceptability of regulations. For example, it will be meaningless to prohibit floodway uses raising flood heights one-tenth of a foot at any point on a stream if hydrologic evaluation techniques are precise only to one-half foot. Of course, more precise standards may be adopted as refinements, in evaluation methodologies become available.

5-18 *Goals and procedures for special permits should be drafted with care to guide agency action and insure due process where precise quantified standards are not practical or feasible.*

A clear statement of regulatory goals and findings of fact is particularly important for processing special permits. The factors relevant to a permit decision should also be listed. Courts have recognized regulatory goals and findings of facts as an integral part of use standards.[20]

Clear permit processing procedures are also important. Procedures should be: (1) spelled out with certainty; (2) provide an expeditious review of proposed development; (3) involve data gathering by the developer or the regulatory agency or

---

[20]*See, e.g.,* J.M. Mills Inc. v. Murphy, 352 A. 2d 661 (R.I. 1976); MacGibbon v. Board of Appeals of Duxbury, 356 Mass. 635, 255 N.E. 2d 347 (1970).

both; and (4) provide public notice and review, including public hearings, wherever major developments or policy issues are involved.

5-19 Data gathering and administrative mechanisms should reflect special permit needs.

Sensitive area programs utilizing special permits apply several approaches to facilitate permit processing:

(1) A portion of data gathering funds is reserved for use during program administration.

(2) Gradations and subzones are identified for some areas (*e.g.*, floodways within broader flood plains) to aid permit evaluation.

(3) Detailed air photos are acquired and carried into the field to help evaluate applications.

(4) Lists of interested agencies and individuals are prepared. Notices of permit applications are sent to them soliciting opinions and attendance at public hearings. Interested individuals and agencies may also review environmental impact statements and help monitor and enforce regulations.

(5) Decision-making processes are structured to include important policy discussions at public hearings. Final decisions concerning these issues are made by regulatory boards or legislative bodies rather than staff.

(6) In state/local cooperative programs, copies of proposed permits are forwarded to the responsible state agency for multi-level review.

(7) Administrative appeals to state appeal boards[21] or commissions are provided for local special permit decisions in some instances. This facilitates expert review of technical issues.

5-20 Combined permit processing procedures should be developed where several agencies or local units of government issue permits for a single use.

Delays and expenses are considerable when multiple, sequential reviews for permit applications occur. Some programs, such as the North Carolina coastal wetland protection program, circulate permit applications to many agencies for comment and simultaneous review.

5-21 Added research is needed to assess the impacts of types of development in various circumstances and develop impact minimization techniques.

Very little research has been done concerning impact minimization techniques. This has hindered the establishment of standards consistent with land capability and sensitivity. New studies are needed on such priority topics as techniques for minimizing septic tank impact on ground water, impacts of adjacent development on wetlands, and impacts of residential development on forestry and agricultural lands.

5-22 State and federal technical assistance and grants-in-aid should be provided to assist local units of government in developing and administering regulatory standards.

Successful state critical area programs have emphasized technical assistance and education efforts to strengthen local land use control capability. Assistance has included guidebooks, reports, and other materials on standard-setting and administration. Model ordinances and guidelines have been prepared for many flood

---

[21]Such an approach is used in the Washington shoreline program and the wetland programs of Massachusetts, Delaware, and Maryland.

plain[22] and shoreland programs.[23] Training sessions have been held for regulatory administrators and local governmental officials. Technical data gathering and analysis assistance has been provided for evaluating special permits, particularly for floodway and wetland uses with multijurisdictional impact.

5-23 *Research and monitoring should evaluate the success of standards in achieving short- and long-term critical area goals.*

To date, the effectiveness of adopted standards has rarely been evaluated. Monitoring efforts are time-consuming and expensive but essential for testing alternative approaches. Regulations should be adopted with a clear understanding that modifications may follow monitoring efforts.

[22] *E.g.,* Minnesota, Wisconsin.
[23] *E.g.,* Maine, Vermont.

Table 18

Principal onsite and offsite use factors determining appropriate use for an area.

Area	Management Objectives	Use Factors On-Site Factors		Off-Site Factors	
		Natural Resource	Cultural	Natural Resource	Cultural
Prime agricultural lands	1. Manage areas to meet present and future local regional, national, and international food needs. 2. Shape urban growth. 3. Preserve as a land bank with options for future development and non-development uses. 4. Control development to meet wildlife management needs, preserve groundwater recharge areas, preserve water supply areas, convey flood flows (flood plains), etc. See discussion of other types of areas.	1. Soil type and areal extent, slope, depth to ground water, climate, water supply limitations such as flooding, erosion, salts. *Comment:* Specific evaluations must relate land characteristics to the requirements of particular types of crops or livestock. Many lands have some potential for food production with fertilization, irrigation or other land management. Acceptable cost levels are important.	1. Existing land ownership, lot size, land values, taxes, etc. *Comment:* Areas committed to commercial or industrial use or high density residential use with fragmented and small scale ownership are effectively available for commercial agriculture use although some truck farming and gardening may be possible. This is also true for areas owned by the public as parks or recreational areas. 2. Additional resource parameters. See other areas.	1. Water supply, *Comment:* The availability of irrigation water from sources within or outside of the region is essential for agricultural production in many areas.	1. Urban centers in area. *Comment:* Proximity determines ease of access and transportation costs. Proximity is increasingly important with dwindling national energy supplies, particularly for perishables, *(e.g.,* strawberries) and bulk goods which demand rapid, inexpensive transportation. 2. Air or water pollution which may threaten agricultural uses. 3. Other land in the region which may serve as alternative development sites. 4. Adjacent residential uses. *Comment:* The raising of pigs and other livestock may cause odor nuisances to adjacent residential uses.
Timber Products Areas	1. Protect the long term timber production base to meet present and future demands for lumber, pulp, and misc. wood products. Due to the long growth period from treeplanting to harvest, this requires long-term land use commitments.	1. Tree species (type diversity, condition, age, density, number), size of unit, soil type, slope, climate, water supply, special problems such as erosion, flooding, See discussion of individual critical areas (*e.g.,* recreational areas, scenic areas, etc.)	1. Existing uses, land ownership, taxes. *Comment:* The subdivision of forest lands and their subsequent development for second home use reduces timber production due to reluctance of second home owners to fell trees although timber continues	1. Watershed uses which may interfere with water supply, cause flooding.	1. Proximity to processing centers. Availability of access roads and transport. Low cost transport. Cost is particularly important for pulp.

Table 18 (continued)

Area	Management Objectives	Use Factors On-Site Factors		Off-Site Factors	
		Natural Resource	Cultural	Natural Resource	Cultural
	2. Provide areas for multipurpose, public or quasi-public use such as camping, watershed management, hunting, and so forth. These uses are generally consistent with forest production but conflicts may arise due to vandalism or fires and recreational users may object to clear-cutting or other management techniques, etc. 3. Protect watersheds 4. Provide wildlife and scientific field study areas. 5. Protect floodways, flood storage areas, etc.		to grow on the land. Public ownership or private large-scale forest holdings may be essential for continued production.		
Mineral resource areas for extraction of sand and gravel, crushed stone, clay, metallic ores, oil, gas, and other minerals.	1. Protect deposits from incompatible uses. The subdivision of lands, and construction of residential, commercial, and other uses often effectively prevent extraction of sand and gravel, metallic deposits, and oil and gas. 2. Prevent waste. 3. Prevent water and air pollution, aesthe-	1. Type and quality of deposit, size, depth and type overburden, slope, ground water, seismic activity and other hazards, topography, wildlife, scenic qualities.	Existing uses and their compatibility with extractive activities; land ownership; land values; zoning. *Comment:* Major impediments to mineral extraction include: incompatible uses, public ownership, and prohibitory local zoning ordinances.	1. Availability of water and other materials needed for extraction and processing. 2. Habitat of rare and endangered species, wetlands, lakes, and other sensitive lands which may be damaged by runoff, dust, and other impacts of mineral extraction or processing. 3. Alternative deposits in the region, state,	1. Adjacent commercial, residential, industrial uses which may be disturbed by effects of extraction including dust, glare, odor, noise subsidence, hauling, and so forth. 2. Location in relationship to users is particularly important for sand and gravel and other aggregates where

Table 18 (continued)

Area	Management Objectives	Use Factors On-Site Factors		Off-Site Factors	
		Natural Resource	Cultural	Natural Resource	Cultural
	tic blights, (*e.g.,* strip mining), erosion, subsidence, and nuisances to adjacent uses from noise, trucking, etc. 4. Require reclamation and rehabilitation. 5. Control local zoning which unreasonably prohibits mineral extraction.			nation (issue of relative scarcity).	transportation costs are a major consideration. 3. Availability of labor force, electrical energy sources transportation systems necessary for extraction, transportation to market, processing.
Flood plains (along coasts, rivers, inland lakes, and including "dry-runs")	1. Prevent damaging increases in flood heights and velocities at upstream and downstream locations and on adjacent lands due to destruction of flood conveyance capacity, flood storage, or natural storm protective barriers such as coastal dunes by structures, fills, grading, or other uses. 2. Reduce losses to damage prone uses within flood hazard areas and the need for public relief, and construction of dikes, dams, and levees, by either prohibiting damage prone uses or requiring individual flood proofing.	Topography, vegetation, aerial extent of flooding, depth, velocity, duration, and pollution content, rainfall, soils. Where flood records are lacking, flood heights, extent, etc. must be calculated based upon rainfall projections, and flood routing techniques. Floodway areas are calculated for riverine areas. *See* discussion of wetland, scientific areas.	Existing uses such as dikes, levees, or other protective works, bridges, houses, etc. which may block flood flows, displace storage, or otherwise modify the natural regime. *See* discussion of wetland, scientific areas.	Soils, topography, vegetation, rainfall, throughout the watershed.	1. Adjacent land uses which may be damaged by increased flood heights due to flood plain development. 2. Lands throughout a locality, region which may serve as alternative development sites.

Table 18 (continued)

Area	Management Objectives	Use Factors On-Site Factors		Off-Site Factors	
		Natural Resource	**Cultural**	**Natural Resource**	**Cultural**
	3. Reduce the cost of sewer, water, roads, and other public facilities for flood prone areas. 4. Protect prime wetlands, recreation areas, areas of special scenic beauty, areas of special scientific interest, and so forth. 5. Protect prime agricultural lands, forestry areas, sand and gravel deposits which often lie within flood plains.				
Erosion Areas	1. Protect development from erosion, flooding. 2. Protect soils for future agriculture and other uses. 3. Protect water quality and reduce sedimentation in lakes, ponds, streams.	1. Geology (types, characteristics), soil type including permeability and porosity, topography including degree of slope, climate including total rainfall and rainfall characteristics, stream flows and runoff characteristics, fluctuations in water levels, wave action (along coasts), vegetation.	1. Existing use of land; land treatment or erosion control measures.	1. Soils, geology, vegetation in watershed which determine runoff characteristics. 2. Downstream lakes, wetlands, which may be impacted by sediment.	1. Groins, sea-walls, dams, other works which may alter stream flows, wave action.
Shore-lands (lake, stream, coastal)	1. Protect water quality, wetlands and fish and other aquatic life. *Comment:* Protection of water resources is a major objective of most shoreland programs.	1. Water quality and quantity, including the size of water body, depth, hardness, acidity, total dissolved solids, odor, color, oxygen level, clarity, fish and other aquatic life, vi-	1. Existing use of waters including dams, piers, channelization, control of water regime by reservoir, commercial and recreational uses, water extraction for water supply or	1. Regional surface water and ground water flow systems. 2. Typography, soil type and other characteristics of adjacent lands which may be impacted upon by	1. Highway access, water supply users in the area, point and nonpoint pollution, sources in the watershed.

Table 18 (continued)

Area	Management Objectives	Use Factors On-Site Factors		Off-Site Factors	
		Natural Resource	**Cultural**	**Natural Resource**	**Cultural**
	2. Protect and manage shoreland areas of special significance such as areas of special scenic beauty, areas of special scientific interest, flood hazard areas, erosion areas, wetlands, historic archaelogical sites, etc. 3. Promote public recreation opportunities (beaches, marinas, etc.) 4. Promote shoreland uses requiring a water front location (marinas, resorts) and compatible with natural values. 5. Prevent incompatible uses.	ruses, fecal coliforms, biological oxygen demand levels, temperature, bottom type, rooted aquatics, flow, sediment levels, nutrient levels, fluctuation in levels. 2. Soils, geology, slope, vegetation and other factors related to the capability of "subzones" for particular uses.	irrigation, pollution sources. Land ownership, existing uses, lot sizes.	or impact upon shoreland uses.	
Wild, scenic, recreational rivers	1. Preserve river and adjacent lands to meet local, regional, statewide recreational demands for canoeing, hiking, picnicking. 2. Protect wildlife, scenic beauty. 3. Reduce flooding, other hazards.	1. Size, length, depth of river, water quality, aquatic special features such as aquatic life, rapids, water falls. 3. Shoreland topography, geology, soils, climate, vegetation.	1. Dams, channel alterations, existing shoreland uses, historic and archeological sites paralleling and crossing roads, landownership, lot sizes. *Comment:* Scenic, wild, and recreation rivers are usually distinguished based upon degree of disturbance and access. Wild rivers are undisturbed and without access; scenic rivers may have some distur-	1. Scenic beauty of adjacent areas, historic sites, other special attractions. 2. Similar areas in the region, state, etc. (relevant to scarcity).	1. Adjacent uses such as industries, airports or mining operations which may may disturb the river corridor due to air, water, or noise pollution, destruction of scenic beauty, and so forth.

Table 18 (continued)

Area	Management Objectives	Use Factors On-Site Factors		Off-Site Factors	
		Natural Resource	**Cultural**	**Natural Resource**	**Cultural**
			cess; recreation rivers may have some impound-ment as well as considerable existing devel-opment and ac-cess.		
Area of special scientific interest (flora, fauna, geology)	1. Provide edu-cational oppor-tunities (primary, secondary, uni-versity). 2. Provide benchmarks for measuring cul-tural impact on the environment. 3. Provide re-search areas (private groups, agencies, universities). 4. Protect nat-ural diversity and gene pools for possible fu-ture use. 5. Provide psy-chological and philosophical benefits.	1. Flora and fauna present: number, condition, diver-sity, rarity, rep-resentative na-ture of species, degree of dis-turbance. Size of unit. Topo-graphy, climate, soils, geology.	1. Existing uses, land ownership, land values.	1. Similar areas in the region, state (relevant to uniqueness, scarcity)	1. Urban areas or other sources of potential users (research groups, schools, etc.) in the re-gion. 2. Adjacent uses which threaten areas.
Wetlands (coastal and inland)	1. Protect fish spawning grounds and other waterfowl and wildlife hab-itats; preserve areas of special scientific inter-est including habitat for rare and endangered species. 2. Protect water quality and the natural pollution reduction func-tion of wetlands. 3. Preserve flood storage, flood convey-ance, and wave action reduction	1. Soils, topo-graphy, vegeta-tion, wildlife, size of wetland, depth. Relation-ship to streams, ground water, recharge areas. Frequency, velo-city, depth of flooding.	1. Land owner-ship, lot sizes, existing uses, land values.	1. Regional eco-systems. 2. Regional ground and sur-face water sys-tems. 3. Erosion po-tential of adja-cent lands, other natural features which may threaten wet-lands.	1. Adjacent land uses such as agriculture or commercial uses which may threaten wet-lands due to sedimentation, erosion, air pol-lution, lowering of groundwater table, etc. 2. Dikes, dams, levees and drainage ditches which deter-mine or modify regional water resources sys-tem. 3. Potential users in area

Table 18 (continued)

Area	Management Objectives	Use Factors On-site Factors		Off-site Factors	
		Natural Resource	**Cultural**	**Natural Resource**	**Cultural**
	areas (*e.g.,* mangroves). 4. Reduce threats to structures due to inadequate structureal bearing capacity of soil; insure adequate operation of on-site waste disposal systems.				including hunters, school groups, etc.

Part **6**

REGULATORY
DATA GATHERING

The accuracy and scale of sensitive area maps and other data are major political, legal, and administrative issues in many programs. Areas must be mapped at relatively large scale to satisfy statutory and administrative requirements. It is difficult to apply rational performance standards without detailed information about specific natural resource values and hazards at particular sites, specifications of proposed uses, and the manner in which uses are to be conducted. Lack of accurate, high resolution data and analysis mechanisms have sometimes led to simplistic definition and standard setting criteria, poor political acceptability, and administrative problems.

Common data deficiencies include:[1] (1) flood, vegetative, existing use, or other essential data types are missing; (2) data lacks sufficient scale or resolution (often a minimum map scale of 1:24,000 is essential for rural regulations and larger scales for urban areas); (3) data is inaccurate; (4) data is inaccessible to regulatory decision-makers; (5) data is insufficiently geo-referenced, *i.e.*, it is not linked to particular points on the ground; and (6) data lacks manipulative capability.

---

[1] *See* J. Kusler *et al., Data Needs and Data Gathering for Areas of Critical Environmental Concern,* Part I: Summary Report, University of Wisconsin, Institute for Environmental Studies, Report 53 (1975).

Figure 26

Three approaches for mapping wetland areas are illustrated below for Port Arthur North Quadrangle, Texas.

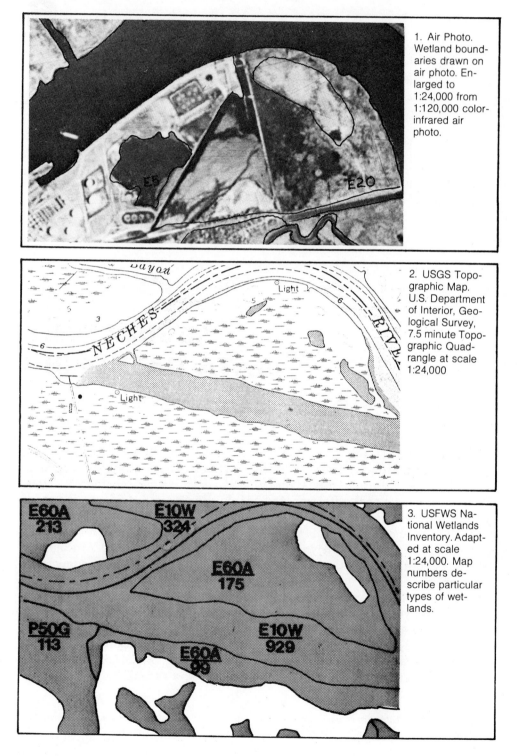

1. Air Photo. Wetland boundaries drawn on air photo. Enlarged to 1:24,000 from 1:120,000 color-infrared air photo.

2. USGS Topographic Map. U.S. Department of Interior, Geological Survey, 7.5 minute Topographic Quadrangle at scale 1:24,000

3. USFWS National Wetlands Inventory. Adapted at scale 1:24,000. Map numbers describe particular types of wetlands.

Table 19

Some principal sensitive data sources: (Source: This table is based upon a somewhat similar table prepared by the Wetland Project, Massachusetts Audubon Society, Lincoln, Mass.)

Data Source	Information Displayed	Scale	Uses	Sources	Cost
USGS Topographic Maps (7½' & 15')	Topographic contours, major roads, railroads, utility lines, contours, water bodies, houses, town names, county and town boundaries, vegetated and non-vegetated wetlands	1"=2000'	1. Enlarged for use as sensitive area base maps 2. Interim wetland maps 3. Watershed boundaries 4. Source of topographic information for calculating flood plain and floodway boundaries, erosion areas, slope areas	USGS Geological Division	$.75 - .95 a sheet
SCS Soil Survey Maps	Soil types	1"=2000' 1"=1320' 4"=1 mile	1. Mapping of wetland, floodplain, slope, erosion, prime agricultural land, forestry and mineral resource areas 2. Determination of soil suitability for onsite waste disposal 3. Determination of soil structural bearing capacity	SCS USDA	Local units get field sheet (aerial photos) & 1 map free; extra copies cost a few dollars
State Wetlands, Floodplain, Geologic Maps	Sensitive area boundaries. Varied (depending on state and type of area).	1"=2000' to 1"=100'	1. Interim or permanent regulation of areas.	State programs	Varied
USGS, HUD, Corps of Engineers, SCS Flood Hazard Maps.	Flood prone areas	Approx. 1"=2000'	1. Interim regulation	HUD and USGS	Free
	Standard project flood plain, 100 year flood evaluation, wetland boundaries (some maps)	Range from 1"=500' to 1'=1000'	1. Used as zone maps for flood plain zoning, and other regulation	Army Corps of Engineers Flood Plain Management Services	Free

Table 19 (continued)

Data Source	Information Displayed	Scale	Uses	Sources	Cost
USGS Hydrologic Investigations Atlas: Hydrology & Water Resources Maps	Each map is different - may contain: wells, test holes, bedrock, ground water info., recharge areas, water quality	1"=2000'	1. Determine ground water flow systems 2. Determine aquifer recharge areas	Geological Division Distribution Office 1200 S Eads St. Arlington, Va. 22202	Less than $2/sheet
Local Subdivision Maps	Dimensions of property, roads, sewers, size and location of houses, and topographic contours, boundaries of watercourses. Wetland and flood plain boundaries (some circumstances)	1"=40' 1"=60'	1. Help determine precise sensitive area boundaries (some instances) 2. Evaluate development proposals	Municipal offices	Varied
Air Photos: USGS USDA Other Sources	Roads, houses, vegetation, topography, watercourses, structures, fills, flooding, etc. (all features visible from air).	Varied; 1"=2000' common	1. Map sensitive area boundaries (*e.g.*, wetlands, flood plains) 2. Evaluate development proposals	USGS USDA state transportation offices, consultants	Often free
Surficial Geology: USGS quad.	Everything on USGS topographic maps plus geologic deposits, bedrock, fill sites	1"=2000'	1. Determine ground water flow systems 2. Determine bedrock 3. Map mineral resource area.	USGS Geological Division 1200 S. Eads St. Arlington, Va. 22202; *see also* Geologic and Water Supply Reports & Maps	Less than $2/sheet
Town, City, County, Borough Zoning Maps	Varied. Information can include: roads, property lines, zoning districts, and sensitive areas	Range from 1"=500' to 1"=1000'	1. Determine existing uses 2. Determine compatibility of proposed wetland uses with zone classification and adjacent uses 3. Use as base maps (or sensitive area mapping)	Municipal Offices	Varied
Assessor Maps, Plat Books'	Property lines, owners' names, easements, roads, buildings	1"=100' or 1"=200'	1. Determine land ownership	Each town, city county	Varied

In some instances, minor modifications in existing data gathering and mapping efforts are sufficient for regulatory needs. For example, wetland regulation may be facilitated through access to basic air photo data sources. More often, major modifications in scale, format, and accuracy are required.

There are, of course, practical and rational limits to scale and precision and sound data are not a guarantee of rational development policies if faulty analytical procedures are applied. Results can be biased and policies not enforced.

6-1 *Data gathering design for a given program should address data types, scales, formats, and manipulative capability. It should reflect legal, planning, political, budget, and natural resource factors.*

Data needs are determined by many factors discussed in the recommendations below: (1) data gathering requirements in statutes; (2) types of areas and diversity within them; (3) tests, criteria, and analytical approaches selected to define critical areas and establish use standards; (4) policy-setting and political requirements; (5) anticipated regulatory use standards; (6) court cases in the jurisdiction pertaining to certainty in zoning boundaries, specificity in use standards, discrimination in regulations, and the taking issue; (7) data needed for regulatory administration; (8) data required for court enforcement; (9) available funds; (10) data refinement procedures anticipated during administrative phases; (11) existing data; and (12) available data gathering techniques.

6-2 *Data gathering should focus on essential data—its absence would prevent program implementation—rather than merely desirable data.*

Enormous quantities of natural resource, social, and economic data may be useful in the design and implementation of critical area regulations. (See table 16.) However, budgetary, staff, and equipment limitations prevent the gathering of all relevant data.

For this reason, data gathering efforts have usually focused on essential data. One criterion used to judge essential data is, can a program be implemented in its absence? Essential data often includes large scale sensitive area maps and data required for case-by-case evaluation of development proposals.

6-3 *Ideally, data gathering efforts should develop several data scales and formats for use in the four steps of regulatory program implementation.*

Each step in sensitive area implementation favors slightly different data types, scales, and formats.

(1) A modest data base is often sufficient for adopting basic enabling structures, including goals, and formulating criteria and procedures for more specific definition of areas in later program stages. Extensive data gathering has rarely preceded adoption of existing enabling statutes. However, generalized surveys and compilations of existing data have sometimes been used to document the need for regulations. Statistical resource profiles—how many acres, at what location, with what demand—have also been used.

(2) Specific maps and research information are useful in formulating detailed definition criteria including subclassification, such as in the Minnesota lakeshore land classification scheme. It defines three classes of lakes and adjacent shorelines and sets criteria for mapping of gradations and subzones in areas. (See figure 7 and table 15.) However, extensive data gathering rarely precedes formulating specific criteria or adopting administrative regulations.

Figure 27

Typical zoning map before and after addition of flood regulations using a two-district approach. (Source: J. Kusler, *A Perspective on Flood Plain Regulations for Flood Plain Management,* Department of the Army, Office of the Chief of Engineers, Washington, D.C., 1976.)

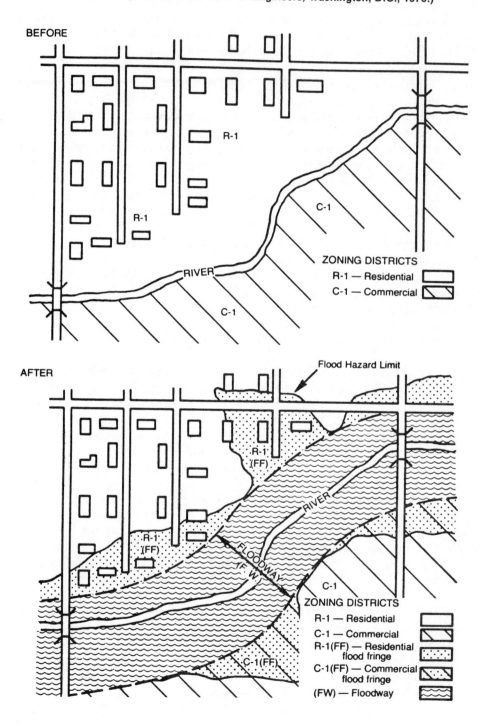

(3) Detailed maps are almost always needed prior to formal designation of areas due to statutory requirements and administrative needs. These maps may be prepared by a state agency working alone or in combination with local units of government, regional planning agencies, federal agencies, or other groups. Initial maps may be refined by subsequent efforts. Maps must usually be prepared at a minimum scale of 1:24,000 for rural areas and up to 1:12,000 for urban areas.[2] Identification of gradations and subzones may also be required.

(4) Site-specific data gathering is required for processing individual regulatory permits at state or local levels, enforcing regulations, and monitoring development. Site specific data is needed to evaluate the special values or hazards at particular sites and the impact of the proposed development. The impacts include principal uses, associated development such as roads, transmission lines, and accessory structures, and the cumulative impact of future uses. Usually data contained in data banks and soil and topographic maps are at an inadequate scale to provide the required site-specific information. For this reason, regulatory agencies must rely on field surveys conducted by staff on a case-by-case basis or information provided by developers and consultants through preparation of environmental impact statements and permit applications. Data acquired at a site is sometimes translated into large scale maps.

While data must be sufficient to implement all phases of a regulatory program, the data required by the final two steps is most essential. A program ultimately succeeds or fails to the extent that policies and standards translate into control of uses on the ground. Large scale data required for the final steps may be generalized to meet the needs of earlier steps. However, data for the first two steps is often at insufficient scale for the final steps.

6-4 *A variety of techniques should be used to minimize high data gathering costs, maximize efficiency, and allocate available dollars to essential data.*

To reduce costs, programs often incorporate a number of measures discussed in later recommendations.

(1) Data is gathered on a priority area basis.

(2) Federal and local cost-sharing and technical assistance is utilized.

(3) Existing data sources are used.

(4) Data suitable for regulatory mapping is generated without prior stages of generalized data gathering.

(5) Data is gathered on an area-by-area or case-by-case basis where development will occur in only a small portion of a total area and an overall review of the resource is not essential.

(6) Air photos are used.

(7) A portion of the data gathering burden is shifted to developers.

(8) Small scale data is used on an interim basis until more detailed data gathering can be carried out.

(9) Detailed data (*e.g.*, high resolution air photos) is initially gathered. This may be interpreted on a first cut basis and used later for more detailed interpretations without new raw data gathering.

---

[2]Not all critical areas require mapping at very large scale. Agricultural and forest zones, which are defined to include large blocks of land in contiguous ownership, may be mapped at smaller scales along roads or property lines.

Required map scale depends not only upon the types of areas, but also on the restrictiveness of anticipated use standards. Large scale maps have often proven necessary for areas where all development is prohibited, such as floodways within a broader flood plain or wetlands within a coastal area. In this way prohibitory controls are applied only when absolutely necessary.

(10) Data is stored in an easily retrievable format so that it may be used for other purposes.

6-5 *Care should be taken not to expend all available funds for a general study of problems on a broad-scale basis. General studies may be of little use in implementation. Often, a substantial portion of the data gathering funds should be used to produce accurate maps of priority areas at minimum scales of 1:24,000 for rural areas and 1:12,000 for urban areas and to gather site-specific data on an area-by-area or case-by-case basis as development proposals are submitted.*

Legislators and landowners demand increasingly detailed, accurate, and quanitified data to justify regulations. This reflects increased competition for land, a "hard-headed" look at environmental arguments, and advances in sensitive area definition and data gathering. Existing data sources can locate and define a sensitive area in a preliminary sense, but are often insufficient for detailed policy setting and planning, land use regulation, and environmental impact analysis. For example, available flood data such as historic flood records, soil surveys, or air photos of flood conditions may initially serve to define flood plains. But they may be insufficient in themselves to quantify flood threat—needed for regulatory definitions and standard-setting purposes.

Small scale environmental or critical area inventories have been of some use in developing political support for programs and setting data gathering and regulatory priorities. However, they have not been sufficient for regulatory mapping. Programs have found it wasteful to expend substantial data gathering funds on small scale and low resolution products.

6-6 *Emphasis should be placed on dissemination as well as acquisition of data.*

Too often, large sums have been spent on data acquisition with little attention to distribution. Distribution of data to users may be encouraged through: (1) preparing data lists and inventories;[3] (2) reproducing reports, air photos, topographic maps, and the like through low-cost techniques; (3) sponsoring workshops, adult education courses, and seminars by universities and agencies; and (4) adopting an "open files" policy for state agencies.

6-7 *Zoning boundary lines must be drawn with relative precision to avoid attack on due process grounds. However, there are limits to required scale, and a two-step procedure may be used to locate boundaries precisely.*

Accuracy and scale of boundary maps has been a principal issue in many programs. Relative precision in zone boundaries has been necessary to meet statutory requirements and give landowners certainty in their use of lands, thereby avoiding due process objections. Failure to accurately map areas at relatively large scale has resulted in landowner confusion and administrative problems. For example, a boundary line 1/32 inch wide on a map at the scale of one inch per mile represents 165 feet on the ground.

Despite the need for relatively large scale data, map scales and accuracy have sometimes been carried to illogical and impractical extremes. There is, for example, no legal requirement that zone boundaries be drawn with mathematical precision.[4] In addition, allocation of too much money to mapping may result in inadequate funding for administration and enforcement. Even where detailed maps are available, supplementary field surveys are necessary in the case of boundary

[3]These lists have been prepared in Wisconsin, Maine, and Washington.
[4]*See* for example, Turnpike Realty Co. v. Town of Dedham, 362 Mass. 221, 284 N.E.2d 891 (1972), *cert.*

disputes. Undue emphasis on map scale and accuracy detracts from the ultimate regulatory objective—maintenance of resource value or protection from natural hazard.

Due to limitations in map scale and accuracy, most programs utilize a two-step procedure to define critical area boundaries and evaluate project impact. First, maps determine the general boundaries. Second, written definition criteria are incorporated in regulations, (*e.g.*, vegetation lists for defining wetland areas) and field investigations are carried out to apply the written criteria if disputes arise.[5]

Other techniques to facilitate location of map boundaries on the ground include: (1) delineating boundaries on air photos which show natural and cultural features; (2) using boundaries coincident with political jurisdiction boundaries; (3) locating boundaries through metes and bounds description or referring to a defined distance from water bodies (common in coastal and shoreland programs); and (4) locating boundaries in relationship to particular elevations such as in flood mapping.

6-8 *Data gathering should be related to anticipated use standards.*

Particularly accurate and detailed data is needed to define boundaries and document the importance of areas or subzones where most or all private development must be prohibited.[6] However, once regulations have been adopted, little additional data gathering may be required.

In contrast, less precise and detailed data may suffice to define initial regulatory boundaries where development is to be permitted, consistent with performance standards. Mapping of gradations and subzones may be required for the application of performance standards. In addition, large quantities of site-specific data are needed to determine the appropriateness of particular development proposals within the areas.

6-9 *The delineation of gradations and subzones is needed for some areas.*

Maps or other identifications of gradations and subzones are desirable in some circumstances to help sustain regulations against constitutional attack and provide appropriate development controls for specific areas. Very tight controls are more easily justified if applied only to the most sensitive or hazardous areas.[7] The application of tight development policies on a broadscale basis undermines the unique and special concept of critical areas.

Identification of gradations is particularly important in coastal and shoreland areas where a broad, arbitrary boundary, such as the 1,000 foot corridor, is used for initial definition of the areas. (See figure 28.) It is less important for areas with maps reflecting specific natural resource values or hazards.

The extent to which mapping gradations and subzones is desirable (as opposed to the identification of such areas on a case-by-case basis as individual permits are submitted) depends on many factors including the type of area, natural diversity of the area, regulatory approach used, size of the area, regulatory objectives, and

---

denied, 409 U.S. 1108 (1973) in which the court upheld flood plain regulations based upon a map which included in the flood plain district several hills above the regulatory flood elevation. The court observed that the ordinance special exception procedure was available to remedy map inaccuracies.

[5] *See* note 29 in Part 8, *infra.*

[6] *See* note 29, Part 8, *infra.*

[7] *See* note 32 in Part 8, *infra.*

Figure 28

Three-district zoning approach suggested in the Wisconsin Model Shoreland Ordinance. Wisconsin lakeshore areas are often divided into three districts. Very restrictive "conservancy" district regulations are applied to wetland areas. Moderately restrictive "recreation-residential" restrictions limiting the types of permissible uses and establishing minimum lot sizes and width are applied to most other areas. "General purpose" district restrictions imposing minimum land use requirements are applied to low quality areas.

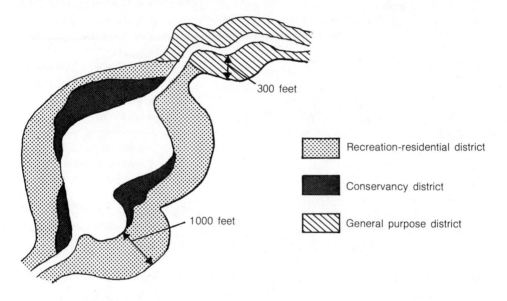

300 feet

1000 feet

Recreation-residential district

Conservancy district

General purpose district

whether the regulations require more detailed data gathering during administrative phases of a program.

6-10 *Data gathering should anticipate the principal regulatory approach for an area.*

The regulatory technique determines the required scale and format of data gathering:

(1) Very specific, quantified hazard information is usually needed for adoption and administration of building codes requiring flood-proofing and other hazard-protection measures. This establishes the minimum standard for protection.

(2) Less precise information is required for some types of zoning, but maps are usually essential for identification of sensitive area boundaries. Site-specific data is needed to apply minimum standards for structures within the critical area zone or zones.

(3) Generalized initial information may be adequate to adopt subdivision controls and other special permit regulations, such as a large scale development site review. A major portion of the data gathering burden can then be shifted to the developer or data gathering can be carried out by the agency on a case-by-case basis.

6-11 *Sufficient data must be gathered to satisfy the criteria and tests selected for defining critical areas.*

In many instances, the type, scale, and format of available data has determined the criteria used to define areas rather than vice versa. Unfortunately, this has limited the sophistication and acceptability of some programs.[8] Criteria and tests for defining

[8]For example, local flood plain regulations based upon generalized, unquantified flood maps have often encountered strong objections from landowners.

sensitive areas have emphasized natural resources such as soils, topography, vegetation, wildlife, water resources, and geology. However, some programs have taken into account existing uses, the path of development, and accessibility of areas for particular uses.

Principal data types needed in definition and regulation of individual types of areas include:[9]

(1) *Flood Plains.* Hydrologic data (stream flow, flood records, rainfall records), topographic maps (5- foot or 2-foot contour intervals), vegetation data (to calculate roughness coefficients), and information concerning existing uses;

(2) *Seismic areas.* Earthquake records, seismic risk or hazard maps, physical evidence of earthquakes (air photos, damage reports).

(3) *Landslide areas.* Records of landslides, air photos, seismic risk or hazard maps, geologic and hydrologic maps, topographic maps, seismic records;

(4) *Erosion areas.* Soil maps, topographic maps, air photos, vegetation maps. Time series information is sometimes used to indicate erosion rates;

(5) *Coastal areas.* Air photos, topographic maps, soil maps, other maps, and data to define subzones including flood areas, wetlands, recreation areas, wildlife areas, *etc.*;

(6) *Shorelands of inland lakes and streams.* Many types and see coastal areas above;

(7) *Wetlands.* Air photos, vegetation maps, high water information, and tidal records. Soil maps have also been used for inland wetland areas;

(8) *Scientific areas.* Air photos, soil maps, vegetation maps, and topographic maps. Primary reliance on field surveys;

(9) *Prime agricultural land.* Soils, topography, land ownership (type of owner, acreage), inventories of existing uses, and assessors maps;

(10) *Mineral areas.* Air photos, soils, geologic maps, maps of land ownership, and existing uses;

(11) *Forestry areas.* Soil maps, topographic maps, climate, timber inventories (size, diversity, condition, other factors), ownership, and existing uses.

Data gathering addressing a single class of area must emphasize the data required for that type of area. However, data gathering for comprehensive programs addressing many types of areas may gather common denominator data: (1) detailed and high resolution air photos, (2) topographic maps, (3) soil maps, (4) hydrologic maps, and (5) geologic maps.

6-12 *Data gathering for hazard areas should, as the long-term goal, quantify the severity and frequency of hazards.*

Flood hazard and to some extent erosion and seismic area programs have stressed quantified data gathering concerning hazard frequency and severity. Quantified information is needed to evaluate the probability of harm to proposed uses and to apply performance standards. Quantified flood data is also required by most state flood hazard statutes which adopt the 100-year flood as the basis for regulation.

Although quantified data is desirable for the administration of programs, generalized unquantified data such as flood photos, soil maps, and historic flood maps have been used with success on an interim basis in urban areas and on a long-term basis in rural areas. This is particularly true where procedures incorporated in

[9]*See also* table 16.

the regulations help to carry out detailed, quantified hazard analysis on a case-by-case basis as individual development proposals are submitted.[10]

In some instances, data gathering has also been conducted for hazard areas to determine wildlife areas, areas of special scenic beauty, erosion problems and other factors related to the suitability of lands for particular uses over and above the hazard problems. This results in a series of overlapping maps which are very useful in standard-setting and program implementation.

6-13 *Ideally, data gathering for non-hazard areas should involve both qualitative and quantitative resource assessment.*

Uniqueness or scarcity is a consideration in definition and standard-setting for virtually all types of non-hazard areas including prime agricultural lands, mineral resource areas, forestry areas, wetlands, scientific areas, coastal areas, and shorelands. However, formal supply and demand analysis has rarely been conducted to determine scarcity due to complexity and the lack of funds. Despite the costs and problems, determination of scarcity through supply and demand analysis is desirable for long-term, systematic resource analysis.

A formal determination of scarcity is unnecessary for large, unique areas such as the Grand Canyon or for areas known to be in short supply such as bald eagle nesting sites. It is more important for more abundant areas such as agricultural lands, forestry lands, sand and gravel deposits, certain types of wetlands, and so forth. The Wisconsin Critical Resources Information Program has suggested the use of sampling techniques as an alternative to blanket data gathering to develop at reasonable costs estimates of total supply. Such techniques do hold potential. For example, if generalized information is available concerning total wetland acreage in a state, the sampling of wetlands could suggest qualitative and quantitative totals for sphagnum bogs.

6-14 *Regulations should not be delayed until the completion of all data gathering.*

Interim regulations based on existing data are sometimes adopted for areas threatened by immediate development.[11] Interim regulations may either freeze all development until more detailed data gathering is possible or incorporate procedures for refining the data base during the implementation phases of a program. Data used for interim mapping often include existing data, no matter how imprecise, data gathered pursuant to nomination procedures, and generalized data gathered on a priority area or case-by-case basis.

6-15 *Relatively imprecise data may be used for mapping when more detailed data gathering is undertaken on a case-by-case basis for individual permits.*

Sensitive area programs with imprecise initial maps often incorporate procedures for site-specific data gathering on a case-by-case basis. This approach is used in flood plain, wetland, shoreland, and coastal area programs. (See figure 28.)

The key regulatory data is developed on a case-by-case basis. However, the regulatory agency must have the necessary expertise and consider cumulative effects of development. Problems can be minimized through careful data-gathering standards.

[10]Such an approach is applied in many single district flood plain zoning efforts. *See* Vol. 1, Water Resources Council *et al., Regulation of Flood Hazard Areas to Reduce Flood Losses,* Part IV, Chapter IV, U.S. Government Printing Office (1970), for such a model single district ordinance.

[11]Interim local flood plain regulations have been adopted by many communities seeking national subsidized flood insurance. These have been based upon historic flood records, soils maps, and other sources of data. *See* note 8 of Part 5, *supra,* for example of statutes authorizing interim regulations.

Figure 29

Use standards for single-district flood plain zoning ordinance. With a single-district approach the flood plain is often mapped based upon available flood data such as historic flood records or soils maps. More detailed data gathering is carried out on a case-by-case basis as individual development proposals are submitted to determine (1) the 100 year flood protection evaluation and (2) the necessary floodway at the proposed development site. (Source: J. Kusler, *A Perspective on Flood Plain Regulations for Flood Plain Management,* **Department of the Army, Office of the Chief of Engineers, Washington, D.C., 1976.)**

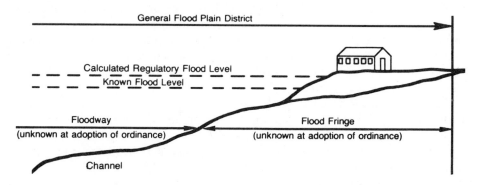

Prohibited Uses: None (initially) except those prohibited by comprehensive underlying zoning ordinance. However, structures, fill, and storage of materials with substantial flood damage potential are prohibited in floodway areas determined by case-by-case analysis of flood areas. See "Special Exception Uses" below.

Permitted Uses: Open space uses permitted in the floodway district with a two-district ordinance such as farming, forestry, wild crop harvesting, parking areas, golf courses, recreation areas, lawns, gardens, and parks.

Special Exceptions: All major structures, fill and storage of materials. A landowner is required to submit plans for a proposed use to the zoning board of adjustment, river cross sections, and stream slope at the site. The board will, with expert assistance, calculate the regulatory flood discharge and floodway limits at the site taking into account equal degree of encroachment and the cumulative effect of existing and similar future uses. This fact-finding will determine whether the proposed use is located in the floodway or flood fringe portion (initially undifferentiated) of the general flood plain district. Based upon this fact-finding, the board will apply the ordinance standards pertaining to the floodway portion or flood fringe portion of the general flood plain district. These standards are identical to use standards for floodway and flood fringe districts established by a two-district ordinance. In short, virtually all structures and fill are prohibited in the floodway portion. Virtually all structures, fill, and other uses are permitted in the flood fringe portion if protected to the calculated regulatory flood protection elevation.

6-16 *Initial data gathering should focus on areas threatened by development.*

Mapping efforts are usually conducted on a priority basis. This maximizes resource protection consistent with budgetary and staff limitations. Formal or informal priorities are set based on: (1) available knowledge concerning location of critical areas; (2) development pressures and other threats; (3) the adequacy of existing controls including land ownership and regulations; and (4) the willingness of local units of government to use data. Mapping efforts usually focus on urbanizing areas, transportation corridors, coastal and shoreland areas, and sites of major proposed development such as power plants.

6-17 *Case-by-case or area-by-area gathering of detailed resource data may be efficient on a long-term basis for some areas.*

Detailed data gathering on a blanket basis may be impractical or unnecessary: (1) where large quantities of site-specific data are required but the specifics depend on the features of proposed uses; (2) where the resource base is rapidly changing (*e.g.*, changes in vegetation, flood runoff, and water quality) and blanket data gathering at a detailed scale would quickly become dated; and (3) where low density development is proposed and only a small percentage of the total area will ever be impacted.

6-18 *Regulations should shift a portion of the data gathering burden for evaluating special permit uses to developers through environmental impact statements and other data gathering requirements.*

Enabling statutes, ordinances, and administrative regulations commonly require that developers prepare environmental impact statements or supply data concerning topography, vegetation, existing uses, soils, water, depth to bedrock, and other factors.[12] Private or public developers are often in a unique position to generate a portion of the site-specific data through onsite investigations or surveys conducted during early phases of a project.

Attempts to shift the data gathering burden generally require careful supervision. The quality of the data generated differs, depending on the objectivity of the developer, his expertise, and financial resources. Generally, large scale developers are in a better position to generate sophisticated data due to available expertise and funds. The quality of data generated may be improved if the regulatory agency adopts precise data gathering standards and criteria.

6-19 *Data gathering may focus on natural resource characteristics during initial definition efforts, but should also identify existing uses and other cultural characteristics in setting standards and administering permits.*

With little exception, sensitive area maps have been based on natural resource characteristics. However, subsequent standard-setting and permit-processing often require broader data. Existing uses, for example, will not affect the designation of an area as a flood plain but may determine its appropriate use once designated. Land ownership, adjacent uses, highway access, and other factors are also relevant to appropriate use.

6-20 *Existing federal, state, and local data sources should be assessed prior to gathering new data.*

In general, sensitive area programs have carefully examined and, in some instances, compiled existing data prior to new data gathering. Compilation of existing data may be cost effective, depending on the accuracy of the available data, scale, data types, base mapping, and other factors. As noted earlier, data is often sufficient to permit interim definition of critical areas although there may be insufficient data for detailed zone mapping or site analysis.

6-21 *High resolution air photos should be used for sensitive area regulatory information to the extent practical.*

High resolution and large scale (1:24,000 and larger) air photos (black and white, stereoscopic, color, color-infrared) have been widely used in sensitive area definition and data gathering efforts due to their low cost and multiple uses. Photos often serve as base maps and as data sources for standard-setting, administration, and enforcement.

Some principal uses of photos include: (1) documenting the extent of flooding; (2) development of detailed topographic maps for flood plain and other critical area delineation (stereo photos); (3) identifying erosion areas and estimating rates of erosion (time sequence photos); (4) identifying landslide areas, landslide damage,

[12]*See* note 2 in Part 2, *supra,* and Appendix D.

and detecting faults for seismic area identification; (5) identifying scenic areas; (6) documenting existing uses; (7) identifying vegetation types and wetland boundaries; (8) surveying timber; (9) identifying agricultural areas; (10) identifying sand and gravel deposits; (11) identifying habitat areas for rare and endangered species; (12) monitoring changes in the environment; and (13) determining violations of critical area regulations.

Despite their multiple uses and low cost, air photos must usually be supplemented by field surveys.

6-22 *Low resolution and small scale satellite imagery or air photos should not be acquired for regulatory purposes.*

Satellite imagery (ERTS and Sky-Lab) has been quite widely investigated in recent years for use in sensitive area programs. However, little actual use has been made by such imagery in implementation efforts due to inadequate scale, resolution, and geo-referencing. Some attempts have been made to use imagery to flag areas requiring more investigation. But larger scale existing air photos can often better serve this purpose.

Many critical area managers feel that vast sums of federal money are being wasted on data with limited regulatory value and that limitations of imagery have not been fairly publicized. This is not to criticize satellite imagery altogether. Future satellite data at larger scale with finer resolution will likely play important roles in critical area definition and standard-setting, particularly if techniques can be developed for direct processing of digital tapes to identify vegetation types, existing uses, changes in the environment, and other parameters.

6-23 *Field surveys must usually be used to supplement air photos.*

Field surveys, including site inspections and detailed scientific and engineering studies, have proven essential for most sensitive area mapping and permit processing efforts. Field surveys are required for subsurface soils investigations, stream flow monitoring, geologic investigations, studying rare plants and animals, forestry inventories, groundwater investigations, and other highly technical and detailed determinations which are not possible from an air photo.

The major restraint of field survey techniques is their high cost. However, costs are often reduced by combining air photo interpretation and limited site visits to identify existing uses, locate areas of scenic beauty, locate erosion areas, and so forth.

6-24 *Data gathering efforts should be carefully documented and time-series information provided to facilitate enforcement and defense of regulations in court.*

Careful records on data gathering have facilitated the defense of regulations. Records are needed concerning the date and location of data gathering, who conducted it, and methods used.

For enforcement purposes, time series aerial photos and inventories of existing uses are needed. Documentation of conditions at the time of adoption of regulations is important to indicate whether uses or structures are in violation of regulations.

6-25 *Assuming limited funds, computerized information systems should receive low priority in sensitive area data gathering and management efforts. However, data should be systematically collected and geo-referenced to facilitate long-term computerization.*

Computerized information systems have rarely been applied in sensitive area regulatory programs.[13] Despite an interest in such systems, limited critical area

---

[13] A computerized data base was used, in part, to classify lakes in the Minnesota shoreland zoning program. Computers have also been used to calculate floodway areas in flood hazard programs.

program funds are often best spent on traditional maps and site-specific data gathering.

Experience to date with computerized information systems has generally been discouraging because: (1) data often becomes dated before the system is operational; (2) information is stored and retrieved at too small a scale (40-acre, square kilometer, or square mile cell size); (3) geo-referencing is not sufficiently precise for regulatory purposes; (4) information is stored in a format unsuitable for aggregation or disaggregation; (5) the computerized system is not available for use by local officials who administer and enforce regulations; (6) the system is too expensive; and (7) there is insufficient expertise for operation of the system.

Computerized programs have potential in combination with traditional map and site-specific data gathering techniques for state level sensitive area regulation where:[14] (1) sufficient funds are available for both maps and information processing devices; (2) a large number of factors are considered simultaneously with a regional or statewide perspective; (3) regulations are drafted or administered by a centralized state regulatory agency with trained personnel; (4) updating procedures are provided; and (5) sufficient lead time is available for data gathering and encoding.

Even where computerized systems are not presently justified, it may be advisable to gather data in an objective format with careful geo-referencing. This process will facilitate later computerization [15] (if this becomes practical) and help meet other sensitive area regulatory needs.

[14]Such conditions may exist for state level regulation of power plant and transmission line siting, water and air pollution, large scale development site review, and strip mining.

[15]Niemann *et al.*, Faculty Land Use Seminar, Subgroup Four, *Data Needs and Data Manipulation,* Faculty Land Use Problem Definition Seminar, Institute for Environmental Studies, University of Wisconsin, Madison (1972) provided a useful outline of characteristics desirable for a geo-information system for land use planning. It concluded that such a system should have the capability to geographically (1) store data, (2) retrieve data, (3) analyze data, (4) output data, (5) integrate data to create new data, and (6) create information from data. The system should have the following characteristics:

(1) As far as is possible, the data should *represent* the planning problem rather than simply *indicate* the planning problem.

(2) The data should be *objective.* An automated geo-information system has the potential of maintaining data without professional bias, thereby assuring utilization of the data for planning by a multiplicity of users. As an example, the ultimate geo-information system should consist of objective data which both the Department of Natural Resources and the Department of Transportation could utilize to locate a highway and determine its environmental impact. This sharing of a common objective data bank would provide a clear documentation of the assumptions utilized by each of the two State agencies.

(3) The data should represent *dynamic* characteristics. For the data to be descriptive and representative of the environment it must be inventoried and organized in a format which assures interrelatability and describes change.

(4) The data should be spacially *interrelatable.* To provide for a spatial or geographical representation, the inventory and storage of the data must retain the geographical character of the data.

(5) The data should be maintained in a format which provides for *quantification.* Extraction and storage of data should be in some form of real amounts so that patterns can be accounted for.

(6) The data collection and manipulation system should be *efficient.* To assure use, economical and efficient utilization of hardware and software systems is critical.

(7) The data should be *uniformly* available. Because of the characteristics of spatial information systems, uniformity, specificity, and vintage of data are critical collection concerns.

(8) The data should *account* for the components of the environment. For example, data should be collected which describes the system in terms of land cover, land activity, land ownership, etc., and does not mix classifications such as land use and land ownership.

(9) The data should be stored with *error statements.* Because of the varying levels of error specificity that will exist in a geo-information system, it will be important to the user to know the error levels so that he may have a basis for judging the output results.

6-26 *Data gathering for sensitive area regulatory programs should be coordinated with broader data gathering efforts.*

Considerable similarity exists between the data needs, formats, and manipulative capability for sensitive area regulatory programs and broader natural resource policy setting, planning, and acquisition programs. Consequently, some multi-purpose data-gathering efforts have been carried out. However, experience indicates that regulatory programs must not compromise scale requirements or the combined effort may be useless. In addition, regulatory data must be made accessible to the decision-makers at local levels who adopt regulations and process individual permit applications.

6-27 *In states attempting comprehensive definition of sensitive areas, it may be desirable to authorize a single agency to act as coordinator for all data gathering efforts and to assemble data into a statewide sensitive areas inventory. However, individual line agencies should be principally responsible for carrying out critical area definition and other data gathering efforts.*

Centralization of all natural resource data gathering efforts in a single state agency has not been accomplished in any state, despite theoretical attractions of economies of scale, standardization of data, and improved analysis capability. Centralization has not been possible for several reasons. First, it creates unacceptable concentrations of political power. Second, centralization separates data gathering from implementation functions and existing expertise in individual line agencies.[16]

Despite the political and practical necessity of a multi-agency data gathering approach, it is important that some lead agency, perhaps the state planning agency, coordinate data gathering efforts between various state agencies, regional planning agencies, and local units of government. This agency could establish minimum standards of compatibility for data gathered by individual agencies, help disseminate data to local units of government and the private sector, compile and distribute a list of data gathering efforts underway in the state, conduct special data gathering efforts for state or federal agencies or local units of government, and make budgetary recommendations concerning data gathering priorities to the governor and legislature. A lead agency approach incorporating some or all of these elements and a measure of centralization of data gathering powers has been used in New York, Minnesota, and Connecticut.

6-28 *Strong local participation is desirable in state data gathering to capture local expertise and knowledge.*

State program personnel often discover that citizens and local governments are the best source of certain types of data based upon intimate, long-term familiarity with an area's resources or hazards.[17] An observant landowner, local birdwatcher, hunter,

---

[16]For example, a state geological survey may be in the best position to undertake earthquake area identification, identification of erosion areas, identification of mineral sites, and so forth. A state natural resources agency may best identify wetlands and areas of special scientific interest. A historic society can identify historic sites. A water resources agency may best identify food plains. *See* note 4 in Part 9, *infra.*

[17]Strong local involvement is required by some statutes such as Mont. Rev. Code Ann., §89-3504(1) (Supp. 1977) which provides:

(b) Before the board establishes by order a designated floodplain or a designated floodway, the department shall consult with the affected political subdivisions. Consultation shall include, but not be limited to, the following:

(i) specifically requesting that the political subdivisions submit pertinent data concerning flood hazards, including flood experiences, plans to avoid potential hazards, estimates of economic impacts of flooding on the community, both historical and prospective and such other data as considered appropriate:

or teacher often has years of experience to draw on in identifying wildlife, trees, caves, and geologic sites of special interest. This data may be compiled through the use of nomination procedures, workshops, public hearings, and other techniques.[18]
6-29 *An initial state strategy for comprehensive sensitive area data gathering can often begin with a subjective assessment of areas involving local units of government, state and federal agencies, universities, interest groups, and concerned citizens. Later, more specific delineations should be carried out for regulatory purposes on a priority area basis.*

Initial subjective identification of sensitive areas on an *ad hoc* basis has been used in many flood plain, shoreland, and coastal area programs to locate data sources, facilitate compilation of existing data, establish data gathering priorities, and permit the adoption of interim regulations. Nomination procedures and workshops are often used to gain information on potential critical area sites. These procedures offer multiple benefits in: (1) drawing on local expertise in identifying particular classes of critical areas such as prime agricultural lands, wetlands, historic and archaeological sites, scenic areas, and recreation areas; (2) educating the public and helping to coalesce public support for programs; and (3) developing information concerning public needs and preferences. Nomination procedures and workshops are particularly useful in soliciting information concerning the observable ground features such as historic sites, scenic areas, and agricultural lands. They are less satisfactory for identifying scientific areas, flood hazard areas, and mineral deposits which require special expertise.

"Interactive" data gathering approaches have also been used. Here the state develops and submits preliminary information concerning sensitive areas to local units of government. Local governments then examine the nominations in light of their own expertise and knowledge. This approach was used with considerable success in the Minnesota Shoreland Zoning Program where the state submitted air photos and lakeshore data to county officials accompanied with tentative lake-shoreland classifications. The county officials then supplemented this data and modified classifications according to their own information and needs.

Once initial subjective data gathering and critical area delineation is completed, more detailed "objective" data gathering, based upon air photos and field surveys, may be carried out.

6-30 *Data generated through permit procedures, public works projects, and environmental impact statements may be used to monitor development, establish data gathering priorities, and supplement local, state, and federal data banks.*

Data contained in regulatory permits and environmental impact statements prepared by private and public developers have potential for supplementing more

---

(ii) notifying local officials, including members of the county commission, city council and planning board, of the progress of surveys, studies and investigations and of proposed findings, along with information concerning data and methods employed in reaching such conclusions; and

(iii) encouraging local dissemination of information concerning surveys, studies and investigations, so that interested persons will have an opportunity to bring relevant data to the attention of the department.

[18]For example, the Wisconsin critical resources information program conducted highly successful workshops in six counties to identify critical areas. Local participants were able not only to identify areas with considerable accuracy, but to rank them in importance. For a report developed with this approach *see* Environmental Monitoring and Data Acquisition Group, Institute for Environmental Studies, *Crawford County Critical Resource Information Booklet,* Institute for Environmental Studies, University of Wisconsin, Madison (1974).

conventional data gathering efforts. This data has rarely been compiled but holds promise for: (1) assisting in the gradual development of data banks; (2) updating existing data; (3) monitoring change; and (4) establishing data gathering priorities for areas under development pressure. To serve these purposes, rigorous data gathering standards pertaining to data scale, type, and format will be necessary to insure the objectivity and consistency of the data supplied through regulatory permit procedures.

6-31 *States should define priorities for federal natural resource data gathering, cost share in such efforts, make recommendations for improvements, coordinate federal and state data gathering, and otherwise encourage the federal government to play a continued, principal role in natural resource data gathering.*

State and local sensitive area regulatory efforts rely to a considerable extent on federal natural resource mapping efforts. Soil surveys developed by the Soil Conservation Service, topographic maps developed by the Geological Survey, and air photos developed by the Agricultural Stabilization and Conservation Service and the Geological Survey are widely used as base maps and for identifying individual areas. Flood maps developed by the Department of Housing and Urban Development, the Corps of Engineers, and other agencies form the basis for most flood plain regulatory efforts.

States and localities can encourage a continued strong federal role (see table 24) in sensitive area data gathering through a better definition of data gathering priorities, cost-sharing, and cooperation. For example, Connecticut has established a natural resources center within the Department of Environmental Protection which coordinates and facilitates state, federal, and local natural resources data gathering efforts. This center has been highly successful in identifying user needs and establishing priorities for federal efforts.

6-32 *States should make use of interest groups, universities, and consultants to aid sensitive area definition and case-by-case evaluation of development proposals.*

Interest groups have often aided state and local data gathering efforts by providing specialized information on the location of rare and endangered species, beaches suitable for surfing, water skiing areas, and so forth. For example, the Nature Conservancy has established natural heritage programs in at least 12 states to identify natural areas of special interest.[19] In addition, they have been helpful in evaluating development proposals by testifying and submitting evidence at public hearings.

Universities have also played important data gathering roles by conducting data related research, compiling critical areas data in cartographic laboratories, and assisting state agencies and local units of government in conducting case-by-case efforts.

Consultants often assist federal, state, and local efforts by providing air photos and, in some instances, specialized critical area maps such as flood maps. In addition, they often prepare environmental impact statements and generate other data concerning individual development proposals.

---

[19]*See* The Nature Conservancy, *The Preservation of Natural Diversity: A Survey and Recommendations,* Alexandria, Va. (1975), for recommendations concerning protection of natural areas through public and private actions.

Table 20

Data characteristics.

Factor	Characteristics	Use in Programs
1. Type of Data	A) Resource data (soils, geology, flora, fauna, climate, hydrology, topography) B) Cultural data (existing uses, public facilities, population, income, economic data)	Regulatory efforts have focused upon natural resource data in original definition of areas. However, cultural data such as existing uses, land ownership, and adjacent uses play important roles in standard-setting and evaluating individual development proposals.
2. Location in Relationship to Sensitive Area	A) Onsite data (natural resource, cultural data) B) Offsite data (natural resource, cultural data)	Onsite natural resource data play the major role in defining sensitive areas and establishing use standards. However, offsite data such as ground water flow systems, ecosystem interrelationships, and adjacent uses have been relevant to some definition and standard-setting efforts and to the evaluation of the compatibility of proposed uses with adjacent uses.
3. Source of Data	A) Air Photos B) Field Surveys C) Other	Air photos, including high, intermediate, and low level black and white, stereoscopic, color, and color-infrared, are used for a wide variety of regulatory purposes including the inventory of existing conditions and uses and the preparation of natural resource surveys such as soil surveys and topographic maps. Field surveys serve as the principal base for environmental impact analysis and evaluation of individual development permits. These include engineering, biological, geological, chemical, and other site surveys. Satellite data has played a limited role in existing programs. Its role will be increased if scale and resolution are improved. Nomination procedures have been used in some programs.
4. Scale	A) Small scale 1:100,000 B) Intermediate scale 1:24,000 to 1:100,000 C) Large scale 1:6,000 to 1:24,000 D) Very large scale 1:6,000 and larger	Small scale data receive some use in identifying critical areas, for general education, to help assess the total quantity of a resource available in a state or region, and to identify areas for more detailed data gathering. Scales smaller than 1:24,000 have rarely been used for regulatory purposes. Large scale data are widely used for regulatory mapping. Very large scale data are used for site planning, environmental impact analysis, evaluation of individual development proposals, and monitoring of the compliance with regulations.
5. Accuracy	A) High level (high correlation between data and existing conditions)	Needed for restrictive regulations with severe impacts upon private land-

Table 20 (continued)

Factor	Characteristics	Use in Programs
	B) Intermediate level (some errors due to changed conditions since data gathering, inadequate spatial referencing, inaccuracies in basic data sources, data analysis, or compilation techniques)	owners and for enforcement of regulations. May be used for some regulatory purposes, particularly where additional data are gathered on a case-by-case basis or where the regulations impose only limited financial burden upon landowners.
	C) Low level (many errors, low level of resolution)	May be used for limited purposes such as the adoption of interim regulations or where extensive additional data are gathered on a case-by-case basis.
6. Degree of Objectivity	A) Objective (qualitative, and in some instances, quantitative evaluation of geologic, water resources, vegetation and other parameters through air photo analysis, engineering surveys, etc.)	Quite widespread use in critical area mapping and evaluation of permits.
	B) Partially subjective data-gathering (generalized evaluation of steep slopes, water quality, existing uses, etc., through air photo analysis, field inspections)	Quite common in case-by-case data gathering for special permit uses to determine compatibility with existing uses, impact upon wildlife, erosion potential, etc.
	C) Subjective (little application of objective standards (*e.g.,* personal statement that an area is "beautiful" to someone, "important," subject to flooding)	Some use in regulatory programs through nomination procedures and site visits. Used in evaluating impact of uses upon scenic beauty in shoreland, flood plain, similar areas. Serious problems with aggregation and disaggregation.
7. Specificity in Geo-Referencing	A) Low level of specificity (*e.g.,* general description of the location in terms of city, town, county, township and range, square miles)	Of limited use in planning and regulatory efforts, but may serve educational goals and help define data gathering priorities.
	B) Intermediate level of specificity (*e.g.,* 40 acre cell, general description in terms of landownership)	Of some use for general zoning classifications, educational purposes, policy setting.
	C) Ground truth within 50-100 feet	Needed for zone definitions, particularly where boundaries cross lot lines.
	D) Site specific data (ground truth within 10's of feet)	Needed for evaluation of development proposals in terms of their impact upon critical area values and hazards.
8. Display Format	A) Maps (black and white, color, three dimensional, etc.)	Two dimensional maps have been widely used to delineate critical area boundaries.
	B) Written descriptions of particular critical areas by metes and bounds) parcel descriptions, other types of descriptions	Written description of flood heights, water quality standards, wildlife and flora to be preserved, etc. have been used to define areas. More often written material is used in policy formation.
	C) Tables, charts, graphs (produced through manual, machine, or computer techniques) indicating total acreage of critical areas, elevations, characteristics	Flood plains are often defined by flood profiles (*i.e.,* a graph showing flood elevations at particular locations).

Table 20 (continued)

Factor	Characteristics	Use in Programs
	D) Simulation models or computers with display through video screens, physical models, coded tape output, etc.	Some use to date to study impact of development upon particular areas, water quality, etc. Modelling costs are high. Likely to have greater use in the future.
9. Manipulation	A) Manual (inspection of maps, use of overlays) B) Limited machine manipulation (*e.g.*, figures manipulated through adding machines, use of map projection techniques, etc.) C) Computer manipulation	Manual data analysis and manipulation are used in most efforts. Flood data are often subjected to statistical analysis. Use of map projection techniques is also common. A few regulatory efforts use computers to determine impact of proposed uses upon air and water quality, and to determine floodways. Computer mapping has rarely been used for regulatory purposes. Computerized manipulation of data holds potential but is also subject to limitations of costs and complexity.
10. Update Requirements	A) Permanent—little update needed (*e.g.*, geologic, topographic, for the definition of areas, soils) B) Relatively permanent—periodic update needed (*e.g.*, water resources, climate, general vegetation and wildlife) C) Changing—frequent update desirable (*e.g.*, existing uses, landownership, specific vegetation and wildlife)	Permanent data are widely used in definition efforts. Gathering of such data is largely "once and for all" proposition. These data are often placed in a map format. Relatively permanent data are also widely used in sensitive area definition and standard-setting. They are placed in a map format but may also be gathered on a case-by-case basis through field surveys and used directly in project evaluations. Quickly changing data are used, to a limited extent, for definition of areas. They receive more common use in standard-setting and processing of permits. Often they are gathered on a case-by-case basis to evaluate development permits.
11. Degree to Which Data are Gathered in Advance of Regulation	A) Blanket data gathering in advance of regulation (*e.g.*, soils or topographic mapping of an entire community, region, state) B) Area-by-area data gathering in advance of regulation (*e.g.*, identification of a particular flood plain, wetland) C) Data gathering on a site-specific basis after regulation (*e.g.*, evaluation of the impact of a proposed subdivision upon a particular wetland)	Although soils or topographic maps are available on a community-wide basis in some areas, few sensitive area programs have delineated all critical areas prior to adoption of regulations. Soil and topographic maps are not in themselves sufficient for definition efforts. Most programs have mapped areas on a priority area basis (*i.e.*, one at a time, a region at a time, etc.). A single area or small number of areas may be mapped in advance of regulation. Others are mapped afterwards. Most programs have combined limited data gathering in advance of regulation with case-by-case data gathering as individual proposals for development are submitted. Some of the data gathering burden is shifted to developers.

Table 21

Data used in selected programs. The information is the result of a survey conducted in 1975 with some updating in 1977. For additional profiles the reader is referred to a report prepared by the American Society of Planning Officials, *Analysis of Information/Data Handling Requirements for Selected Critical Area Programs.* **(Source: This table was extracted from a similar table prepared by the author and his colleagues in** *Data Needs and Data Gathering for Areas of Critical Environmental Concern: Part 1, Summary Report,* **University of Wisconsin, Institute for Environmental Studies, Report 53, Madison, 1975.)**

The following profiles were compiled through interviews or telephone conversations conducted primarily during 1975. The information is, therefore, somewhat dated. Nevertheless, a partial update indicated few changes in the 1975-1977 period. For additional profiles the reader is referred to a report prepared by the American Society of Planning Officials, *Analysis of Information/Data Handling Requirements for Selected Critical Area Programs.*

State	Type of Area	Statutory Data Gathering Requirements	Data Acquisition During Program Administration
		Flood Plain Programs	
California	Floodway	None	800 miles of floodway mapped by state (100-year flood). Mapping at scale of 1″=200′ or 1′=100′. Use air-photo base. Use federal data (Corps, FIA, USGS) where available.
Colorado	Flood plain	None	Designate 100-year flood plain. Use federal data where available (Corps in most instances.) State mapping at scales of 1″=200′ or 1″=400′ on air-photo base or detailed base map (2-foot contour).
Connecticut	Floodway	Agency shall establish encroachment lines	State has established approximately 250 miles of stream encroachment lines at the scale of 1″=100′ on own map base. Use USGS topographic and stream flow information where available. No new encroachment studies underway due to lack of funds. Corps and HUD flood studies have been coordinated.
Indiana	Flood plain and floodway	Agency shall make comprehensive studies and investigations of flood areas	Mapping of 100-year flood plain. 33 streams have been mapped for urban areas with 2-foot contour intervals at a scale of 1″=200′. Use air photo base. Assistance is being provided to 19 counties and 15 cities to prepare generalized maps based upon flood of record, initial Corps data, etc. Use of federal studies where available. Case-by-case evaluation of proposed floodway uses (30 to 50 per month).
Iowa	Flood plain, and floodway	Agency shall determine characteristics of floods, establish encroachment limits and protection elevations	Mapping of 100-year flood plain. State has participated in 2-foot contour mapping for ten floodplain information studies (Corps). State has done 7 floodplain encroachment studies on its own at scales of 1″=100′, 1″=200′. Primary reliance upon federal data gathering (Corps, FIA, Etc.), case-by-case evaluation of permits.
Michigan	Flood plain	None	Mapping of 100-year flood plain. Principal reliance upon Corps, HUD studies, and SCS flood studies. Varied scales, depending upon base mapping and specific circumstances. Case-by-case evaluation of subdivisions and other alterations of floodway areas. Developers required to supply valley cross sections (at minimum).
Minnesota	Flood plain, floodway	Agency is directed to collect and disseminate flood information	Mapping of 100-year flood plain and floodway. State has undertaken its own studies in some areas but is now relying primarily upon data gathering of federal agencies including Corps, FIA, USDA. Some use of

Table 21 (continued)

State	Type of Area	Statutory Data Gathering Requirements	Data Acquisition During Program Administration
			soil maps and flood photos of flood plain delineation. Case-by-case data gathering is conducted for specific projects (*e.g.*, bridges).
Montana	Flood plain, floodway	Agency shall delineate all flood plains and floodways in the state	Extensive use of existing federal data including flood flows and valley cross sections. Some limited mapping by state at various scales, principally 1"=1000'. Anticipate almost exclusive reliance upon federal mapping in the future. Some case-by-case evaluation of development.
Nebraska	Floodway	Agency shall designate all commission floodways in the state	Statewide mapping of 100-year flood plain on air photos or topo maps underway at scale of 1:12,000. Only small portion of state completed, but anticipate complete state coverage in 19 years.
New Jersey	Flood plain, floodway	Agency shall study the nature and extent of flood plains in the state	Mapping of 100-year plus flood plains and floodways. State has delineated 668 mile of stream (145 on an initial basis and the rest more detailed). Detailed mapping has been done at 5-foot contour intervals with scales of 1"=200'. Floodways delineated areas with detailed maps. In addition, state has been using federal data (USGS, Corps, SCS, and HUD) wherever available. Anticipate principal future reliance upon federal efforts. Case-by-case data gathering for some types of development (*e.g.*, bridges).
Washington	Flood plain, floodway	Agency shall designate flood control zones	Mapping of 100-year flood plain. Primary reliance upon federal flood data (Corps, HUD, USGS, SCS). No new state flood control zones have been designated for four years. Case-by-case analysis if individual development proposals within flood control zones where it is warranted. Developers are required to provide much of the required information.
Wisconsin	Flood plain, floodway	None	Mapping of 100-year flood plain. Primary reliance upon federal data-gathering efforts. All floodways mapped by state, usually through use of federal data. State is checking federal efforts. Case-by-case evaluation of bridges, fills, and other rural flood plain developments.

Scientific Area Programs
(Note: these use acquisition rather than regulation for implementation)

State	Type of Area	Statutory Data Gathering Requirements	Data Acquisition During Program Administration
Indiana	Nature preserves	Agency is authorized to make surveys and maintain registries and records of unique materials areas within the state	Air-photos and topographic maps used provided by transportation department for preliminary definition. Nomination procedures. Field surveys to specifically evaluate areas. Detailed evaluation sheet prepared for each area. Areas are ranked.
Illinois	Nature preserves	Agency must designate areas for preservation and protection	Extensive use of ASCS air photos for preliminary studies. Some use of soil maps, USGS quadrangles. Field surveys are conducted initially from the air. More detailed studies are later conducted on the ground. Pilot study is underway for six counties using air photos. Nomination procedures. An information system is being developed.

Table 21 (continued)

State	Type of Area	Statutory Data Gathering Requirements	Data Acquisition During Program Administration
Ohio	Nature preserves	Agency must prepare and maintain surveys and inventories of natural areas and habitats of rare and endangered species of plants and animals	ASCS photos and USGS 7½ minute quadrangles are used on a preliminary basis, also nomination procedures. Field surveys are the primary source of detailed information. Some in-house development of air photos at 1″=200′ or 1′=400′.
Wisconsin	Scientific areas	State must prepare and publish an official state list of scientific areas	ASCS air photos and USGS quadrangles are used for preliminary surveys, also nomination procedures. Field surveys are the primary source of information.
Comprehensive Critical Area Programs			
Colorado	Areas of state interest	Inventory of state (public) land required. Local units designate critical areas on private land	Primary reliance upon local data gathering. Technical assistance is provided to local units.
Florida	Areas of critical concern	No state inventory mandated. However, local units and regional planning agencies are to nominate areas. The state is to map areas as a prerequisite to state establishment of standards for local regulation.	Use of existing data, nomination procedures. Air photos and field surveys are used to generate detailed data on an area-by-area basis. Only three areas have been designated so far, others are under consideration.
Maine	Areas of critical concern	State is to establish a register of critical areas. State planning office is to carry out a statewide inventory.	Use of existing data including a natural areas inventory prepared prior to adoption of law. Nomination procedures. Case-by-case data gathering for particular areas through air photos, field surveys.
Maryland	Areas of critical state conern	None. However, the state is to establish statewide standards for referencing all planning data.	Extensive use of existing data, particularly detailed soils information at scales of 1:15,000′-1:21,000′ and high-resolution air photos provided by NASA. A geographic information system with 2000 square foot cells has been developed.
Minnesota	Areas of critical concern	See Florida	Use of existing data. Nomination procedures. An attempt is being made to use the Minnesota Land Information System. Only one critical area has been designated so far (St. Croix wild river) other areas are under consideration.
North Carolina	Areas of environmental concern	None	Primary reliance upon existing data including USGS 7½ minute quadrangles, ASCS air-photos, and detailed soil maps. A statewide base map at a scale of 1″=2000′ is proposed. Orthophotos at that scale are anticipated for the state as a whole and will soon be

Table 21 (continued)

State	Type of Area	Statutory Data Gathering Requirements	Data Acquisition During Program Administration
			available for the coastal zone. High-resolution air photos as well as field surveys have been used for selected areas.
Coastal Zone Programs			
California	Coastal zone	None. However, coastal plans must be prepared.	Use of existing data from federal, state, and local sources. Coastal zone commissions have compiled inventories for individual sections of the coast. Co-ordinated data-gathering program recently initiated at state level. Anticipate a variety of map scales. Case-by-case data gathering on individual development proposals.
California	San Francisco Bay	San Francisco Bay Commission is to prepare a bay plan	Use of existing data from many state, federal, and local sources. Inventory of marshes, seismic areas. Various levels of aerial photography. Assistance from USGS in providing a variety of types of maps. Case-by-case data gathering on individual development proposals.
Michigan	Shorelands (Lake Michigan shores)	Inventory required for high-risk erosion areas, flood plain areas, and marsh areas within 1000 feet of shoreline	Detailed state mapping is underway for high-risk erosion areas, based on high-resolution air photos and field surveys. Erosion recession rates and 30-year setback lines are calculated. Environmental inventories have been prepared based on air photos, field sites, other sources of information. Federal Insurance Administration will provide assistance in mapping 100-year flood plain.
North Carolina	Coastal area	State is to designate areas of environmental concern	Use of existing data, including ASCS photos, soil maps, and USGS 7½ minute quadrangles. Acquiring orthophotos at the scale of 1"=2000' for 20 coastal counties. Use of detailed air photo and field surveys to evaluate particular areas and proposed development.
Shorelands of Lakes and Streams			
Maine	Shorelands	State is to identify waterfowl breeding areas	Primary reliance on existing data. Survey of selected lakes. Coastal zone survey at scale of 1'=4000'. Local data gathering on case-by-case basis.
Minnesota	Shorelands	None.	Extensive data gathering for 1,923 lakes over 150 acres was undertaken prior to adoption of program. Primary reliance upon air photos and soil maps. These data were compiled in a computerized form and used to classify lakes for the shoreland law. Local data gathering on an area-by-area and a case-by-case basis.
Vermont	Shorelands	None. However, the State is to prepare a comprehensive water resources plan as a guide for state, regional, or local land use plans	None. However, a guidebook was developed which suggested the use of soil maps. Local data gathering on a case-by-case basis.

Table 21 (continued)

State	Type of Area	Statutory Data Gathering Requirements	Data Acquisition During Program Administration
Washington	Shorelines	Local units of government are required to inventory shorelines when preparing master programs	Little. However, USGS is carrying out an inventory of Washington lakes. The state has compiled a booklet listing data sources. Local and state data gathering on a case-by-case basis for individual development proposals.
Wisconsin	Shorelines	None. However, the state is to prepare a comprehensive shoreline plan, to assist local shoreland programs.	Little. Local units use existing soil, topographic and planimetric maps by local units. Local data gathering on a case-by-case basis for individual development proposals.

Scenic, Wild, Recreational Rivers

State	Type of Area	Statutory Data Gathering Requirements	Data Acquisition During Program Administration
Michigan	Natural rivers including wild, scenic and recreational	None. However, the state is to adopt a long-range comprehensive plan for each river	Studies conducted on five rivers including 160 miles of mainstream and 260 miles of tributaries. Some use of nomination procedures to suggest candidate rivers (36 have been suggested so far). Site analysis for candidate rivers. All available information used in preparation of reports.
Ohio	Scenic rivers including wild, scenic, and recreational		Studies conducted for seven rivers. Extensive use of existing data for land capability and suitability analysis including topographic, soils, geologic maps, air photos. Field studies for candidate rivers. Corridor plans are prepared.
Wisconsin	Wild rivers	None	Plans are being prepared for two rivers. Use of existing soils, topographic, ASCS, air photos, and other information. USGS has prepared a specialized hydrologic report for the two rivers. Field surveys have been used to gather fish and wildlife data, forestry data.

Wetlands Programs

State	Type of Area	Statutory Data Gathering Requirements	Data Acquisition During Program Administration
Connecticut	Coastal wetlands, inland wetlands	Wetland inventory at 1"=200' is required for coastal areas	Air photos field surveys are used to map coastal areas at 1"=200'. Case-by-case data gathering for individual development proposals. Soil maps are being prepared at varied scales (1:15,480' - 1:24,000') by SCS for inland areas.
Georgia	Coastal wetlands	None	Field surveys and frequent air surveillance. Some use of satellite data.
Maryland	Coastal wetlands	Inventory at 1"-200'	Air photos and field surveys used to prepare maps at 1"=200', 1"=2000'. Case-by-case data gathering on permits.
Massachusetts	Coastal wetlands	None	Air photos and field surveys used to prepare maps at 1"=600', 1"=200' (varied). Case-by-case data gathering on permits.
New Hampshire	Coastal and inland wetlands	None	Some use of black and white air photos. Field survey for regulation. Case-by-case data gathering on permits.

Table 21 (continued)

State	Type of Area	Statutory Data Gathering Requirements	Data Acquisition During Program Administration
New Jersey	Coastal wetlands	Make an inventory and maps of all tidal wetlands.	Air photos at 1"=200'. Case-by-case data gathering on permits. Some use of satellite imagery for monitoring regulations.
New York	Tidal wetlands	Inventory of tidal wetlands in order to provide clear and accurate maps. Inventory of all inland wetlands 10 acres or larger in size.	Maps based upon air photos 1"=200', 1"=2000' and 1"=1600'.
North Carolina	Coastal wetlands	None	Low level air photos used for enforcement of dredge and fill laws. Testing of systems underway.
Rhode Island	Intertidal marshes	None	Air photos and field surveys at scales of 1"=1000' and 1"=500'. Case-by-case data gathering on permits.
Rhode Island	Inland wetlands	None	Air photos at scales of 1"=1000', 1"=5000'. Case-by-case data gathering on permits.
Virginia	Coastal wetlands	None	Field surveys and air photos used to prepare 1"=2000' maps. Case-by-case data gathering on permits.

Mineral Resource Areas

State	Type of Area	Statutory Data Gathering Requirements	Data Acquisition During Program Administration
Colorado	Commercial mineral deposits	Colorado Geological Survey is directed to contract for a study of commercial deposits in the populous counties of the state and to complete such a study by July 1, 1974.	Mapping of 16,000 square miles at a scale of 1:24,000' with other smaller map scales also being developed. Extensive use of existing data such as high altitude air photos, rectified photo maps, geologic maps.

Part 7

GOVERNMENTAL ROLES
IN REGULATING
SENSITIVE AREAS

A principal issue in sensitive areas implementation is the appropriate role for each level of government. Despite some early indications that the "quiet revolution" would shift land use control responsibility to the states, most critical area regulatory efforts have been cooperative state and local programs. A state agency typically maps areas and establishes minimum overall standards. Local general purpose units of government adopt regulations meeting state standards and administer and enforce controls. Regional planning agencies usually play data gathering and planning roles but lack implementation powers. Special purpose units of government also gather data and provide technical assistance, but do not have regulatory roles.

The sharing of data gathering, sensitive area definition, standard-setting, and program administration and enforcement responsibilities among several levels of government has been motivated by: (1) the desirability of combining statewide, regional, and federal perspectives in critical area definition and standard-setting; (2) the need to draw upon existing data and available expertise presently distributed through several levels of government; (3) the desirability of meeting "home rule" and "state rights" objectives through maximum involvement at local and state levels; (4) the need to coordinate public works decisions with sensitive area definition and standard-setting; (5) the need to involve several levels of enforcement personnel; and (6) the need to share costs.

The continued sharing of responsibilities between several levels of government is desirable as suggested by table 24 and the following recommendations.

7-1 A cooperative approach involving both state and local governments should be used in most sensitive area regulatory efforts.

A cooperative state and local regulatory approach has been used widely in flood plain, shoreland, coastal area, and, to a lesser extent, in wetland programs to capitalize on state and local capabilities while minimizing disadvantages of regulation at either level. With a cooperative approach, the state conducts data gathering, promulgates minimum development standards, and provides technical assistance to local units of government. General purpose units of local government adopt zoning, subdivision codes, building codes, and other regulations meeting state standards and administer and enforce them. The state regulates areas only in the event of local inaction.

This state/local approach helps remedy several of the weaknesses of an exclusively local approach including: (1) inadequate data base and expertise; (2) insufficient geographic perspective; (3) inadequate enabling authority; and (4) indiscriminate issuance of special permits. It also helps meet the weaknesses of an exclusive state approach including: (1) lack of information pertaining to existing uses, land ownership, local economic conditions, local plans, and local public works policies; (2) substantial transportation and communication barriers for evaluating special permits; (3) political objections to state control based on home rule arguments and desire for local autonomy; and (4) monitoring and enforcement problems due to lack of field monitoring devices and inspection staff.

7-2 States should offer both mandates and incentives to strengthen local regulatory programs. They should adopt clear and flexible state minimum standards, improve data gathering, and provide technical assistance and grants-in-aid.

Several lessons have emerged from existing state/local programs:

(1) The state should not demand the impossible of local units of government in terms of planning, data gathering, or administrative responsibilities such as completion of comprehensive planning within a one year period. Local units of government should usually be required to adopt regulations only after state generated data becomes available.

(2) State standards should provide options for local regulations so that the content of final standards depends, at least in part, on local desires.

(3) Local units of government should be required to submit copies of variances, amendments, and other special permits to the state regulatory agency to assist the agency in monitoring and to provide an opportunity for comment.

(4) The state should provide technical assistance, workshops, and training programs for local regulatory officers and administrative personnel in combination with standard-setting.

(5) Incentives should be offered to local units such as grants-in-aid for local planning and administration or regulations meeting state standards.

(6) State public facilities planning and other activities which impact upon land use should be coordinated with critical area management policies through executive order or statutory doctrine.

On the other hand, local units of government should be encouraged to take the initiative in critical area management. They should: (1) suggest potential sensitive areas through nomination procedures; (2) aid the state in initial mapping of areas by providing base maps, existing use data, and land ownership information; (3) evaluate the impact of proposed critical area uses on adjacent uses, traffic, community services, and the tax base; (4) carry out public education efforts; (5) adopt regulatory and other policies meeting or exceeding state standards; (6) monitor development and enforce regulations; and (7) coordinate critical area management with local public facilities planning and comprehensive land use management.

7-3 Direct state regulation may be desireable for certain limited classes of uses and in areas with clear multijurisdictional impact or exceedingly complex technical issues.

Local units of government often lack the data gathering and technical capability, perspective, or political clout needed for regulating certain floodway uses, coastal wetland uses, large scale mining operations, power plants, and other types of uses and areas. Further, it may be impractical to develop technical evaluation capability in each local unit of government. Direct state control may be advisable in these limited circumstances.

Even where direct state regulation is required, a local public hearing is advisable on each major application. Local plans should be considered. In addition, local government should generally be permitted to adopt more restrictive regulations.

7-4 Regional planning agencies should continue to play an important role in sensitive area data gathering, planning, and technical assistance to aid both states and local units of government.

Regional planning agencies have aided state agencies and local sensitive area regulatory efforts by: (1) defining sensitive areas; (2) suggesting development policies; (3) carrying out specialized public facilities and comprehensive land use planning; (4) coordinating state and local efforts; (5) preparing manuals and model ordinances; (6) providing technical assistance programs to local units of government; (7) conducting workshops and public education; and (8) commenting on development proposals. However, regional agencies have rarely regulated sensitive lands.

The political acceptability of a regional planning agency regulatory role is questionable. It adds an additional level of regulation and would require relinquishment of local control—contrary to strong home rule traditions. Exercise of regulatory powers would require restructuring of these agencies from appointed, advisory bodies to elected, governmental bodies. However, additional powers may be warranted and acceptable in metropolitan areas *(e.g.,* the Twin Cities Metropolitan Council)[1], and certain critical areas requiring regional management *(e.g.,* the Lake Tahoe Planning Agency).

---

[1]Precedent for a strengthened regional role in critical area regulation can be found in the Minnesota Twin Cities Metropolitan Council. Minn. Stat. Ann. §473.204 (1977) requires the Council to promulgate standards and criteria and suggests model ordinances by January 1, 1976 for the regulation of the use and development of the land and water within the metropolitan area which provide for:

(a) the protection and preservation of those wetlands and lowlands permanently or intermittently covered with waters such as marshes, swamps, bogs, meadows, potholes and sloughs which are essential to hydrological or ecological systems or for flood control;

(b) the protection of groundwater recharge areas which contribute significantly to the recharge of groundwater aquifers;

(c) the minimum erosion of those slopes which are subject to severe or moderate erosion because of their degree of slope and soil type;

(d) the maximum retention of existing forests and woodlands, the minimum removal of trees for development, and the encouragement of replanting where removal is unavoidable;

(e) the determination of the suitability of soils or bedrock for development, design and construction measures for development which would compensate for existing soil or bedrock problems, and the prevention of the type of development for which such soils or bedrock are unsuitable;

7-5 Special purpose districts should provide data gathering and technical assistance to general purpose units of local government and states. They should also carry out non-regulatory land-management functions such as constructing sewers.

Special purpose units of government such as sanitary districts have assisted state agencies and units of local government in forming and implementing sensitive area policies. They have rarely been vested with regulatory powers. Even where special purpose units, such as soil conservation districts, have been authorized to adopt regulations, few have done so.

The creation of special purpose units of government to carry out sensitive area policies has advantages. It can insure control by an expert body. It can establish planning and regulatory boundaries and management needs. However, it also has disadvantages: (1) creation of special units results in a proliferation of governmental entities; (2) special units often lack the broad-based political support necessary to carry out tough resource management policies; and (3) special units fragment planning and implementation functions. The latter problem is particularly serious since it is desirable to integrate critical areas with broader land use management programs already excercised by general purpose units of local government. For this reason the role of special purpose districts in comprehensive planning and regulation should be limited.

7-6 The federal government should continue to play a major support role for state and local sensitive area programs through data gathering, technical assistance, research, and grants-in-aid. In very limited instances, it should regulate lands directly to protect national interests.

Federal data gathering, technical assistance, research, and grants-in-aid have been a major incentive for state and local programs. They should be continued and strengthened through: (1) accelerated programs for soils, topographic, and geologic mapping at scales necessary to meet state and local regulatory needs *(e.g., 1:24,000 or larger)*; (2) mapping of flood and other hazard areas; (3) the acquisition of high resolution orthophotos for the nation with relatively frequent updates; (4) additional critical area mapping for wetlands, scientific areas, prime agricultural lands, and other areas; (5) greater emphasis on coordination of federal data gathering areas; (6) added technical assistance to train sources through workshops, manuals, and other technical aids; (7) direct technical assistance in evaluating development proposals; and (8) additional research pertaining to selected aspects of critical area implementation.

The political acceptability of a strong direct federal regulatory role is questionable except for very limited areas such as regulation of wetlands and watercourses.[2]

(f) the protection and preservation of the natural water courses, intermittent or permanent, and minimizing the discharge of pollutants into water bodies and water courses by storm runoff and otherwise;

(g) the protection and preservation of areas containing unique or endangered species of plants and animals;

(h) the prevention of premature development for nonagricultural use of prime agricultural lands where such land is essential for agricultural purposes;

(i) the regulation of the extraction of minerals, including sand and gravel, to minimize undesirable environmental effects and provide for future utilization of the lands involved;

(j) the preservation of natural resource areas of particular historical significance.

[2]*E.g.,* Corps of Engineers regulation of fills in navigable waters and wetlands. 33 U.S.C.A. §§401-466, 1251-1524 (1970, Supp. 1977). However, *see* articles proposing federal control of lands adjacent to federal parks. J. Kusler, *Public/Private Parks and Management of Private Lands for Park Protection,* University of Wisconsin, Institute for Environmental Studies, Report 16 (1974); Sax, "Helpless Giants: The National Parks and Regulation of Private Lands," 75 *Mich. L. Rev.* 239 (1976).

Table 22

Suggested roles in sensitive area regulation.

Level of Government	Recommended Role	Improvements in Existing Efforts
Federal Government	1. High resolution aerial photos should be produced on a periodic basis and distributed for the country as a whole to states and localities. Resolution and scale should exceed that of USGS orthophotos and ASCS photos for some, but not all, areas.	1. Declassified military photography might satisfy state and local needs without massive new data gathering. Scale and resolution of satellite imagery must be enhanced.
	2. Existing natural resource mapping should be continued and accelerated including 7½ minute topographic maps, detailed soil surveys, detailed geologic maps, flood hazard area maps, seismic area maps, erosion area maps (coastal and inland) and historic, archaeological and natural area thematic studies and maps. *New* major mapping efforts should be initiated for wetlands (already begun by Fish and Wildlife Service), prime agricultural lands (in discussion stages by USDA), and habitat (proposed by Fish and Wildlife, also USGS LUDA program).	2. Larger scale and more accurate maps (minimum scale of 1:24,000) are needed for many areas. Maps should be rectified and at compatible, although not necessarily identical, scales. Basic data as well as map products should be made available. Rapid production and distribution is needed since maps are often not completed until several years after initial data gathering.
	3. Increased technical assistance to states and local units should be provided including: (a) preparation of guidebooks, manuals, model regulations; (b) conduct of workshops and training sessions for state and local officials concerning use of federal data sources, development of sensitive area program, and impact analysis; and (c) field assistance in evaluating environmental impact of individual projects.	3. Efforts should be more "nut and bolt" and enlarged in scope. Added effort should be made to tailor technical assistance to state and local needs.
	4. Additional research should be conducted or grants-in-aid provided to states and universities to carry out research on land suitability analysis, environmental impact of particular types and densities of development techniques, and the administration and enforcement of sensitive area regulations.	4. Duplication in research should be reduced. Additional emphasis should be placed upon implementation issues.
	5. Federal public land use management, grants-in-aid, regulatory research, and other planning and land management efforts should be better coordinated with those of the states and localities.	5. Improved coordination between federal and state land use management is particularly important for the western states where much of the land is in federal ownership.
	6. Federal regulation of wetlands and navigable waters under Corps "404" permit procedures and federal standard-setting for private uses in national recreation areas applying the Cape Cod formula should be continued and improved. Possible federal standard-setting for regulation of other types of areas such as mineral resources areas and lands adjacent to national parks may be necessary if states and localities fail to adopt and administer regulations meeting national needs. This should be approached cautiously.	6. Impact evaluation and policy-setting methodologies should be improved.

Table 22 (continued)

Level of Government	Recommended Role	Improvements in Existing Efforts
	7. National land and water use legislation might be adopted with a focus upon data gathering, technical assistance and grants-in-aid for the states and localities rather than all-encompassing standards. Local and state initiatives and priorities should be encouraged.	
States	1. New enabling acts or amendments to existing acts authorizing individual area programs or comprehensive programs are needed where existing acts are inadequate or the stimulation of new legislation is needed.	1. Local zoning and subdivision control enabling acts should often be amended to make them more responsive to regulatory needs.
	2. Individual areas should be defined and mapped in cooperation with local units of government, regional planning agencies, and federal agencies. State mapping should focus on areas without adequate federal efforts. State should coordinate federal and local mapping efforts.	2. Existing sensitive area definitions should be refined through studies and monitoring of regulations. Mapping should be extended to areas not presently covered. Gradations and subzones should be identified in some areas. Public involvement in definition and mapping should be improved.
	3. State standards should be developed for local regulation of most types of areas with direct state regulation only in the event of local inaction. However, direct state regulation may be appropriate for some areas such as floodways and for major uses such as power generation plants, governmental uses, strip mining and large scale subdivisions where local units lack expertise or sufficient geographical perspective.	3. Administration and enforcement should be improved through increased budgets, field staff, and periodic field surveys. Improved planning, policy-setting and standard setting mechanisms should be applied. States should adopt administrative regulations to refine statutory policies.
	4. Technical assistance should be provided to local units of government in the adoption and administration of programs including (a) the preparation of guidebooks, want-ads and model regulations, (b) the conduct of workshops and training sessions, and (c) the evaluation of individual permits.	4. See federal technical assistance above.
	5. Additional research should be conducted in sensitive area policy-setting, planning, implementation. See description of federal research above.	5. See federal research above.
	6. State public work and regulatory activities should be coordinated with local sensitive area programs through statutory mandate or executive order.	
	7. A framework of short-term and long-term state land and water development and conservation policies should be developed, taking into account growth, resource carrying capacity, future development needs, etc. Critical area policies should be developed within this broader framework.	7. Improved techniques for projecting or controlling population growth and estimating resource carrying capacity should be developed.
Regional Planning Agencies	1. Continued technical assistance and data gathering should be provided to states and localities in sensitive area definition, mapping, evaluation of development proposals.	1. Expertise in hydrology, biology, zoology, botany, and other resource disciplines should be improved.
	2. Local, state, and federal programs should be coordinated.	
	3. Regional water quality, transportation, sewer and water, flood control, recreation and other types of plans should be prepared.	3. Plans should be implementation-oriented and based upon sound data.

Table 22 (continued)

Level of Government	Recommended Role	Improvements in Existing Efforts
	4. Comprehensive land use plans with sensitive area components should be prepared on a regional or community-by-community basis. These plans should integrate land capability analysis with broader planning techniques.	4. Plans should be designed to accomodate changing conditions and emphasize priority areas.
	5. Regional agencies might be vested with implementation powers for some areas such as metropolitan regions and resource areas of national or multistate significance (e.g., Lake Tahoe). However, the political acceptability of this approach is doubtful for most areas.	5. Governing bodies should be elected rather than appointed.
Local Units (General Purpose Units)	1. Assist the states and federal agencies in the definition and mapping of areas by supplying base maps such as sewer and water maps, providing local data through workshops and use of nomination procedures, checking state maps for accuracy, conducting specialized field studies, and refining state and federal maps for urban areas.	1. Local sources of information should be inventoried and compiled. Individuals with special expertise should be identified and involved in data gathering efforts.
	2. Adopt specialized critical area zoning, subdivision controls, building codes, and other regulations meeting or exceeding state and federal standards.	2. Local land and water regulations should often be amended to more clearly reflect natural resource capability.
	3. Administer and enforce critical area regulations by gathering data needed to evaluate special permit uses, conducting public hearrings, employing consultants to prepare and evaluate development proposals, inspecting sites, inspecting and enforcing regulations in court.	3. More funds should be appropriated to land use control functions. Local conservation commissions should be delegated planning and regulatory powers (where this is statutorily acceptable).
	4. Local public works, acquisition, and real estate taxation policies should be coordinated with sensitive area regulatory policies by adoption of overall community sensitive area protection and management policies.	4. Coordination between local governmental functions should be improved.
	5. Comprehensive land uses plans should be adopted and implemented with sensitive area regulation as one component. Natural resource carrying capacity should be determined to serve as the basis for growth limits.	5. Local comprehensive planning should be based upon improved natural resources data.
Special Purpose Units	1. Continued data gathering and technical assistance should be provided to states and local units of government. For example, soil conservation districts should provide continued assistance concerning erosion and watershed management with the possibility of broadened functions.	1. Added expertise in land use planning is needed.
	2. Special districts should be, in limited circumstances, vested with regulatory powers where general purpose governments lack the expertise or perspective for such regulations. However, the general political acceptability and advisability of regulation by special district is questionable.	2. Amendments to existing enabling statutes or new enabling statutes would be needed.

Part **8**

LEGAL RESTRAINTS

Sensitive area regulations raise the same constitutional issues posed by broader planning and regulation efforts. The taking issue is best known and most controversial. Other issues common to both sensitive area and broader programs include: (1) Are federal constitutional or statutory provisions vesting local units with home rule powers an impediment to state or conjunctive state/local critical area regulation? (2) Must statutory procedures, including data gathering, prior planning, notice and hearing, publication, and adoption requirements be strictly followed? (3) Do zoning and subdivision control enabling acts authorize local critical area regulation? (4) Are sensitive area regulatory objectives, such as protection of health and safety and protection of the natural suitability of land, valid? (5) How closely must regulatory standards reflect variations in the natural resource base and impacts of particular types of uses? (6) What scale and accuracy is required in data gathering, including specificity in boundary definition? (7) To what extent must similar uses be treated alike to avoid discrimination arguments? (8) Must regulatory standards be specific in delegating discretionary powers to an administrative body?

Extensive discussion of legal issues is beyond the present report. The reader is referred to more detailed texts.[1] Nevertheless, a brief overview of applicable law can be provided.

A broad examination of sensitive area courts decisions reveals some judicial disapproval of sensitive area regulations. But regulations are sustained in the majority of cases. (See Appendix E.) Courts are more receptive to resource protection regulations than they were a decade ago and may accept in the future what they consider unconstitutional today. In other words, the spectre of legal challenge is overdone. Nevertheless, it is useful in preparing and administering regulations to take into account judicial findings and attitudes in order to avoid serious legal pitfalls.

In determining the consistency of sensitive area regulation with the federal constitution and state constitutions, courts look first to the general validity of regulations (adequacy of statutory powers, compliance with statutory procedures) and then to their specific validity as applied to particular land (reasonableness, discrimination, taking). The majority of attacks upon sensitive area regulations are upon the application of regulations to particular property.[2] In other words, a landowner may concede the general validity of a flood plain, wetland, or other regulation but argue its unconstitutionality as applied to specific property. A court decision in the landowner's favor will not invalidate the regulations as applied to other lands. Understandably, this case-by-case approach has led to a great deal of litigation and varying court decisions. Nevertheless, decisions consistently apply certain broad tests or principles.

Based upon these tests or principles, several recommendations may be made for future efforts.

8-1 *To reduce the possibility of home rule challenge, legislation should: (1) emphasize the multijurisdictional nature of sensitive areas and their statewide importance and (2) maximize local participation in definition, data gathering, standard-setting, and enforcement.*

Thirty-three states now authorize cities and villages or boroughs to exercise home rule powers through constitutional or statutory provisions and eight states authorize county home rule.[3] Home rule provisions permit local governmental units to develop and implement policies concerning matters of local concern without specific statutory enabling authority. However, local home rule policies must, in most states,

[1]*See,* for example, R. Anderson, *American Law of Zoning,* 3 Vols., published by the Cooperative Publishing Company, Rochester, New York (1968); Emmet Yokley, *The Law of Subdivision,* Michie Company, Charlottesville, Virginia (1968).

[2]This "pinpoint" approach to the determination of the constitutionality derives from two United States Supreme Court decisions in the 1920's. In a 1926 decision, Euclid v. Ambler, 272 U.S. 365 (1926), the Court upheld the basic concept of zoning involving the division of a community into various districts and the application of different land use standards to each of the districts. A year later, the Court in Nectow v. Cambridge, 277 U.S. 183 (1928), faced a dilemma when it considered the validity of a zoning ordinance which made sense as applied to community lands as a whole, but was unreasonable as applied to a particular parcel. To have struck down the ordinance as a whole would have left the community without zoning and would have destroyed the good elements of zoning along with the bad. Taking a compromise position, the Court held that zoning regulations were valid in general, but invalid as applied to the particular property. This "pinpoint" approach has been followed by the state courts across the nation.

[3]*See* table 4 at p. 19 of E Strauss and J. Kusler, *Statutory Land Use Control Enabling Authority in the Fifty States,* U.S. Department of Housing and Urban Development, Federal Insurance Administration, Washington, D.C. (1975) for a listing of home rule statutes and constitutional provisions.

be consistent with general statutes or laws and must comply with other constitutional requirements.[4]

It is sometimes argued that statutes authorizing state regulation of sensitive areas violate local home rule powers. However, no court has invalidated state sensitive area regulations on this basis and successful challenge is unlikely for several reasons: (1) sensitive areas are of greater than local concern due to the multijurisdictional location of areas such as flood plains which cross municipal and state boundaries and the multijurisdictional importance of areas such as agricultural lands which must meet the food requirements of the state or nation and (2) sensitive area statutes often strongly involve local units of government and provide options to local governments, rather than preempting them, thereby maintaining a measure of home rule.

Home rule provisions may give rise to political objections even if they do not pose legal challenges.[5] For this reason sensitive area enabling statutes often emphasize the statewide importance of sensitive areas in findings of fact and require involvement of local units of government in regulatory administration. Local involvement is particularly important for matters of local concern such as protecting the local tax base, evaluating impacts on community services, and determining compatibility with existing uses and plans. In addition, local units are usually authorized to adopt regulations more restrictive than those of the state.

8-2 *Modifications in local subdivision control and zoning enabling acts are desirable in some instances to increase their responsiveness to sensitive area needs.*

Forty-eight states authorize cities and 40 authorize counties to adopt zoning controls.[6] Forty-one states authorize cities and 30 authorize counties to adopt subdivision regulations.[7] Authority to adopt critical area regulations may usually be found in these acts, which authorize regulations to serve the broad "health, safety and general welfare."[8] In addition, most zoning acts authorize regulations to promote the most suitable use of land throughout a community.[9] Many of these zoning and subdivision enabling acts have been amended to specifically authorize flood plain, lakeshore, agricultural zoning, or other sensitive area controls.[10]

Apart from this broad enabling authority, many states have adopted special statutes authorizing local units to adopt one or more types of sensitive area regulations.[11] Home rule powers noted above may provide an independent basis for adoption of critical area regulations in the absence of statutory enabling authority.

[4]*See* R. Anderson, *American Law of Zoning,* Vol. 1, Section 3.06, 3.07 at p. 134 *et seq.* (1968) and cases cited therein.

[5]As legislative acts, sensitive area regulations depend upon the will of legislators and, ultimately, upon the voting public. The question, then, is not simply what regulations courts will uphold, but also the political acceptability of particular types of regulations.

[6]*See Statutory Land Use Control Enabling Authority in the Fifty States,* note 3 *supra,* for a listing and description of these statutes.

[7]*Id.*

[8]This language has been incorporated in the Department of Commerce, *Standard State Zoning Enabling Act* (1926), and adopted in many states.

[9]*Id.*

[10]*E.g.,* Calif. Gov't Code, §65502 (West 1966); S.D. Code Annot., §11-1-13 (1967 and Supp. 1977). *See also, Statutory Land Use Control Enabling Authority in the Fifty States,* note 3 *supra,* for a listing of state statutes authorizing local flood plain and shoreland regulations.

[11]*See, e.g.,* Vernon's Tex. Code Annot., Article 28:8280-13 (1972 and 1973 Supp.) which authoizes local

No state supreme court has invalidated sensitive area regulations due to insufficient regulatory powers and a successful challenge is unlikely in light of the array of general and specific enabling and home rule powers available in the states.[12] However, a small number of general purpose units of government—some counties in Oklahoma and cities in Alaska—do not have general land use control enabling power and therefore could not rely upon such powers for adoption of sensitive area regulations.

Despite the minimum sufficiency of existing enabling authority, modifications could be made through amendment or new statutes to encourage local adoption of regulations, clarify powers, and provide more satisfactory sensitive area control mechanisms. These modifications could: (1) specify resource management and protection goals; (2) tighten exemptions for agricultural and existing uses; (3) require resource inventories and assessments as part of planning and regulatory processes; (4) authorize the use of resource protection regulatory mechanisms such as special permit uses, impact zoning, natural resource districts, or planned unit development permits issued by expert boards; (5) require developers to file environmental impact statements and other information required by the regulatory agency; (6) authorize piecemeal flood plain, wetland, and other sensitive area regulation without prior comprehensive land use planning; (7) require special procedures for issuing variances such as referral to a state administrative agency to discourage arbitrary decision-making; (8) require coordination of regulatory, tax, acquisition, and public work policies; and (9) require local units of government and state agencies to comply with regulatory standards.

8-3 *Regulations must be adopted in close conformance with statutory, ordinance, or administrative regulation requirements and procedures to satisfy due process requirements.*

Courts generally demand close compliance with notice and hearing, formal adoption, amendment, and appeal procedures.[13] These requirements are generally set forth in enabling acts but may also be included in ordinances and administrative regulations.

Few local zoning, subdivision control, and special sensitive area enabling acts establish formal data gathering requirements. However, some statutes establishing state critical area programs require very specific data gathering such as the Connecticut Coastal Wetland Act which requires mapping of areas at a scale of one inch equals 200 feet.[14]

Virtually all enabling acts authorizing state and local critical area programs require notice and hearing prior to adoption of local ordinances or state administra-

---

governments to adopt flood plain regulations in order to qualify for participation in the flood insurance program and Wis. Stat. Ann. §144.26 (1974) which authorizes municipal adoption of shoreland regulations.

[12]For example, the Massachusetts Supreme Court in Turnpike Realty Co. v. Town of Dedham, 362 Mass. 221, 284 N.E. 2d 89 (1972), *cert. denied,* 409 U.S. 1108 (1973), observed that the broad zoning enabling language of the Massachusetts statute (similar to that of many other states) was sufficient to authorize adoption of flood plain regulation even before it had been amended to expressly authorize flood plain zoning.

[13]*E.g.,* Morris v. Public Service Commission, 7 Utah 2d 167, 321 P. 2d 644 (1958); Hampton v. Arkansas State Game & Fish Commission, 218 Ark. 757, 238 S.W. 2d 950 (1951).

[14]Conn. Gen. Stat. Ann., §22a-30 (1975).

tive regulations. In addition, most acts, ordinances, and administrative regulations require notice and hearing prior to issuance of a development permit. Statutes typically require notice through a local newspaper prior to adoption of regulations. A small number of acts, such as the Massachusetts Wetland Act, require written notice to landowners prior to adoption of orders.[15]

Most acts specify that formal adoption of regulations requires a majority of legislators or an administrative body at a formally called meeting. Many zoning enabling acts require a 2/3 or 3/4 majority vote, as opposed to a simple majority, if a certain percentage of landowners protest a zoning change.

Most acts establish appeal procedures for aggrieved parties either directly to a court, or to a special hearing board and then to a court, if the aggrieved party remains unsatisfied.

Most acts authorizing direct state regulation of sensitive areas establish specific procedures for the processing of development permits. Local zoning and subdivision control enabling acts and special acts are usually less specific.

Although courts require close conformance with statutory procedures, an exception is found in comprehensive planning requirements for zoning.[16] Courts have not enforced comprehensive planning requirements strictly, in part because of the ambiguous nature of the requirements. Courts have often found a plan within the zoning regulations themselves where a separate plan had not been prepared.[17] No state supreme court has struck down sensitive area regulations adopted under general enabling authority without prior planning. However, prior planning requirements can be expected to gain teeth with the adoption of statutes such as Florida's Comprehensive Land Use Planning Act of 1975, which describes in detail the content and specifics of comprehensive plans.[18]

8-4 *Sensitive area regulatory standards should emphasize health, safety, and prevention of nuisances since courts give great weight to these regulatory objectives.*

Courts afford legislative bodies broad discretion in determining legislative goals.[19] However, courts have traditionally disapproved of regulations designed solely to protect aesthetics although this position is changing.[20] For this reason, natural

---

[15]Mass. Gen. L. Ann., §130-105 (Supp. 1977-78).

[16]Most local zoning enabling acts require regulations to be adopted "in accordance with a comprehensive plan" or preceded by prior planning. Subdivision enabling acts also typically require prior planning. However, acts establishing state critical area programs do not.

[17]*E.g.,* Kozesnik v. Montgomery Township, 24 N.J. 154, 131 A. 2d 1 (1957); DeMeo v. Zoning Com. of Bridgeport, 148 Conn. 167 A. 2d 454 (1961); Cleaver v. Board of Adjustment, 414 Pa. 367, 200 A. 2d 408 (1964).

[18]Fla. Stat. Ann. §163.316 *et seq.* (Supp. 1977).

[19]*E.g.,* Berman v. Parker, 348 U.S. 26 (1954).

[20]*See, e.g.,* Barney and Casey Co. v. Milton, 324 Mass. 440, 87 N.E. 2d 9 (1949); Cooper Lumber Co. v. Dammers, 2 N.J. Misc. 289, 125 A. 325 (1924). This position has been based, in part, upon a conviction that beauty is purely subjective and not subject to objective evaluation. However, aesthetics is recognized as a valid secondary objective in all states. Some courts have upheld aesthetic protection regulations by emphasizing the tangible benefits of such beauty including property values, tax base, and the regional recreation. *E.g.,* Jordan v. Village of Menomonee Falls, 28 Wis. 2d 608, 137 N.W.2d 442 (1965), *appeal dismissed,* 385 U.S. 4 (1966). Even where beauty or its benefits are accepted as a valid object, the further question remains: "How tightly may private property be controlled in the name of beauty?" Cases to date suggest that some restriction, but not total prohibition of uses, may be justified. *See,* for example, Bismark v. Bayville, 49 Misc. 2d 604, 267 N.Y.S. 2d 1002 (Sup. Ct. 1966) in which the court generally endorsed the adoption of regulations to protect aesthetic values but held that regulations that reduced property values by 58 percent to serve aesthetic objectives were unreasonable.

resource issues related to public safety,[21] such as flooding, seismic hazard, landslide, and erosion should be documented with particular care in defining areas and subzones.

In determining the reasonableness of regulations, courts are increasingly sympathetic to the protection of the natural suitability of land and possible irreversible effects of development on natural resources.[22] Data gathering should document suitability and project irreversible effects.

In some instances courts have invalidated zoning regulations designed to hold land in an open condition until public purchase is possible.[23] Courts have also struck down regulations allocating private lands to active public recreation uses.[24] Alternative bases for regulation should be emphasized when these are among the several regulatory objectives.

8-5 *In order to insure a reasonable relationship between the regulatory standards (the means) and the regulatory goals (the ends), regulations should be based on sound natural resources data and employ case-by-case data gathering and performance standards where diversified resources are encountered.*

The most common ground for judicial attack on traditional land use regulations and critical area controls is the failure of standards to bear a reasonable relationship to regulatory goals.[25]

---

[21]As noted by the U.S. Supreme Court in Queenside Hills Reality Co. v. Saxl, 328 U.S. 80, 83, when threats to human life are involved a legislature may adopt "the most conservative course which science and engineering offer." Regulations related to protection of health and safety are almost invariably sustained even where they regulate existing uses or prevent essentially all private use of land. *See, e.g.,* Cleaners Guild v. Chicago, 312 Ill. App. 102, 37 N.E. 2d 857 (1941); Denver & Rio Grande R.R. Co. v. City of Denver, 250 U.S. 241 (1919).

Courts have also strongly endorsed regulations to prevent nuisances or uses with nuisance characteristics. *E.g.,* Hadacheck v. Los Angeles, 239 U.S. 394 (1915); Reinman v. Little Rock, 237 U.S. 171 (1915); Pierce Oil Corp. v. City of New York, 248 U.S. 498 (1919).

However, health and safety considerations are not relevant to the definition of some areas, such as scenic areas. Efforts should not be attempted to relate standards to health and safety where they are not relevant.

[22]*See* cases cited in notes 51, 56, 60, 61, *infra.*

[23]*E.g.,* Long v. Highland Park, 329 Mich. 146, 45 N.W. 2d 10 (1950); Miami v. Romer, 73 So. 2d 285 (Fla. 1954); Galt v. Cook County, 405 Ill. 396, 91 N.E. 2d 395 (1950). However, official mapping to preserve sites for future roadways until purchase is possible has been sustained. *E.g.,* Headley v. Rochester, 272 N.Y. 197, 5 N.E. 2d 198 (1936); State *ex rel.* Miller v. Manders, 2 Wis. 2d 365, 86 N.W. 2d 469 (1957). In addition, the California court in Turner v. County of Del Norte, 24 Cal. App. 3d 314, 101 Cal. Rptr. 93 (1972), upheld highly restrictive flood plain regulations for an area subject to extreme flood hazards that was contemplated for public purchase. Plans for long term public purchase should not undermine the validity of present regulation based upon independent objectives such as protection of floodway areas.

[24]*E.g.,* Sanderson v. City of Wilmar, 282 Minn. 1, 162 N.W. 2d 494 (1968).

[25]The United States Supreme Court in Welch v. Swasey, 214 U.S. 91, 105 (1909) stated this requirement:
The statutes . . . passed under the exercise of so-called policy power . . . *must have some fair tendency to accomplish, or aid in the accomplishment of some purpose,* for which the legislature may use the power. If the statutes are not of that kind, then passage cannot be justified under that power.

These principles have been so frequently decided as not to require the citation of many authorities. *If the means employed, pursuant to the statute, have no real, substantial relation to the public object which government can accomplish; if the statutes are arbitrary and unreasonable and beyond the necessities of the case; the courts will declare their invalidity.* (emphasis added).

The court further noted in Stephenson v. Binford 287 U.S. 251, 272 (1932), that "(i)t is enough if it can be seen that any degree or under any reasonable circumstances, there is an actual relation between means and the end."

To achieve regulatory goals and stave off legal attacks, standards must take into account actual hazards and values encountered at sites and the probable impact of particular uses. Sound data, including, in some instances, identification of gradations in areas and subzones, is needed to provide the basis for reasonable standards. However, there are practical limits to which resource variations and impact can be taken into account. The extent to which regulations must be modified to reflect special conditions depends on the impact of regulations upon landowners,[26] capability of the governmental body to carry out necessary surveys, and susceptibility of the subject to quantified analysis.

Because of the diversity in the factual base, most sensitive area programs employ special permit procedures combined with performance standards and detailed case-by-case data gathering to evaluate individual development permits.

8-6 *Accurate, large scale maps are needed to define sensitive area boundaries. Site-specific data gathering is needed to analyze individual development permits.*

While state supreme court land use control cases rarely focus on the sufficiency of the available data, the types and accuracy of data clearly play an important role in judicial balancing of public and private interests. Sensitive area cases suggest several conclusions. (1) Statutory data gathering requirements with respect to scale, type, and format must be followed.[27] (2) In general, critical area mapping requires relatively large scale and accurate maps to fix the location of zone boundaries on the ground.[28] However, a two step procedure using relatively large scale maps (1:24,000) to define general boundaries, combined with field investigations to determine precise boundaries in boundary disputes, may suffice.[29] (3) Data must be sufficiently accurate and at large enough scale to justify boundaries and regulations as they apply to individual lands.[30] Most landowners concede the general validity of regulations but challenge their sufficiency as applied to particular properties. (4) Data gathering programs should document with particular care health, safety, and

---

[30]*See* cases cited in note 28, *supra. See also* Sturdy Homes, Inc. v. Township of Redford, 30 Mich. App. 53, 186 N.W. 2d 43 (1971), in which the court held that a flood plain zoning ordinance which prohibited dwellings was unreasonable as applied in part because there was little evidence that the land was subject to flooding.

[26]Courts demand particularly sound classifications where use standards severly restrict private uses and affect property values. The Connecticut court in Strain v. Mims, 123 Conn. 275, 286, 193 A. 754, 759 (1937) observed:

(W)here the value of property of an individual is seriously affected by a zoning regulation especially applicable to it, this fact imposes an obligation to carefully consider the questions where the regulation does in fact tend to serve the public welfare and the recognized purposes of zoning.

[27]*See generally* cases cited in note 13, *supra.*

[28]*See* Annot., "Validity of Zoning Regulations, With Respect to Uncertainty and Indefiniteness of District Boundary Lines," 39 A.L.R.2d 766 (1955) and cases cited therein. *See specifically* Auditorium, Inc. v. Board of Adjustment of Mayor and Council, Del, 91 A.2d 428 (1952); Slattery v. Caldwell, 83 N.J. Super. 317, 199 A.2d 670 (1964). However, *see* Lebannon v. Woods, 143 Conn. 182, 215 A.2d 112 (1965).

[29]In Just v. Marinette Co., 56 Wis. 2d 7, 201 N.W. 2d 761 (1972), the Wisconsin Supreme Court upheld the use of U.S. Geological Survey topographic maps for wetland mapping combined with a written definition of wetland areas:

[A]reas where groundwater is at or near the surface much of the year or where any segment of plant cover is deemed an aquatic according to N.C. Fassett's "Manual of Aquatic Plants."

A landowner contested the regulations arguing, in part, that the wetland maps were not sufficiently specific and that his land was not a wetland. The Court did not specifically discuss the validity of the maps, but sustained the regulations, noting that the land was clearly wetland by the written test.

nuisance problems where prohibitory or very restrictive standards will be applied.[31] (5) Gradations and subzones in areas, in some instances, should be mapped to insure the application of reasonable regulatory standards and permit application of highly restrictive use standards in areas with severe hazards or highest values.[32] (6) Often a major emphasis should be placed on detailed case-by-case data gathering, since the real meat of most controls is found in the application of performance standards to areas. (7) Courts are likely to defer to administrative discretion concerning the use of a specific data gathering or evaluation approach when an expert agency has undertaken the data gathering effort.[33] However, a court may find an expert determination inadequate when there is little or no data to support a determination or a clear abuse of discretion.[34]

8-7 In order to avoid discrimination, regulations should provide similar treatment to similarly situated properties. However, it is clear that: (1) more restrictive standards can be applied to new uses than existing uses; (2) all lands need not be regulated at once; and (3) differing standards can be applied to areas with similar natural resource characteristics where differences in cultural features or planning goals exist.

Sensitive area standards must afford equal treatment to similarly situated landowners to comply with the 14th Amendment guarantees of due process and prohibition of discrimination.[35] While discrimination is an increasingly common issue in traditional zoning contexts because of exclusionary intent or result, critical area regulations have rarely been invalidated on discrimination grounds.

Despite a general requirement that regulations apply equally to similarly situated property, courts have usually sustained regulations which apply only to new uses[36]— the common sensitive area regulatory approach. Courts have reasoned that it is one matter to design and locate a new use consistent with regulatory standards and another to modify and relocate existing uses in compliance with new laws.

[31]*See* notes 21, 25 *supra* and note 32 *infra. See specifically* MacGibbon v. Duxbury (1976), in which the Massachusetts Supreme Court held that threat of pollution or erosion hazard would be sufficient to deny a special exception for a wetland area, but that broader ecological considerations might not be.

[32]No court has required that gradations or subzones be identified in areas. However, courts have invalidated highly restrictive regulations applying to an entire flood plain area. *See, e.g.,* Dooley v. Town Plan and Zoning Comm'n., 151 Conn. 304, 197 A. 2d 770 (1964) (Court invalidated a flood plain zoning ordinance applying to an entire estuarine area); Morris County Land Imp. Co. v. Parsippany-Troy Hills Tp., 40 N.J. 539, 193 A.2d 232 (1963) (Court invalidated a conservancy district designed to preserve wildlife and flood storage). In contrast, they have upheld regulations applying to narrow floodway areas subject to extreme flooding. *See, e.g.,* Turner v. County of Del Norte, 24 C.A. 3d 311, 101 Cal. Rptr. 93 (1972) (Court upheld county ordinance tightly controlling area subject to extreme flooding); Vartelas v. Water Resource Comm'n, 146 Conn. 650, 153 A. 2d 822 (1959) (court upheld Connecticut state-level floodway encroachment statute.)

[33]Courts do not generally require that expert agencies use one method rather than another in performing expert determinations. As noted by a New York Court in Chiropractic Ass'n of New York, Inc. v. Hilleebee, 12 N.Y. 2d 109, 187 N.E. 2d 756 (1962):

It is not for the courts to determine which scientific view is correct in ruling upon whether the police power has been properly exercised. The judicial function is exhausted with the discovery that the relation between means and end is not wholly vain and fanciful, an illusory pretense.

[34]*See* Sturdy Home, Inc. v. Township of Reford, 30 Mich. App. 53, 186 N.W. 2d 43 (1971) (no evidence of flooding); A.H. Smith Sand and Gravel Co. v. Dept. of Water Resources, 313 A. 2d 820 (Md. App. 1974) (agency was required to redefine flood plain boundaries in light of new flood information); National Land Inv. Co. v. Kohn, 419 Pa. 504, 215 A. 2d 597 (1965) (insufficient evidence of water pollution to justify large lot sizes).

[35]*See generally* Yick Wo v. Hopkins, 118 U.S. 356 (1886).

[36]*E.g.,* Zahn v. Board of Pub. Works, 195 Cal. 497, 234 P. 388 (1925), *aff'd,* 274 U.S. 325 (1927).

Courts have not required all sensitive areas to be regulated at once within a state or region.[37] This is consistent with the widespread practice of mapping and regulating wetlands, flood plains, prime agricultural lands, and other types of areas on an area-by-area basis as data gathering is completed.

Finally, courts have recognized that lands with identical or similar natural resource characteristics need not always be treated alike.[38] Valid differences may exist between such lands due to cultural features, such as existing uses, and varied planning goals.

8-8 *Sensitive area statutes, ordinances, and administrative regulations should establish relatively specific standards for the delegation of regulatory powers to administrative boards.*

Courts have upheld sensitive area regulations as providing sufficiently specific standards despite the widespread application of unquantified nuisance, environmental, or general welfare standards.[39] However, in traditional zoning, courts have held invalid broad delegation of special permit powers to boards of adjustment where standards fail to establish legislative intent and place restraints on administrative actions.[40] Judicial disapproval usually occurs where a non-expert agency is authorized to determine the consistency of proposed permits with the "general welfare" or some other poorly defined criterion. These cases suggest that sensitive area standards need not be quantified but should offer real guidance for acceptable uses.

Courts have upheld broad delegation of powers to expert agencies where varied circumstances prevent iron-clad rules.[41] Where diverse factual circumstances prevent

---

[37]*E.g.,* Scarborough v. Mayor and Council of Town of Cheswold, 303 A. 2d 701 (Del. Ch. 1973); Ann Arundel Co. v. Ward, 186 Md. 330, 46 A. 2d 684 (1946); Town of Marblehead v. Rosenthal, 316 Mass. 124, 55 N.E. 2d 13 (1944); *In Re* Sports Complex in Hackensack Meadowlands, 62 N.J. 248, 300 A. 2d 337 (1973), *cert. denied,* 414 U.S. 989 (1973); Sands Point Harbor, Inc. v. Sullivan, 136 N.J. Super. 436, 346 A. 2d 612 (1975); Potomac Sand and Gravel Co. v. Governor of Maryland *et al.,* 266 Md. 358, 293 A. 2d 241 (Md. Ct. App., 1972), *cert. denied,* 409 U.S. 1040 (1972); J.M. Mills, Inc. v. Murphy, 352 A. 2d 661 (R.I. 1976).

[38]*See, e.g.,* Kozesnik v. Montgomery Township, 24 N.J. 154, 131 A.2d complete cite (1957).

[39]In a recent wetland decision, J.M. Mills, Inc. v. Murphy, 352 A. 2d 661 (R.I. 1976), the Rhode Island Supreme Court upheld a statute that authorized the director of Rhode Island Department of Natural Resources to deny permits for inland wetlands "if in the opinion of the director granting of such approval would not be in the best public interest" or if the city council or town council within whose borders the project lies had disapproved the project. The court held that the purposes section of the statute, which listed in some detail wetland functions and the need for protection, sufficiently defined the "public interest" for the purposes of delegating regulatory powers and establishing a policy for evaluation of permits by local governments. Similarly, the Massachusetts Supreme Court has upheld quite broad standards for local issuance of special exceptions in wetland areas in MacGibbon v. Board of Appeals of Duxbury, 356 Mass. 635, 255 N.E. 2d 347 (1970) and Turnpike Realty Company v. Town of Dedham, 362 Mass. 221, 284 N.E. 2d 891 (1972), *cert. denied,* 409 U.S. 1108 (1973).

[40]*See generally,* "Annot., Attack on the Validity of Zoning Statute, Ordinance, or Regulation on the Ground of Improper Delegation of Authority to Board or Officer," 58 A.L.R. 1083 (1958), and cases cited therein.

[41]Courts have upheld broad standards where the subject matter is diverse and each situation must be considered individually, for example, in City of Utica Water Pollution Control Board, 5 N.Y. 2d 164, 156 N.E. 2d 301 (1959). The New York Court of Appeals noted, 156 N.E. 2d at 304-305:
The Legislature may constitutionally confer discretion upon an administrative agency only if it limits the field in which that discretion is to operate and provides standards to govern its exercise ... That does not, however, mean that a specific or specific formula must be furnished in a field "where flexibility and the adaptation of the (legislative) policy to infinitely variable conditions constitute the essence of the program." It is enough if the Legislature lays down "an intelligible

the adoption of very specific standards, emphasis should be on (1) a clear statement of goals, (2) specification of the factors and considerations in permit processing. (3) regulatory procedures providing for full notice, and (4) clear and prompt hearing and appeal procedures.

8-9 *Sensitive area regulation should avoid rather than confront the taking issue.*

The taking issue remains an obstacle for highly restrictive regulations.[42] But the taking issue is more than a legal question. It is the focus of broad philosophical and political debates concerning public versus private interests in land and the role of government versus private landowners in determining land uses.

Courts use a variety of tests to determine whether regulations take property.[43] A determination of taking is often closely related to a determination of reasonableness of regulations and compliance with other constitutional requirements.[44] Regulations that lack sufficient factual basis are often considered both unreasonable and a taking since unreasonable restrictions, however slight, are unjustified. Similarly, regulations that do not serve valid police power objectives impose an undue restraint on private

---

principle," specifying the standards or guides in as detailed a fashion as is reasonably practicable in the light of the complexities of the particular area to be regulated . . . Obviously, the Legislature cannot "constitutionally (be) required to appraise beforehand the myriad situations to which it wishes a particular policy to be applied and to formulate specific rules for each situation. Necessity therefore fixes a point beyond which it is unreasonable to compel (the Legislature) to prescribe detailed rules."

[42]For more extensive discussion of the "taking" issue the reader should consult, F. Bosselman and D. Callies, *The Taking Issue*, U.S. Government Printing Office (1973); J. Kusler, "Open Space Zoning: Valid Regulation or Invalid Taking," 57 Minn. L. Rev. 1 (1972); and recent articles listed in the bibliography of this book.

[43]Common tests for determining whether regulations take property include:

1. *Physical invasion.* Almost without exception, courts hold that government cannot physically invade property and put it to public use (*e.g.,* hiking, picnicking, roadways, public access) without payment of compensation. Government use of private critical areas is rarely an issue although one case held that public flooding of private land was a taking. Pumpelly v. Green Bay Company, 80 U.S. 166 (1871). Similarly, the New Jersey Supreme Court held that the construction of a large sand dune by the Army Corps of Engineers on private property to protect the surrounding area against hurricane damage was a taking. Lorio v. Sea Isle City, 88 N.J. Super. 506, 212 A. 2d 802 (1965). Borderline situations exist, however, such as the zoning of private property for public park use.

2. *Prevention of threats to public safety and prevention of nuisances.* On the other hand, courts universally uphold regulations to prevent real threats to public safety or nuisances, in part because landowners have no right to threaten safety or make nuisances of themselves. *See* cases cited in note 21, *supra.* Courts have upheld tight control of existing as well as prospective uses to achieve these objectives. *Id.* Regulations to serve these objectives have been sustained even where they inadvertently prevent all private economic use of land. *See* note 47, *infra.*

3. *Diminution in value.* Traditionally courts compare the value of property before and after regulation. *E.g.,* Pennsylvania Coal Co. v. Mahon, 260 U.S. 393 (1922); Morris County Land Imp. Co. v. Parsippany-Troy Hills Tp., 40 N.J. 539, 193 A. 2d 232 (1963). Although courts consider the impact of regulations upon landowners, this test is rarely applied as a final measure of taking.

4. *Denial of all reasonable or practical use of land.* Courts usually determine whether sensitive area regulations deny all reasonable or practical use of land. *See* cases in note 46, *infra.* This is usually final. A distinction between "reasonable" and "practical uses" is made in some instances. For example, highly restrictive coastal wetland regulations for an area subject to severe flood hazards may prevent all practical uses (*i.e.,* profitable uses) such as residences or marinas. However, regulations do not take property if these uses are considered unreasonable due to flood hazards or incompatibility with adjacent uses.

A use may be reasonable and practical in one instance and not in another depending upon land values, taxes, existing uses, and other factors. Courts have qualified the reasonable or practical use tests through the application of additional tests.

[44]*See* Sax, "Takings and the Police Power," Yale L.J. 36 (1964); Kusler, "Open Space Zoning: Valid Regulation or Invalid Taking," 57 Minn. L. Rev. 1, 13 (1972).

property. Finally, regulations that discriminate may be held a taking, based on the rationale that tight restrictions are acceptable if they affect all in like circumstances but unacceptable if they single out a few.

Courts agree that regulations may substantially reduce land values without a taking.[45] Typically, courts balance the public need for regulation in a particular circumstance with the impact of the regulations upon private property owners when they determine whether regulations take property. This means that they may uphold regulations as to one property but not the next.

While several tests are often combined to determine the validity of regulations, courts are usually less concerned with overall diminution in value and instead ask "Do the regulations prevent all economic use of land?" In general, regulations are held a taking when they prevent all "practical" or "reasonable" use of land.[46] However, there are important exceptions. (1) Courts consistently uphold regulations to protect public safety or prevent nuisances even if these restrictions inadvertently prevent all practical use of the land.[47] (2) Courts sustain the control of narrow strips of lands such as setbacks, where usable sites remain on lots.[48] (3) Courts often uphold large minimum lot sizes for low density residential uses.[49] (4) Courts generally uphold building moratoria and other highly restrictive regulations for limited periods.[50] (5) Courts often uphold restrictions protecting public rights in navigable waters,[51] (6) Courts quite often uphold regulations where landowners fail

[45]*See, e.g.,* Chevron Oil Company v. Beaver County, 22 Utah 2d 143, 449 P.2d 989 (1969) (Court upheld a grazing district zoning classification for land apparently worth $20-30 per acre for grazing purposes but $10,000 per acre as "highway service land"); Turnpike Realty Co. v. Town of Dedham, 284 N.E. 2d 891 (Mass. 1972), *cert. denied,* 409 U.S. 1108 (1973) (court upheld flood plain zoning despite testimony that land was worth $431,000 before regulations and $53,000 after regulations).

[46]*See, e.g.,* Arverne Bay Construction Co. v. Thatcher, 278 N.Y. 222, 15 N.E. 2d 587 (1938); Morris County Land Imp. Co. v. Parsipanny-Troy Hills Tp., 40 N.J. 539, 193 A. 2d 232 (1963); Dooley v. Town Plan and Zoning Commission, 151 Conn. 304, 197 A. 2d 770 (1964).

[47]*See, e.g.,* Consolidated Rock Products Co. v. Los Angeles, 57 Cal. 2d 515, 370 P. 2d 342 (1962), in which the California Supreme Court sustained an ordinance prohibiting sand and gravel operations in a dry stream bed where no other economic use could be made of the land because nearby residential areas would be affected by the dust and noise of mining operations. *See also* Filister v. Minneapolis, 270 Minn. 53, 133 N.W. 2d 500 (1964), *appeal dismissed* and *cert. denied,* 382 U.S. 14 (1965), in which the Minnesota Supreme Court sustained a single family residential classification for a swampy area surrounded by residences in part because proposed apartments would have been incompatible with adjacent uses.

[48]*See, e.g.,* Gorieb v. Fox, 274 U.S. 603 (1927) (Supreme Court upheld 35 foot setback); Flinn v. Treadwell, 120 Colo. 117, 207 P. 2d 967 (1949) (upheld 25 foot setback); State *ex rel* McKusick v. Houghton, 171 Minn. 231, 213 N.W. 907 (1927) (upheld 30 foot setback); Gitlin v. Rowledge, 36 Misc. 2d 933, 123 N.Y.S. 2d 812 (Sup. Ct. 1953) (upheld 50 foot setback); Sierra Constr. Co. v. Board of App., 12 N.Y. 2d 79, 187 N.E. 2d 123, 236 N.Y.S. 2d 53 (1962) (upheld 60 foot setback).

[49]*See, e.g.,* Zygmont v. Planning and Zoning Comm'n, 152 Conn. 550, 210 A. 2d 172 (1965) (upheld 20,000 square foot minimum lot sizes for an area with onsite waste disposal limitations); Honeck v. Cook County, 12 Ill. 2d 257, 146 N.E. 2d 35 (1957) (upheld five acre minimum for hilly land full of ravines); County Comm'rs v. Miles, 246 Md. 355, 228 A. 2d 450 (1967) (upheld five acre minimum for coastal area).

[50]*See, e.g.,* Fowler v. Obier, 224 Ky. 742, 7 S.W. 2d 219 (1928); Campana v. Clark Tp., 82 N.J. Super. 392, 197 A. 2d 711 (L. Div. 1964); Walworth County v. Elkhorn, 27 Wis. 2d 30, 133 N.W. 2d 257 (1965).

[51]*See, e.g.,* Sibson v. State, 336 A.2d 239 (N.H. 1975); Township of Grosse Ile v. Dunbar & Sullivan Dredging Co., 15 Mich. App. 556, 167 N.W. 2d 311 (1969); Zabel v. Tabb, 430 F. 2d 199 (5th Cir. 1970); Just v. Marinette County, 56 Wis. 2d 7, 201 N.W. 2d 761 (1972).

to protest restrictions in a timely manner.[52] (7) Finally, courts sometimes uphold highly restrictive regulations where special permits are potentially available for structures, fill, or other practical uses.[53]

Regulatory objectives and other factors are relevant to a determination of taking. In balancing public and private interests, courts give great weight to the protection of public health and safety and prevention of nuisances despite severe economic impact upon property owners.[54] Thus regulations may validly prevent all economic use of lands if all economic uses are unsafe or nuisances.[55] Several courts have sustained tight wetland regulations to protect the natural suitability of land.[56] In contrast, courts give less weight to aesthetic values although this position is slowly changing.[57]

One emerging line of cases should be noted. Illustrated by the landmark wetland protection case, *Just v. Marinette County*, [58] they sustain sensitive area regulations on the theory that public rights in natural resources are paramount to the rights of private landowners. In *Just*, the Wisconsin Court reasoned that "the shoreland zoning ordinance preserves nature, the environment, and natural resources as they were created and to which the people have a present right." Regulations do not take property where a landowner has no property right or where public rights supercede private interests. Most cases using this approach similarly involve land uses with impact upon public waters.[59] However, public interests have been recognized in cases sustaining the regulation of forestry operations and oil and gas extraction.[60]

---

[52]*See, e.g.,* Hodge v. Luckett, 357 S.W. 2d 303 (1962); Filister v. City of Minneapolis, 270 Minn. 53, 133 N.W. 2d 500 (1964), *cert. denied,* 382 U.S. 14 (1965).

[53]Where special permits are potentially available for structures, fills, or other practical uses, regulations do not on their face deny all practical uses. For example, the Connecticut Supreme Court in Vartelas v. Water Resources Commission, 146 Conn. 650, 153 A. 2d 822 (1959) upheld the denial of a permit under a state floodway protection law. The Court observed that the denial of one permit for a proposed use was not equivalent to denial of all possible uses. Similarily, the Wisconsin Supreme Court in Just v. Marinette County, 56 Wis. 2d 7, 201 N.W. 2d 761 (1972), upheld very restrictive wetland conservancy regulations, noting that special exceptions were potentially available under the terms of the ordinance. The potential for special permits was also considered significant by the Massachusetts Supreme Court in upholding flood plain regulations in Turnpike Realty Co. v. Town of Dedham, 362 Mass. 221, 284 N.E. 2d 891 (1972), *cert. denied.* 409 U.S. 1108 (1973).

[54]*See* cases cited in note 21, *supra.*

[55]*See* cases cited in notes 21 and 47 *supra,* and in notes 164-179 of Kusler, "Open Space Zoning: Valid Regulation or Invalid Taking," 57 *Minn. L. Rev.* 1, 47-51 (1972).

[56]*E.g.,* Sibson v. State, 336 A. 2d 239 (N.H. 1975); Just v. Marinette County, 56 Wis. 2d 7, 201 N.W. 2d 761 (1972).

[57]*See* cases cited in note 20, *supra.*

[58]56 Wis. 2d 7, 201 N.W. 2d 761 (1972). The court observed at 201 N.W. 2d 768:
Is the ownership of a parcel of land so absolute that man can change its nature to suit any of his purposes? The great forests of our state were stripped on the theory man's ownership was unlimited. But in forestry, the land at least was used naturally, only the natural fruit of the land (the trees) were taken. The despoilage was in failure to look to the future and provide for the reforestation of the land. An owner of land has no absolute and unlimited right to change the essential natural character of his land so as to use it for a purpose for which it was unsuited in its natural state and which injures the rights of others. The exercise of the police power in zoning must be reasonable and we think it is not an unreasonable exercise of that power to prevent harm to public rights by limiting the use of private property to its natural uses.

[59]*See generally* cases cited in note 51, *supra.*

[60]*E.g.,* State v. Dexter, 32 Wash. 2d 551, 202 P.2d 906, *aff'd,* 338 U.S. 863 (1949) (forestry resources); Lindsley v. Natural Carbonic Gas Co., 220 U.S. 61 (1911) (gas); Ohio Oil Co. v. Indiana, 177 U.S. 190 (1900) (gas).

In the next decade courts will be called upon many times to determine whether specific critical area regulations "take" property. Decisions will likely turn not only upon the impact of the regulations upon private property but the soundness of the factual base and the reasonableness of the overall program. Courts appear particularly willing to sustain controls designed to protect national or statewide as opposed to purely local interests.[61]

Although situations do arise where it is best to confront the taking issue, it is often politically advisable to avoid potential litigation through a conscious attempt to permit private economic land uses while minimizing their impacts and preserving important values. Specific measures for avoiding the taking issues may include: (1) genuine attempts to balance public and private interests and permit some private economic land uses;[62] (2) generation of a sound data base distinguishing most hazardous and valuable areas from other less crucial areas where some development may be permitted; (3) applying special permit approaches combined with performance standards to maximize private land use options; (4) emphasizing health and safety, prevention of nuisances, and prevention of fraud; (5) public education programs to gain landowner support and cooperation; (6) combining large lot zoning with density controls and performance standards to permit some private uses while minimizing impacts; and (7) combining regulations with real estate tax incentives, easements, fee acquisition, or payment for development rights.

[61]*See, e.g.,* Candlestick Properties, Inc. v. San Francisco Bay Conservation and Development Commission, 11 Cal. App. 3d 557, 89 Cal. Rptr. 897 (1970) (court upheld denial of a permit for filling San Francisco Bay); Brown v. Tahoe Regional Planning Agency, 385 F. Supp. 1128 (D. Nev. 1973) (court held that public welfare may require exceptionally restrictive land use classifications to protect Lake Tahoe); Meadowlands Regional Development Agency v. State, 112 N.J. Super. 89, 270 A. 2d 418 (1970) (court upheld general constitutionality of a statute creating the Meadowlands Regional Development Agency).

[62]To illustrate the balancing of public and private interests, consider alternative flood plain zoning policies for a community. A prohibitory approach preventing all development in the flood plain can reduce flood losses and preserve wildlife, open space, and flood storage for community benefit but may severely limit community growth and private use of land. In contrast, a wholly permissive approach maximizes landowner options but increases flood losses. A middle approach, adopted by many communities, balances preservation and development needs by tightly controlling a narrow floodway to prevent increases of flood height while permitting flood-protected development in the outer flood fringes. However, this balancing of conservation and development needs and public and private interests requires sophisticated regulations which recognize gradations in areas and a data-base sufficient to identify gradations. It also requires that critical areas not be viewed as monolithic resources but rather as a gradation of environment with varying land use capability and management needs.

Of course, development policies which reflect both conservation and development interests are impossible in some instances. For example, even limited development may destroy endangered species.

Part **9**

SENSITIVE AREA PROGRAMS IN THE BROADER CONTEXT OF LAND USE MANAGEMENT

The wisdom of a natural resource focus in land management is sometimes disputed. The proper relationship between sensitive area programs and broader comprehensive planning and regulation efforts is another issue. A sensitive area approach clearly does not solve all problems. It is of questionable value in urban areas with disturbed soil, vegetation, and water resources systems. Yet even here important natural areas such as wetlands are found and natural hazards such as flooding and seismic activity threaten public and private uses.

It is difficult to argue with proposals for combining sensitive area programs with one another or with broader land and water management efforts. Ideally, all problems should be approached comprehensively. And yet, sensitive area programs have been adopted in many states and localities only after the inadequacies of comprehensive approaches became apparent.

An overview of both critical area programs and broader land and water efforts suggests several conclusions.

9-1 *State and conjunctive state/local land use management efforts, particularly those for rural areas, should continue to focus upon sensitive areas but with greater emphasis on the interrelationships between areas and the integration of sensitive area programs and broader land use planning and management programs.*

A continued natural resource focus in state land management efforts is justified. This focus is supported by the long-term mathematics of resource supply and demand, and the fixed supply of land, water, and minerals which must meet present and future needs for food supply, fossil fuels, metals, wood, recreation, scientific study, education, and a wide range of public and private development. Population growth and dwindling resources add incentive to a resource-conscious approach.

While comprehensive land planning and regulatory approaches have theoretical attractiveness, they are often beset by political and budgetary problems and hindered by the sheer complexity of issues and analytical needs. Regulations based on tangible needs are less controversial than regulations based on projected development needs. In addition, critical area definition and regulation provides a rational and manageable first step in broader land use planning.

Despite the attractiveness of a resource protection focus, mechanisms are needed to coordinate programs and provide an overall policy framework considering both natural resource protection and broader land use management objectives.

9-2 *The continued adoption of sensitive area programs addressing individual areas has certain advantages and may be politically more palatable than adoption of a comprehensive sensitive area program addressing many types of areas.*

Sensitive area programs have usually been established for individual types of areas, such as flood plains, through separate state legislation for each type of area. This approach contrasts with the critical area approach proposed by section seven of the American Law Institute Model Land Development Code, which authorizes a single agency to designate and adopt management standards for many types of areas.[1] The American Law Institute approach has been substantially adopted in Florida and Minnesota. In addition, Colorado, Nevada, Maine, and Oregon address several types of areas in a single statute, but they have not vested a single agency with as broad regulatory powers.

The American Law Institute comprehensive sensitive areas approach has the potential advantages of economies of scale, centralized and coordinated policy-making, and less chance of duplication in data gathering and other activities. Nevertheless, experience indicates several disadvantages: (1) the centralization of power in a single agency is often politically unacceptable; (2) a single agency approach may not capitalize on the expertise found in existing line agencies, such as expertise concerning agricultural lands found in an agricultural agency, expertise concerning wetlands found in a wildlife agency, and expertise concerning flood problems found in a water resources agency; and (3) it may be more difficult to gain legislative support for the funding required for data gathering and management by a single agency.

Adopting individual sensitive area programs for each type of area is more directly responsive to individual interest groups, such as fishermen, hunters, nature lovers,

[1] American Law Institute, *A Model Land Development Code,* Proposed Official Draft No. 1, Phila., Pa. (1974). Section 7-201 authorizes a state planning agency to designate areas affected by or having significant impact upon major public facilities and areas of public investment (proposed and existing), areas of regional or statewide importance from historical, natural, or environmental resource perspectives, sites of new communities and surrounding lands, and certain other areas not regulated by local governments.

and the scientific community, and may be more politically acceptable. With an individual area approach, conflicting policies must be resolved in a political forum rather than a state planning office or other comprehensive critical area agency. This is preferable to many interest groups and may provide an important measure of public debate and legislative involvement otherwise lacking.

Despite advantages of the individual area approach, careful coordination between existing programs is essential. In addition, comprehensive approaches may become politically palatable over time as many types of sensitive lands become scarce and the technical problems of comprehensive programs are overcome through adequate staffing and funding. Comprehensive approaches, even where underfunded, may also serve an important function in addressing areas not considered by other programs.

9-3 *State sensitive area efforts should be distinguished from programs governing broader critical areas and from state regulations governing developments of regional impact.*

State land use regulatory efforts in recent years have focused on three types of areas or activities: sensitive resource areas, broader critical areas including sites for future public development, and developments of regional benefit or impact. These areas and activities share two characteristics: widescale impact and inadequate regulation at local level. The American Law Institute Model Land Development Code proposes that all three areas and activities be subject to state standard setting for local regulation or direct state regulation. Nevertheless, each is quite different conceptually and requires a somewhat different data base, definition effort, prior planning, regulatory procedures, and legal considerations.

(1) Sensitive resource area maps may be based on relatively permanent natural resource factors. Performance standards may then be promulgated to minimize the impact of development. While natural resource data and expertise are essential, little prior comprehensive planning may be required for the application of performance standards. A natural resources agency may best define areas, establish standards, and administer regulations. Regulation of natural resource areas has strong legal support, based on public rights in natural resources such as navigable waters, as well as legal support from general police powers.

(2) Broader critical areas, such as sites for new towns or proposed roadways, cannot be mapped by natural resources alone since their location depends on cultural factors, such as projected population growth, availability of transportation, and industrial or commercial opportunities in the area. Prior land use planning and specialized public facility planning are essential. The primary regulatory goal is the reduction of costs to government rather than minimizing impact on resources. Legally, efforts to preserve prospective development sites in an open condition face adverse precedent, since courts have, with little exception, held that zoning cannot be used to reduce condemnation costs, and have, in some instances, disapproved attempts to officially map parks.[2] There is little experience in regulating such broader critical areas at the state level. States have not undertaken protection even

---

[2]*See* note 23 of Part 8, *supra*. *See also* Miller v. Beaver Falls, 368 Pa. 189, 82 A. 2d 881 (1968) (court held invalid regulations holding land intended for public parks in an open condition for three years). *But see* New Jersey Lomarch Corp. v. Mayor of Englewood, 51 N.J. 108, 237 A. 2d 881 (1968) (Court upheld a statute which granted municipalities one year periods to decide to purchase officially mapped parks and playgrounds but read into the state law an obligation that municipalities pay for these one year options to purchase.)

where control is authorized. Agencies have instead focused primarily on natural resource areas.[3]

(3) Developments of regional benefit or impact are activities rather than areas and are not mapped prior to submission of development proposals. Proposals are usually evaluated on an *ad hoc* basis, taking into account many factors including natural resources, compatability with adjacent uses, and adequacy of public services. Comprehensive planning and specialized public facilities planning is desireable prior to regulatory control. Broader planning and natural resource expertise is needed. Only a few states, such as Maine and Vermont, have authorized control of regional development impacts at the state level.

Because of these differences, it is often advisable to separate critical resource area definition and regulation functions, and place them in a natural resource agency while vesting a planning or other land use management agency with control of broader areas and development of regional impact.

9-4 *A single agency should play a strong lead agency function in (1) coordinating individual sensitive area programs, gathering data, and broader planning and land use management efforts in a state and (2) developing a state resource data bank and overall framework for development policies.*

The proliferation of sensitive area programs and other land use management efforts at state and regional levels has increased the need for coordinating data gathering, planning, regulation, and other implementation efforts to insure consistency in policies, exchange of information, and to prevent duplication of efforts.[4] It is also essential that state public works decisions, such as those on transportation and pollution control, be coordinated with critical area policies.

In some states, state planning agencies have attempted to serve a general coordinating function with some success. Strong lead agencies (state planning,

[3]For example, the Minnesota critical area program initially focused upon the Saint Croix wild river corridor; the Florida program focused upon Big Cypress Swamp, Green Swamp, and the Florida Keys.

[4]For example, the Colorado critical area act vests the land use commission with coordination power but delegates data gathering and technical assistance roles to a number of agencies. (Col. Rev. Stat. 24-65 and Supp. 1976) provides:

Functions of other state agencies. (1) Pursuant to this article, it is the function of other state agencies to:

(a) Send recommendations to local governments and the Colorado land use commission relating to designation of matters of state interest on the basis of current and developing information; and
(b) Provide technical assistance to local governments concerning designation of and guidelines for matters of state interest.

(2) Primary responsibility for the recommendation and provision of technical assistance functions described in subsection (1) of this section is upon:

(a) The Colorado water conservation board, acting in cooperation with the Colorado soil conservation board, with regard to floodplains;
(b) The Colorado state forest service, with regard to wildfire hazard areas;
(c) The Colorado geological survey, with regard to geological hazard areas, geological reports, and the identification of mineral resource areas;
(d) The Colorado division of mines, with regard to mineral extraction and the reclamation of land disturbed thereby;
(e) The Colorado soil conservation board and soil conservation districts, with regard to resource data inventories, soils, soil suitability, erosion and sedimentation, floodwater problems, and watershed protection; and
(f) The division of wildlife and the department of natural resources, with regard to significant wildlife habitats.

(3) Pursuant to section 24-65.1-202 (1)(d), the oil and gas conservation commission of the state of Colorado may identify an area of oil and gas development for designation by local government as an area of state interest.

natural resource) are needed to exercise policy-making and coordination functions, particularly where individual critical resource definition and standard-setting functions are exercised by other agencies. Such coordination is relatively meaningless unless individual line agencies are required to follow lead agency policies by statute, executive mandate, or some measure of budgetary control.

Initially, the lead agency might: (1) emphasize information exchange and establish mechanisms for coordination among state agencies, local units of government, and regional planning agencies; (2) require standardization in data gathering; and (3) coordinate federal data gathering, technical assistance, and grant-in-aid programs with state and local efforts. Ultimately the agency could, in cooperation with other agencies, develop overall development and resource protection policies and a multi-purpose data bank. These would be applied by other agencies and local governments in their sensitive area programs.

Appendix **A**

STUDY METHODOLOGY

Regulating Sensitive Lands is based upon four sources of information.

First, it reflects the author's work as a consultant over the last decade with the design and implementation of sensitive area programs, including: the Wisconsin coastal zone program; state planning programs in Wisconsin and Minnesota; lake and stream shore programs in Wisconsin, Massachusetts, Minnesota and Maine; flood plain programs in Wisconsin, Massachusetts, Minnesota, and the Delaware river basin. Other efforts include flood plain programs of the U.S. Water Resources Council, the U.S. Army Corps of Engineers, and the National Flood Insurance Program (H.U.D.) and critical area projects for the U.S. Department of Interior and Smithsonian Institution.

Second, it is based on the author's research efforts. Some principal ones include:

Kusler, Jon, Douglas Yanggen, *et al.*, Vols. 1 and 2, *Regulation of Flood Hazard Areas to Reduce Flood Losses,* U.S. Government Printing Office (1971, 1972).

Kusler, Jon and Thomas Lee, *Regulations for Flood Plains,* American Society of Planning Officials, Report No. 277 (1972).

Strauss, Eric and Jon Kusler, *Statutory Land Use Control Enabling Authority in the Fifty States with Special Reference to Flood Hazard Regulatory Authority,* Federal Insurance Administration, United States Department of Housing and Urban Development (1976).

Kusler, Jon, *Zoning for Shoreland Resource Protection: Uses and Limitations,* unpublished Ph.D. dissertation, University of Wisconsin (1970).

Kusler, Jon, *Regulations to Reduce Conflicts Between Recreation and Water Use,* Wisconsin Department of Natural Resources (1970).

Kusler, Jon *et al., Strengthening Lake-Shoreland Management in Massachusetts,* University of Massachusetts Water Resource Center (1976).

Kusler, Jon (contributor and director of seminar series), *Lake-Shoreland Management Programs: Selected Papers,* University of Massachusetts Water Resources Center (1976).

Kusler, Jon, *Flood Plain Regulations in the Broader Context of Flood Plain Management,* U.S. Army Corps of Engineers, Flood Plain Management Services (1976).

Kusler, Jon *et al., Data Needs and Data Gathering for Areas of Critical Environmental Concern,* U.W. Institute for Environmental Studies (1975). A series of 3 reports.

Kusler, Jon, *Survey: Lake Protection and Rehabilitation in the United States,* University of Wisconsin Inland Lake Demonstration and Renewal Project (1972).

Kusler, Jon, *Artifical Lakes and Land Subdivisions,* University of Wisconsin Center for Resource Policy Studies and the Wisconsin Bureau of Commercial Recreation (1971).

Kusler, Jon, *Public/Private Parks and Management of Private Lands for Park Protection,* University of Wisconsin Institute for Environmental Studies (1974).

Kusler, Jon, *Strengthening State Wetland Regulation,* Environmental Law Institute, Washington, D.C. (forthcoming publication, 1978).

Kusler, Jon and Corbin Harwood, *Our National Wetland Heritage: A Protection Guidebook,* Environmental Law Institute, Washington, D.C. (forthcoming publication, 1978).

Third, it draws upon a number of major studies addressing common denominators in critical area definition and management. See the bibliography below.

Finally, it extracts materials from three unpublished reports prepared by the author for the University of Wisconsin Institute for Environmental Studies. The reports were prepared with support from the University of Wisconsin Sea Grant Program, funded by the National Oceanographic and Atmospheric Administration. They include *Definition of Critical Areas, Standard-Setting for Critical Areas,* and *Data Gathering for Critical Areas.* Research for the unpublished reports included: (1) a literature survey dealing with selected issues in sensitive area definition, standard-setting, and data gathering; (2) a statutory survey and examination of court cases to determine constitutional considerations in all phases of sensitive area regulation; and (3) interviews with sensitive area program personnel to determine the successes and failures of existing approaches. Telephone or personal interviews were conducted with regulatory staff for most of the state programs listed in Appendix B.

The author also examined many local sensitive area zoning, subdivision control, building code, and other regulations. These included approximately 400 flood plain ordinances (from states throughout the nation); 200 inland lake, stream, stream shore, or Great Lake shoreland ordinances (principally from Wisconsin and Minnesota but some from Washington and Maine); 80 wetland preservation ordinances; 150 special coastal zone ordinances (California, Florida, and others); several dozen fill and grading ordinances for slope areas (primarily California); several forest-recreation district ordinances (Wisconsin); several dozen tree-cutting ordinances (three states); and several dozen agricultural district regulations (Wisconsin, Illinois). One study was particularly helpful in the survey: Charles Thurow, William Toner, and Duncan Erley, *Performance Controls for Sensitive Lands: A Practical Guide for Local Administrators*, American Society of Planning Officials, Planning Advisory Service Report 307 (1975).

Appendix **B**

PROFILES OF SELECTED STATE SENSITIVE AREA REGULATORY PROGRAMS

The following chart profiles some of the best known state and cooperative state/ local sensitive area regulatory programs.

State	Category	Cite	State/Local Roles	Substance
Alabama	Coastal Areas (includes coastal wetlands, beaches, etc.)	Tit. 8 §§312-320	State regulation	1. After a state plan has been completed, permits are required for activities in the coastal zone, including dredging, dumping, and erection of structures which effect the ebb and flow of the tide or damage flora or fauna.
Arizona	Flood Plain Areas	§45-2342	State standard setting for local regulation	1. Arizona Water Commission develops regulatory criteria for the 100 year flood. 2. The governing board of a city, town, and county must adopt regulations and submit them to the state for approval.

State	Category	Cite	State/Local Roles	Substance
Arkansas	Flood Plain Areas	§21-1903	State and local regulation	1. Local units may regulate flood plain areas. 2. If a local unit is to be denied federal flood insurance due to a failure to adopt regulations, state may adopt regulations.
California	Coastal Area	Pub. Res. Code §§30.000-30.900	Regional regulation. Calif. Coastal Zone Conservation Commission coordinates efforts	1. Permit required from regional coastal zone district commissions for development up to 1000 yards landward from mean high tide. Recent amendments to the act stress protection for coastal wetlands.
	Coastal Area	Govt. Code §§66600-66661	San Francisco Bay Conservation and Development Commission	1. Permit required for filling of Bay or land within 100 feet of the Bay.
	Lakeshore Area	Govt. Code §§67000-67130	Regional regulation. Tahoe Regional Planning Agency	1. In the counties of Placer and El Dorado, the Tahoe Regional Agency establishes regulations which may be superseded by local controls (not actually state regulation).
	Scenic Rivers	Public Res. Code §5093.50	State regulation of dams	1. State designates wild, scenic and recreational rivers, prepares management plan. 2. State regulates dams, reservoirs, and impoundments.
	Floodway	Govt. Code §8400-8415	State standard setting for local regulation	1. State establishes minimum standards for local regulations. 2. Failure of local units to adopt flood plain regulations will result in loss of state funds for cost-sharing in flood control projects.
Colorado	Flood and Other Hazard Areas	§24-65-104 (2)(a)	State regulation (limited). Primary reliance upon local regulations	1. State Land Use Commission can issue cease and desist orders for certain types of development in hazard areas if local units fail to adopt satisfactory regulations.
	Areas of State Interest	§24-65.1-101 *et seq.*	Local regulation consistent with state guidelines	1. Local units of government are to designate areas of state concern consistent with statutory guidelines and guidelines of Land Use Commission. Many types of areas may be included (e.g., flood, geological hazard, mineral resources). 2. Local units are to regulate designated areas consistent with state standards.
Connecticut	Inland Wetlands	§§22a-36 to 22a-45	Local regulation	1. State regulates inland wetlands and watercourses if local units do not. Local regulation resumes upon state approval.
	Floodways	25-4a to 25-4g	State regulation	1. State establishes encroachment lines. 2. State permits are required for delineated floodways.
	Coastal Wetlands	§§22a-28 to 22a-35	State regulation	1. Permit is required for all regulated activities in tidal wetlands. 2. State inventories are required.

State	Category	Cite	State/Local Roles	Substance
Delaware	Beach Protection	§7-6801	State regulation	1. State regulates use of beaches.
	Coastal Wetland	§7-6604	State regulation	1. Permits are required for activities in coastal wetlands.
	Coastal Zone	§§7-7001-7013	State regulation	1. Act prohibits heavy industrial development; requires state permits for light industry.
Florida	"Comprehensive" critical areas act	§§380.05-380.055	State standard-setting for local regulation	1. State designates areas of critical state concern (may include many types of land) and formulates minimum development standards. 2. Local units are required to adopt regulations consistent with state standards. State may directly regulate if local units do not.
	Beach Setback	§161.052	State regulation	1. Beach setback line of 50 feet from mean high water is provided for any construction or excavation.
Georgia	Coastal Wetlands	§40-3519	State regulation	1. State permits are required for activities in coastal marshlands.
Hawaii	Coastal Shoreline Setbacks	§§205-31 to 205-37	State regulation	1. State is to establish shoreline setback lines not less than 20 feet nor more than 40 feet inland from upper wash of waves. Structures and removal of beach materials are prohibited unless a variance is granted by local units of government.
	State Zoning for All lands	§205-2	State regulation	1. State places all lands in one of four zones (urban, rural, conservation, and agriculture). 2. State has exclusive power over conservation districts. Local regulations may apply to other areas.
Illinois	Flood Plain	§19:65f	State regulation	1. State regulates development in defined flood plain areas.
Indiana	Flood Plain	Ind. Code Ann. §§ (Burns) 13-2-22-11 13-2-22-13 13-2-22-15 13-2-22.5-1	State regulation. State standard-setting for local regulation	1. State regulates floodway areas. State adopts standards for local flood plain regulations. All local regulations must first be approved by state but may be more restrictive.
	Scenic Rivers	§13-2-26-8	State regulation of dams	1. State designates natural, scenic, and recreational rivers. 2. Plans for development and use of river require an environmental impact statement.
Iowa	Flood Plain	§455A.35	State regulation	1. State regulates flood plain activities. Local ordinance must be submitted to state for approval.

State	Category	Cite	State/Local Roles	Substance
Kansas	Flood Plain	§12-734	State standard-setting for local regulations.	1. State must establish standards for city or county flood plain zoning. 2. Local regulations must be approved by state before they become effective, but no direct state regulation.
Kentucky	Floodway	§151.220	State regulation	1. Permits are required for obstructions in all floodways and streams.
Maine	Shorelands (lakes, streams, coastal areas	§§12-4811-4814	State standard-setting for local regulation	1. State establishes standards for local regulations of shoreland areas, including lands within. 2. Mandatory local shoreland zoning within 250 feet of high water mark of water bodies. If cities and town do not adopt adequate regulations, the state will.
	Unorganized and Disorganized Areas	§12-865-A	State regulation	1. Maine Land Use Commission regulates land in unorganized territory, plantations and towns.
	Site review large scale development	§38-481	State regulation	1. Maine Board of Environmental Protection regulates development which "may substantially affect the environment" including subdivisions and most development over 20 acres or with structures occupying more than 60,000 square feet.
	Coastal Wetlands	§§12:4701 to 12:4709 and §§12:4751 to 12:4758	State and local regulation	1. Local permits required for filling, dumping, dredging, or sewage discharge into coastal wetlands. 2. State may also disapprove permit.
	Coastal Areas	§38:541	State regulation	1. Discharge of oil, petroleum products or their by-products into or upon any coastal waters, estuaries, tidal flats, beaches, adjoining lands or waters which drain to the coast is prohibited. 2. All oil terminal facilities must have state approval.
	Critical Areas	Tit. 5, §§3310-3314	State regulation	1. State is to inventory and create a register of "critical areas" of significant natural, scenic, scientific, or historic value. 2. State must receive notice of proposed development within such areas, and no development is to take place within such an area for 60 days after notification without approval of the state.
Maryland	Flood Plain	§8-901(a)	State regulation	1. Permits are required for activities in flood plains and waters.

State	Category	Cite	State/Local Roles	Substance
	Areas of Critical State Concern	§8-901(b)	Local regulation	1. State is to establish guidelines for local designation of areas of critical environmental concern. However, the state does not have regulatory powers. The state assists locals in identification of areas, receives notice of proposed development within areas and may appear at public hearings on such development.
	Coastal Wetlands	§9-101	State regulation	1. State and local permits are required for activities in state wetlands. 2. State permits are required for activities in private wetlands except conservation of soil, etc., hunting and fishing and exercise of riparian rights to improve access or fight erosion. 3. Regulated activities include dredging, filling and removing. 4. An inventory of coastal wetlands is to be conducted.
	Scenic and Wild Rivers	§8-401	State regulation of dams, on all rivers, control of land uses on scenic and wild rivers	1. State is to inventory all rivers in the state and recommend scenic and wild rivers. 2. State directly regulates regulation of mining along the Youghiogheny River.
Massachu-setts	Coastal Wetlands	Ch.131-§40 Ch.130 §105	State and local regulation	1. State permits are required in some instances for fill or alteration of coastal wetlands and flood plains. Local permits are also required.
	Inland and Coastal Wetlands	Ch.131-§40 Ch.131-§40A	State and local regulation	1. Local permits are required for alteration of inland wetlands. State permit may be required in some circumstances.
	Flood Plain	Ch.131-§40A	State regulation	1. The state may regulate some flood plains through wetland orders.
Michigan	Flood Plain Areas	Mich. Comp. Laws Ann. §323.5b	State regulation	1. Permits are required for uses in flood plains identified by state.
	Shoreland Areas	§281.631	State standard-setting for local regulation	1. State must identify and establish standards for shoreland flood and high risk erosion areas and environmental areas within 1000 feet of the Great Lakes and connecting waterways. 2. The state regulates areas in the event local units fail to do so.
	Wild Rivers	§281.761	State standard-setting for local regulation	1. The state may enact zoning ordinances along an unincorporated natural river area, after the adoption of a comprehensive plan, if a local unit does not adopt regulation.

State	Category	Cite	State/Local Roles	Substance
	Inland Lakes and Streams	§281.951	State regulation	1. Permits are required for: A. Dredging, filling, and construction on bottomland. B. Creation or interference with an inland lake, stream, or artificial channel.
Minnesota	Flood Plain	§104.04	State standard-setting for local regulation	1. State standard-setting for local regulations. 2. Counties and cities must adopt flood plain and floodway management regulations meeting state standards for 100 year flood within six months of notification by Commissioner of Natural Resources that they have sufficient flood data.
	Shorelands States, Streams, Great Lakes	§105.485	State standard-setting for local regulation	1. Counties are required to adopt shoreland zoning ordinances consistent with state standards for unincorporated areas within 1000 feet of lakes and 300 feet of streams or landward side of the flood plain by 1972. 2. Cities must also adopt regulations by 1975. 3. If local units do not adopt regulations, state will.
	"Comprehensive" Critical Areas Act	§§116G.01 to 116G.14	State standard-setting for local regulation	1. Local governments have one year from designation of critical areas by state to protect area or state may adopt plans for area. 2. No development permits may be issued unless they conform to the plans.
	Wild and Scenic Rivers	§104.31	State standard-setting for local regulation	1. State designates wild, scenic and recreational rivers and adopts development guidelines. 2. Local units have 6 months to adopt regulations meeting or exceeding state standards or the State directly regulates.
Mississippi	Coastal Wetlands	§§49-27-1 to 49-27-69	State regulation	1. Permits are required for regulated activities in coastal wetland including dredging, dumping and erection of structures which affect the ebb and flow of tide or damage flora and fauna. 2. Many exemptions (19) include hunting highways and oil pipelines.
Montana	Floodways and Flood Plains (broadly defined)	§89-3504	State standard-setting for local regulation	1. State designates flood plains and floodways and establishes standards for local regulations (100 year flood). 2. Permits are required from either state or local units. 3. Local units must adopt standards within six months of state designation or state adopts. 4. If necessary for federal flood insurance, state may adopt standards for local areas.
Nebraska	Floodways (broadly defined)	§§2.1506.03 *et. seq.*	State standard-setting for local regulation	1. State designates 100 year floodway.

State	Category	Cite	State/Local Roles	Substance
				2. Local jurisdictions are given one year following designation of an area to enact ordinances consistent with state standards; state regulates if locals fail to act.
				3. Either state or local permits are required depending upon who enforces the act. Local rules may be more stringent than state.
Nevada	Local Comprehensive Zoning (strong critical areas orientation)	§§278.645 to 278.655	State standard-setting for local regulation	1. By July 1, 1975, if the Governor determines that there is unplanned and unzoned land in any county, he may adopt planning and zoning.
New Hampshire	Coastal and Inland Wetlands	§§483-A:1a to 483-A:6	State regulation	1. No one shall excavate, fill or dredge land in or adjacent to tidal or inland waters without a permit from the state water resources commission. 2. Notice to towns, municipalities and abutters is required.
New Jersey	Coastal Wetland	§§13:9A-1 to 13:9A-10	State regulation	1. State permits are required for dredging, removing or filling of wetlands or any structures in the area. Agricultural activities are exempted. 2. An inventory is required.
	Flood Plains	§§58:16A-50 *et seq.*	State regulation, for floodways. State standard-setting for local regulation of flood fringe areas	1. State identifies flood plain and floodway areas and establishes standards for areas. 2. State regulates floodway areas. 3. State may regulate flood plain if local units fail to adopt adequate regulations within 12 months of delineation and adoption of state guidelines.
	Coastal Areas	§13:19-2	State regulation	1. State permits are required for new "facilities" in coastal area. 2. "Coastal area" is defined by roads and highways.
New York	Tidal Wetlands	Env. Cons. Law §§25-0101 to 25-0602	State or local regulation	1. State permits are required for alteration of tidal wetlands. 2. State is directed to inventory tidal wetlands.
	Flood Plains	Env. Cons. Law §36-0101	State regulation	1. The state may enact regulations in order to qualify local units for flood insurance.
North Carolina	Beach and Dune Areas	§§104B:3 to 104B:15	County regulation. State control in limited circumstances	1. State permits are required for activity in the the Outer Banks area, including sand dunes and beaches on the Atlantic shore and coastal waterways.

State	Category	Cite	State/Local Roles	Substance
				2. County regulation is also permitted consistent with state standards.
	Coastal Wetlands	§§113-229, 330	State regulation	1. State permits are required for excavation in estuarine waters, tidelands, marshlands, and state owned lakes. 2. Permits may be denied on grounds including adverse effect on public use of the water, riparian rights, or wildlife. 3. Notice sent to abutting owners.
	Coastal Areas	§§113A-100 to 113A-12B	State supervised city and county regulation	1. State permits are required in some instances for development in coastal areas (coastal counties) of coastal environmental concern. 2. City and county land use plans must be consistent with state guidelines. 3. State may develop land use plan if local unit does not. 4. City and county issue permits.
	Floodway	§§143.215. 51 *et seq.*	Local regulation	1. State may designate 100 year floodway if a stream is in more than one jurisdiction or where it finds delineation necessary and local governments have not acted.
	Areas of Environmental Concern	§§113-150	Local regulation	1. State is to classify lands throughout state, designate critical environmental areas. 2. Local units regulate areas.
Oklahoma	Scenic and Wild Rivers	tit. 82, §1451 *et seq.*	State regulation of impoundment	1. Special legislative approval is required for impoundment on scenic and wild rivers.
Oregon	Beach Areas	§§390.605 to 390.770	State regulation	1. State permits are required from State Highway Commission for improvement in ocean shore area. 2. Vehicles may be banned.
	Lands Throughout state	§§215.505 to 215.535	Local regulation	1. Local units of government must adopt comprehensive plans and zoning or the Land Conservation and Development Commission is authorized to adopt such plans or zones.
	Scenic Waterways	§390.805	State regulation	1. State designates scenic waterways. 2. State approval required for development within 1,320 feet of waterways.
Pennsylvania	Floodways	Tit. 32, §682	State regulation	1. Obstructions in streams including immediate floodways require state permit.
Rhode Island	Coastal Wetlands	§§2-1-13 to 2-1-17; 11-46.1-1	State regulation	1. The state designates coastal wetlands by order and limits uses. 2. Permits are required for dumping and depositing materials on intertidal salt marshes.

State	Category	Cite	State/Local Roles	Substance
	Coastal Areas	§§46-23-1 to 46-23-16	State regulation	1. State permits are required for activities in tidal waters and certain shoreland areas. 2. Shoreland uses subject to state control include power generation plants, desalination plants, chemical or petroleum processing, minerals extraction, sewage treatment and solid waste facilities, shoreland protection facilities, intertidal salt marshes.
	Inland Wetlands	§§2-1-18 to 2-1-25	State regulation	1. State permit required for alteration of inland wetland and flood plain areas.
Tennessee	Scenic Rivers	§§11-1401 *et. seq.*	State regulation (apparently)	1. State designates "natural", "pastoral," and "partially developed" rivers, establishes development standards.
Texas	Coastal Areas	§§5415e-1	State regulation	1. State permits are required for uses in coastal public lands. 2. Permits may include leases, easements, and the right to build structures.
Vermont	Flood Plains	Tit. 10, §751	State standard-setting for local regulation	1. State is to identify 100 year flood plains and promulgate sample ordinances. 2. Local units are to adopt flood plain regulations after the state has designated areas.
	Floodways, Streams, Shorelands, Wildlife Habitat, Agricultural Soils Forest, Soils, Mineral Resources, and Other Lands	Tit. 10, §6081 *et seq.*	Regulation by district commissions	1. District commissions appointed by the Governor regulate certain large scale developments including developments of more than 10 acres for commercial, industrial, state, or municipal purposes; dwellings, apartments, etc. of 10 units or more; commercial and industrial development of more than one acre in municipalities without any zoning or subdivision regulation, or any commercial, residential, or industrial development over 2500 feet in elevation. 2. Detailed standards are provided for protection of floodways, water quality wildlife, prime agricultural lands, forestry areas, mineral resources, etc..
	Shoreland Areas (lakes and ponds)	Tit. 24 §4410a, Tit. 10 §1422 to 1425	State regulation for waters; state supervised regulation of shoreland areas	1. State is to adopt regulations for use of public waters. 2. State is to provide sample bylaws to local units of government to assist them in shoreland zoning. Local units are to regulate shoreland areas (up to 1000 feet from lakes and ponds) by June 1, 1976.
Virginia	Coastal Wetlands	§§62.1-13.1 to 62.1-13.20	State and local regulation	1. State permits are required for activities in tidal wetlands. 2. Local units may adopt the ordinance contained in the statute. 3. State board reviews local decisions under certain conditions. Prior nonconforming uses exempted.

State	Category	Cite	State/Local Roles	Substance
	Critical Environmental Areas	§§10-187 to 10-196	Local regulation	1. State is authorized to define critical areas (*e.g.*, coastal zone, estuaries, flood plains, shorelands, etc.) and recommend standards for land use and development within areas. 2. No direct state regulation without approval of legislature. Local implementation of standards.
	Scenic Rivers	§10-167	Local regulation except for dams and other structures	1. State designates rivers, directly regulates dams and other structures.
Washington	Shoreline Areas (lakeshore, streamshore, coastal, areas, certain wetlands)	§§90.58. 010 to 90.58.930	State regulation; also state standard-setting for local regulation	1. State adopts guidelines for local "master" shoreline programs for shorelines (both salt and fresh) except on lakes less than 20 acres and rivers above the navigable limit. 2. State may adopt regulations in the event units fail to adopt and enforce regulations for shorelines of statewide significance. 3. State directly regulates certain uses of statewide significance.
	Flood Plain Areas	§86.16.020	State regulation, also state standard-setting for local regulation	1. State regulates flood plain areas. 2. State designates flood control zones and issues permits for development therein. 3. Local programs not preempted and state may delegate its powers to local units.
Wisconsin	Shoreland Areas (lake, stream, Great Lakes)	§59.971, §144.26	State standard-setting for local regulation	1. State establishes standards for county regulation of shoreland areas (1000 feet of lakes, 300 feet of streams, flood plains.) 2. Counties must regulate unincorporated shoreland areas consistent with state standards by Jan. 1, 1968 or state will.
	Flood Plains	§87.30	State standard-setting for local regulation	1. See shorelands above (same requirements).
	Wild Rivers	§30.26	State standard-setting for local regulation for one river	1. State is to adopt standards for local zoning of the Lower St. Croix River. 2. Local units are to adopt regulations meeting state standards with 30 days; otherwise state regulates areas directly.
Wyoming	Areas of Critical or More Than Local Concern	§§9-850 to 9-862	Local regulation	1. State is to identify areas of critical or more than local concern, and to establish development guidelines for such areas. However, no direct state regulatory powers. 2. Local units are mandated to adopt land use plans, and, in the event of local inaction, the state is to adopt a plan for a local unit.

Appendix **C**

STATUTORY
DEFINITION CRITERIA

The following table illustrates selected statutory sensitive area definition criteria. Many programs have adopted more specific definitions in rules and guidelines.

Type of Area/State/Statutory Cite	Definition Criteria	Comment
FLOOD HAZARD AREAS		
Flood Plain		
Kansas Kan. Stat. Ann. §12-734 (1975)	The "floodplain" is defined to include "land adjacent to a watercourse subject to inundation from a flood having a chance occurrence in any one year of one percent (1%): Provided, that any county or city may establish floodplain zones and districts and restrict the use of land therein and may restrict the application thereof to lands, adjacent to watercourses, subject to floods of a lesser magnitude than that having a chance occurrence in any one year of one percent (1%) . . . "	All states have a-dopted the "100 year flood" for the purpose of sensi-tive area regula-tion.

Type of Area/State/Statutory Cite	Definition Criteria	Comment
Flood Plain		
Michigan Mich. Compiled Laws §§560.117, 138, 194	State approval is required for subdivisions in the flood plain. If any area of subdivision lies within a flood plain, (1) no building may be undertaken for residential purposes unless there is approval in accordance with the rules of the Water Resources Commission, and (2) restrictive deed covenants must be filed and recorded with the final plot to insure that the flood plain will be left in its essentially natural state. However, the natural flood plain may be altered if its original discharge capacity is preserved and the stream flow is not revised so as to affect the riparian rights of other owners.	This act contains the most detailed regulations for subdivisions in flood hazard areas.
Flood Plain		
Mich. Stat. Ann. §26.430 (Callaghan 1970)	"Flood plain" means that area of land adjoining the channel of a river, stream, water course, lake or other similar body of water which will be inundated by a flood which can reasonably be expected for that region. More specific rules for definition of flood plains by the Water Resources Commission are to be published in the administrative code.	Several states have not defined the regulatory flood as the "regional flood."
Flood Plain and Floodway		
Minnesota Minn. Stat. Ann. §104.02 (West Supp. 1977)	"Flood Plain" means the area adjoining a watercourse which has been or hereafter may be covered by the regional flood. "Floodway" means "the channel of the watercourse and those portions of the adjoining flood plains which are reasonably required to carry and discharge the regional flood." The "regional flood" means a flood representative of large floods known to have occurred generally in Minnesota and reasonably characteristic of what can be expected to occur on an average frequency in the magnitude of the 100 year recurrence interval. State standard-setting for local regulations. Direct state regulatory power in the event of local inaction.	
Floodway		
North Carolina N.C. Gen. Stat. §143-215.52 (1974)	"Floodway means that portion of the channel and floodplain of a stream designated to provide passage for the 100 year flood without increasing the elevation of that flood at any point by more than one foot." State defines floodways. Local government is responsible for issuing permits and enforcing regulations.	The statutes of several states apply only to floodway areas including (with variations in definitions) Connecticut, Nebraska, and Pennsylvania.
WETLANDS		
Tidal Wetlands		
Connecticut Conn. Gen. Stat. Ann. §22a-29 (West 1975)	'Wetland' means those areas which border on or lie beneath tidal waters, such as, but not limited to banks, bogs, salt marshes, swamps, meadows, flats, or other low lands subject to tidal action, including those areas	Most other coastal states define coastal wetlands in terms of tidal in-

Type of Area/State/Statutory Cite	Definition Criteria	Comment
	now or formerly connected to tidal waters, and whose surface is at or below an elevation of one foot above local extreme high water: and upon which may grow or be capable of growing some, but not necessarily all, of the following: salt meadow grass (Spartina patens), spike grass (Distirchlis spicata), black grass (Juncus gerardi), salt marsh grass (Spartina alterniflora), saltworts (Salicornia Europaea, and Salicornia bigelovii), Sea Lavender (Limonium carolinianum), saltmarsh bulrushes (Scirpus robustus and Scirpus Paludosus var. atlanticus), sand spurrety (Spergularia marina), switch grass (Panicum virgatum), tall cordgrass (Spartina Pectinata), hightide bush (Ica frutescens var. oraria), cattails (Typha-angustifolia and Typoa latifolia), spike rush (Eleocharis rostellata), chairmaker's rush (Scrirpus americana), bent grass (Agrostis palustris), and sweet grass (Hierorchloe odorata)."	fluence, elevation in relationship to tidal action, and vegetation lists. These include Georgia, Maine, New Hampshire, Masschusetts, New York, Maryland, Virginia, North Carolina.

Inland Wetlands

Type of Area/State/Statutory Cite	Definition Criteria	Comment
Connecticut Conn. Gen Stat. Ann. §22a-38 (West 1975)	'Wetlands' means land, including submerged land, not regulated pursuant to sections 22a-28 to 22a-35 inclusive, which consist of any of the soil types designated as poorly drained, very poorly drained, alluvial, and flood plain by the National Cooperative Soils Survey, as may be amended from time to time, of the Soil Conservation Service of the United States Department of Agriculture." Local units are to regulate wetlands consistent with statutory standards. State may regulate in the event of local inaction.	Only Connecticut defines inland wet-lands based solely upon soil type.

Inland Wetlands

Type of Area/State/Statutory Cite	Definition Criteria	Comment
Massachusetts Mass. Ann. Laws Ch. 131, §40 (Michie Law Co-op 1972 and supp. 1977)	"Freshwater wetlands" means "wet meadows, marshes, swamps, bogs, areas where groundwater, flowing or standing surface water or ice provide a significant part of the supporting substrate for a plant community for at least five months of the year; emergent and submergent plant communities in inland waters; that portion of any bank which touches any inland water." "Bog," "swamps," "wet meadows" and "marshes" are further defined in the act by vegetation type. Local permit required from conservation commission (local). However, state permit may be required under certain conditions.	The statutes of Rhode Island, New York, and New Hampshire similar-ly define inland wetlands based primarily upon vegetation.

Coastal Area

Type of Area/State/Statutory Cite	Definition Criteria	Comment
Alabama Ala. Code Tit. 8, §314 (Supp. 1973)	"Coastal area" means the coastal waters (including the lands therein and thereunder) and the adjacent shorelands (including the water therein and thereunder) strongly influenced by, and in proximity to, the shorelines of Alabama, and includes transitional and intertidal areas, salt marshes, wetlands and beaches. The area extends seaward to the outer limit of the United States territorial sea and extends inland from the shorelines only to the extent necessary to control shorelands, the uses of which have a direct and significant impact on the coastal waters.	

Type of Area/State/Statutory Cite	Definition Criteria	Comment

Coastal Zone

California
Cal. Pub. Res. Code
§27100
(Deering 1976)

"Coastal zone" defined to include lands extending inland to the highest elevation of nearby coastal mountain range or five miles from the mean high tide, whichever is shorter. Regulatory "permit area" means that portion of the coastal zone lying between the seaward limit of the jurisdiction of the state and 1,000 yards landward from the mean high tide line of the sea . . . However, exclusions are also provided. Regulation by regional commissions.

The coastal zone is defined in terms of a particular distance from the highwater mark, in Maine (250 feet), Minnesota (1000 feet for Great Lakes), Wisconsin (1000 feet for Great Lakes), Michigan (1000 feet for Lake Michigan).

Coastal Zone

Delaware
Del. Code Ann.
Tit. 7,
§7002 (1975)

"Coastal zone" is defined to include "land; water or subaqueous land between the territorial limits of Delaware in the Delaware River, Delaware Bay and Atlantic Ocean, and a line formed by certain Delaware highways and roads as follows. [Detailed listing of roads]." State regulation of coastal facilities.

A similar broad definition of the coastal zone is applied in North Carolina (coastal counties) and New Jersey (determined by roads).

Shorelands

Minnesota
Minn. Stat. Ann.
§105.485
(West Supp. 1977)

"Shoreland" means "land located within the following distances from the ordinary high water elevation of public waters: (1) land within 1,000 feet from the normal high watermark of lake or pond or flowage; and (2) land within 300 feet of a river or stream or the landward side of flood plain delineated by ordinance on such a river or stream, whichever is greater." State is to establish standards for county and municipal regulation of shoreland areas and to directly regulate such areas unless counties adopt adequate regulations by July 1, 1972 and municipalities (cities, villages, and boroughs) by July 7, 1975.

The Wisconsin shoreland zoning act contains a very similar definition, incorporating the 1,000 foot and 300 foot figures. Vermont uses a 1,000 foot figure but applies only to lakes. Maine applies a 250 foot figure to lakes, rivers, and the ocean.

Shorelines

Washington
Wash. Rev. Cod Ann.
§90.58.030
(Supp. 1976)

(Complicated definition) "Shorelines of state-wide significance" are specifically defined to include specified coastal areas seaward of the high water mark (*e.g.,* "Nisqually Delta-from DeWolf Bight to Tatsolo Point), lakes of more than 1000 acres, rivers in unspecified areas, and specified wetlands. "Shorelines" are defined to include all water areas of the state including reservoirs except "shorelines of statewide significance," shorelines of streams upstream of a point where mean annual flow is 20 cubic feet per second or less and the wetlands associated with such segments. Local units of government are to inventory and regulate both "shorelines" and "shorelines of state significance" consistent with state standards and a rather complicated

No set shoreland distance is defined by the Washington acts although wetlands are defined to include lands within 100 feet of specified waters.

Type of Area/State/Statutory Cite	Definition Criteria	Comment

time schedule. The state may directly regulate "shore-lands of statewide significance" if local units fail fail to adopt satisfactory regulations.

SCENIC AND WILD RIVERS

Scenic and Wild Rivers

Minnesota
  Minn. Stat. Ann.
  §§104.33, 104.34
  (West. Supp. 1977)

State is to designate wild, scenic, and recreational rivers and to establish minimum land use standards. Local units must adopt regulations meeting or exceeding those standards within 6 months or the state may directly regulate areas. The river corridor may include "not more than 320 acres per mile on both sides of the river." This would provide a boundary area of about 1300 feet if the boundary were even. Rivers or segments are to be classified as wild, scenic, or recreational consistent with the following criteria:

"(a) 'Wild' rivers are those rivers that exist in a free-flowing state, with excellent water quality, and with adjacent lands that are essentially primitive. 'Free-flowing' means existing in natural condition without significant artificial modification such as impoundment, diversion, or straightening. The existence, however, of low dams, diversion works or other minor structures at the time any river is proposed for inclusion shall not-automatically bar its inclusion as wild, scenic, not recreational river.

"(b) 'Scenic' rivers are those rivers that exist in a freeflowing state and with adjacent lands that are largely undeveloped.

"(c) 'Recreational' rivers are those rivers that may have undergone some impoundment or diversion in the past and may have adjacent lands that are considerably developed, but that are still capable of being managed so as to further the purposes §§104.31 to 104.40."

Natural Rivers

Michigan
  Mich. Stat. Ann.
  §§11.501 to 11.516
  (1974)

The natural resources commission is to designate "natural rivers" and to establish standards for use of such rivers. Local units must adopt regulations meeting or exceeding those standards or the commission is authorized to directly regulate areas. "Natural river" is defined to include a river "which has been desig-nated by the commission for inclusion in the wild, scenic, and recreational rivers system." The commission is to designate rivers and adjacent lands "for the purpose of preserving and enhancing its values for water conser-vation, its free flowing condition and its fish, wildlife, boating, scenic, aesthetic, flood plain, ecologic, historic, and recreation values and uses." A river qualifying as a natural river must possess one or more of these natural or outstanding existing values. The commission is to establish categories of rivers "based on the character-istics of the waters and the adjoining lands and their uses, both as existing and as proposed."

Local zoning ordinances or a rule promulgated by the commission may limit the cutting of trees up to 100

Type of Area/State/Statutory Cite	Definition Criteria	Comment

feet from the water's edge, mining and the drilling for oil and gas up to 300 feet from the edge, and the control of lands up to 400 feet from the edge.

SCIENTIFIC AREA

Scientific Area

North Carolina
  N.C. Gen. Stat.
  §§113A-113
  (1975)

The following types of scientific and natural areas are to be designated by the state and regulated by local units of government consistent with state guidelines. "Fragile" areas and "other areas containing environmental or natural resources of more than local significance, where uncontrolled or incompatible development could result in major or irreversible damage to important . . . cultural, scientific or scenic values or natural systems" which may include:

"(a) Existing national or state parks or forests, wilderness areas, the State Nature and Historic Preserve, or public recreation areas; existing sites that have been acquired for any of the same, as identified by the Secretary of Natural and Economic Resources, provided that the proposed site has been formally designated for acquisition by the governmental agency having jurisdiction;

"(b) Present sections of the natural and scenic rivers system;

"(c) Stream segments that have been classified for scientific or research uses by the Board of Water and Air Resources, or that are proposed to be so classified in a proceeding that is pending before said Board pursuant to G.S. 143-214.1 at the time of the designation of the area of environmental concern;

"(d) Existing wildlife refuges, preserves or management areas, and proposed sites for the same, as identified by the Wildlife Resources Commission, provided that the proposed site has been formally designated for acquisition (as hereinafter defined) or for inclusion in a cooperative agreement by the governmental agency having jurisdiction;

"(e) Complex natural areas surrounded by modified landscapes that do not drastically alter the landscape, such as virgin forest stands within a commercially managed forest, or bogs in an urban complex;

"(f) Areas that sustain remnant species or aberrations in the landscape produced by natural forces, such as rare and endangered botanical or animal species;

"(g) Areas containing unique geological formations, as identified by the state geologist . . . "

Note: this act applies only to the coastal zone.

PRIME AGRICULTURAL LANDS

Prime Agricultural Land

California
  Cal. Gov't Code
  §§51200, 65570
  (Deering 1974)

The state is to inventory but not regulate prime agricultural lands. Prime agricultural lands defined below may be subject to real estate tax incentives and local regulation but there is no direct state regulatory control. "Prime agricultural land" is defined

Type of Area/State/Statutory Cite	Definition Criteria	Comment
	by the California Land Conservation Act of 1965 (Williamson Act) as "any of the following: "(1) All land which qualifies for rating as class I or class II in the Soil Conservation Service land use capability classifications. "(2) Land which qualifies for rating 80 through 100 in the Storie Index Rating. "(3) Land which supports livestock used for the production of food and fiber and which has an annual carrying capacity equivalent to at least one animal unit per acre as defined by the United States Department of Agriculture. "(4) Land planted with fruit- or nut-bearing trees, vines, bushes or crops which have a nonbearing period of less than five years and which will normally return during the commercial bearing period on an annual basis from the production of unprocessed agricultural plant production not less than two hundred dollars ($200) per acre. "(5) Land which has returned from the production of unprocessed agricultural plant products an annual gross value of not less than two hundred dollars ($200) per acre for three of the previous five years."	

Agricultural Districts

Hawaii
  Hawaii Rev. Stat.
  §205-2
  (1968 & Supp. 1975)
	The state land use commission is directed to classify all state lands as (1) urban, (2) rural, (3) agricultural, and (4) conservation. The commission is directed to "group contiguous land areas suitable for inclusion" in particular districts. State and county regulations apply to agricultural districts. The statute directs that in establishing agricultural districts "the greatest possible protection shall be given to those lands with a high capacity for intensive cultivation." The statute provides that in establishing district boundaries the land use commission shall give consideration to the master plan or general plan of the county. The statute further provides that "(a) agricultural districts shall include activities or uses as characterized by the cultivation of crops, orchards, forage and forestry; farming activities or uses related to animal husbandry, and game and fish propagation; services and uses accessory to the above activities including, but not limited to, living quarters or dwellings, mills, storage facilities, processing facilities, and roadside stands for the sale of products grown on the premises; and open area recreational facilities." The districts may also include "areas which are not used for, or which are not suited to, agricultural and ancillary activities by reason of topography, soils, and other related characteristics."	Only Hawaii defines and directly zones agricultural lands at the state level.

Type of Area/State/Statutory Cite	Definition Criteria	Comment

FORESTRY AREAS

Prime Forest Land (as one type of area of environmental concern within the coastal zone)

North Carolina
   N.C. Gen Stat.
   §113A-113
   (Michie 1975)

The state is to designate coastal areas of particular environmental concern and to adopt guidelines for local regulation of such areas. Areas of environmental concern are defined to include "Prime forest land (site capable of producing 85 cubic feet per acre-year, or more, of marketable timber), as identified by the Department of Natural and Economic Resources."

Forest and Water Reserves

Hawaii
   Hawaii Rev. Stat.
   §183-41
   (1968 & Supp. 1975)

State definition and regulation is provided for forest and water reserves. Forest and water reserves are defined to "initially encompass all of those areas in the various counties, either government or privately owned, contained within the forest reserve boundaries as established on January 21, 1957." The department of land and natural resources is further directed to, "after notice and hearing as herein provided, review and redefine the boundaries of forest and water reserve zones as established by or under the authority of this part. The department may establish subzones within the forest and water reserve zones, which subzones shall be restricted to certain uses."

GEOLOGICAL HAZARD AREA

Geological Hazard Area

Colorado
   Colo. Rev. Stat.
   §24-65.1-103

"Geological hazard area" is defined to include an "area which contains or is directly affected by geologic hazard." "Geologic hazard" is defined as "a geologic phenomenon which is so adverse to past, current, or foreseeable construction or land use as to constitute a significant hazard to public health and safety or to property. The term includes, but is not limited, to:

   "(a) Avalanches, landslides, rock falls, mudflows, and unstable or potentially unstable slopes;
   (b) Seismic effects;
   (c) Radioactivity; and
   (d) Ground subsidence."

The latter terms are further defined as:
   "(1) 'Mudflow' means the downward movement of mud in a mountain watershed because of peculiar characteristics of extremely high sediment yield and occasional high runoff.
   (2) 'Unstable or potentially unstable slope' means an area susceptible to a landslide, a mudflow, a rock fall, or accelerated creep of slope-forming materials.
   (3) 'Seismic effects' means direct and indirect effects caused by an earthquake or an underground nuclear detonation."

Comment (Geological Hazard Area): California and Nevada require local regulation of seismic areas.

Type of Area/State/Statutory Cite	Definition Criteria	Comment

(4) 'Radioactivity' means a condition related to various types of radiation emitted by natural radioactive minerals that occur in natural deposits of rock, soil, and water.

(5) 'Ground subsidence' means a process characterized by the downward displacement of surface material caused by natural phenomena such as removal of underground fluids, natural consolidation, or dissolution of underground minerals or by man-made phenomena such as underground mining."

MINERAL RESOURCE AREAS

Mineral Resource Area

Colorado
  Colo. Rev. Stat.
  §24-65.1-104

"Mineral resource area" means an area in which minerals are located in sufficient concentration in veins, deposits, bodies, beds, seams, fields, pools, or otherwise, as to be capable of economic recovery. The term includes, but is not limited to, any area in which there has been significant mining activity in the past, there is significant mining activity in the present, mining development is planned or in progress, or mineral rights are held by mineral patent or valid mining claim with the intention of mining."

" 'Mineral' means an inanimate constituent of the earth, in solid, liquid, or gaseous state which, when extracted from the earth, is usable in its natural form or is capable of conversion into usable form as a metal, a metallic compound, a chemical, an energy source, a raw material for manufacturing, or construction material. This definition does not include surface or ground water subject to appropriation for domestic, agricultural, or industrial purposes, nor does it include geothermal resources."

Only Colorado requires local regulation of mineral resource areas.

Appendix **D**

STATUTORY
USE STANDARDS

The following table summarizes selected statutory standards for development and other uses. Most statutes are quite general. The administering agency generally has wide discretion to adopt more specific administrative regulations.

Regulatory Area/State/Statutory Cite	Standards	Comment

FLOOD HAZARD AREAS

Floodway

Regulatory Area/State/Statutory Cite	Standards	Comment
Indiana Ind. Ann. Stat. §§13-2-22-11; 13-2-22-13; 13-2-22-15 (Burns 1973)	State permits are required for uses in floodway areas. It is unlawful to erect or maintain in or on any floodway a permanent abode or to erect or maintain any structure, obstruction, deposit or excavation in or on any floodway or to permit any of the above which will adversely affect the efficiency or unduly restrict the capacity of the flooodway or which will create an unreasonable hazard to the safety, life, or property.	Similar standards are incorporated in the floodway statutes and administrative regulations of other states.

Regulatory Area/State/Statutory Cite	Standards	Comment

Flood Plain

Kansas
  Kan. Stat. Ann.
  §12-735
  (1975)

The state identifies flood plain areas and reviews local flood plain regulations but does not excercise state regulatory powers. The statute establishes minimum standards for local regulations:

"(a) Human habitation shall be prohibited unless adequately protected within the floodplain zone or district.

"(b) Suitable flood proofing to the elevation level established by the county or city and approved by chief engineer shall be required for new construction subsequent to this act.

"(c) Structures and other encroachments shall not be permitted on a floodplain if they will raise the flood height so as to unreasonably affect another.

"(d) Uses that are not specifically prohibited, that will not cause undue restriction of flood flows upon a floodplain, and that are not inconsistent with the purposes of this act shall be permitted."

Comment: These standards are some of the most detailed for local regulation.

Floodway

Nebraska
  Neb. Rev. Stat.
  §2-1506.06
  (1974)

State standards are provided for local control of floodway areas. Direct state regulation takes place in the event of local inaction. In considering permits for uses in floodway areas the state or local unit "shall consider (a) the danger to life and property by water which may be backed up or diverted by such obstruction or land use, (b) the danger that the obstruction or land use will be swept downstream to the injury of others, (c) the availability of alternate locations, (d) the construction or alteration of the obstruction in such a manner as to lessen the danger, (e) the permanence of the obstruction or land use, (f) the anticipated development in the foreseeable future of the area which may be affected by the obstruction or land use, (g) hardship factors which may result by approval or denial of the application, and (h) such other factors as are in harmony with the purpose of [the act] . . . ."

Comment: This is a particularly detailed list of criteria for floodway uses.

Flood Plain and Floodway

Minnesota
  Minn. Stat. Ann.
  §104.03
  (West Supp. 1977)

The state establishes standards for local regulation of flood plain and floodway areas. The regulatory flood is defined by statute to be the 100 year flood. Once a local flood plain ordinance has been established, "no major alteration to a structure in existence on the effective date of the ordinance and no new land fill, structure, deposit or other flood plain use that is reasonably hazardous to the public or that unduly restricts the capacity of the flood plain to carry and discharge the regional flood (100 year flood) shall be permitted . . . "

Comment: This approach is common where the state establishes standards for local regulation of both flood plain and floodway areas. Similar approaches are applied in Wisconsin, Iowa, New York, and New Jersey.

Regulatory Area/State/Statutory Cite	Standards	Comment

Flood Plain and Floodway

Montana
  Mont. Rev. Codes Ann.
  §89-3506
  (West Supp. 1975)

Permits are required from local units or the state (in the event that local units fail to adopt adequate regulations) for uses in defined 100 year flood plain or floodway. Prior artificial obstructions and non-conforming uses are excepted except "(1) any building for permanent use by human beings, and (2) any structure that will cause water to be diverted or reduce the capacity of the floodway. Alterations to non-conforming uses require a permit. The following uses are ordinarily permitted within the floodway: (1) agricultural uses, (2) industrial, commercial uses such as parking lots, loading areas, and emergency landing strips, (3) recreational uses such as golf courses, tennis courts, archery ranges, picnic grounds, etc., (4) forestry, including processing of forest products with portable equipment, (5) residential uses such as lawns, gardens, parking areas, (6) excavation subject to issuance of a permit.

This is a particularly detailed listing of permitted uses.

WETLANDS

Coastal Wetlands

Connecticut
  Conn. Gen. Stat. Ann.
  §22a-33
  (1975)

A state permit is required for activities in coastal wetlands. In considering a permit application, the state "shall consider the effect of the proposed work with reference to public health and welfare, marine fisheries, shellfisheries, wildlife, the protection of life and property from flood, hurricane and other natural disasters, and the public policy" . . . (set forth in this act).

A similar broad list of criteria is provided for coastal wetland uses in the statutes of Maine, Maryland, and Massachusetts.

Inland Wetlands

Connecticut
  Conn. Gen. Stat. Ann.
  §22a-40
  (West Supp. 1975)

Local units are to regulate wetlands consistent with state standards. State may regulate in the event of local inaction. Some uses are permitted as of right in wetlands: "(1) Grazing, farming, nurseries, gardening and harvesting of crops and farm ponds of three acres or less; (2) A residential home (i) for which a building permit has been issued or (ii) on a subdivision lot, provided the permit has been issued or the subdivision has been approved as of the effective date of promulgation of the municipal regulation; (3) Boat anchorage or mooring; (4) Use incidental for the enjoyment and maintenance of residential property (such property defined by statute) . . . (5) Construction and operation, by water companies of dams, reservoirs, and other facilities necessary to the impounding, storage and withdrawal of water in connection with the public water supplies . . . ." Other operations and uses permitted as a nonregulated use in wetlands and water courses, provided they do not disturb the natural and indigenous character of the land. These include:
(1) Conservation of soil, vegetation, water, fish, shell fish, and wildlife and (2) Outdoor recreation including play and sporting area golf courses, field trails, nature study, hiking,

This is a particularly detailed list of standards for uses in inland wetland areas.

Regulatory Area/State/Statutory Cite	Standards	Comment

horseback riding, swimming, skin diving, camping, boating, water skiing, trapping, hunting, fishing and shellfishing where otherwise legally permitted and regulated.

In carrying out policies of the act the state is to take into consideration all relevant facts and circumstances, including but not limited to:

(a) The environmental impact of the proposed action;

(b) The alternatives to the proposed action;

(c) The relationship between short-term uses of the environment and the maintenance and enhancement of long-term productivity;

(d) Irreversible and irretrievable commitments of resources which would be involved in the proposed activity;

(e) The character and degree of injury to, or interference with, safety, health or the reasonable use of property which is caused or threatened; and

(f) The suitability or unsuitability of such activity to the area for which it is proposed.

Coastal Marshes

Virginia
  Va. Code Ann.
  §62.1-13.5
  (1973)

State permits are required for lands owned by the state. Towns must regulate other wetlands consistent with statutory standards. Wetlands of primary ecological significance shall not be altered so that the ecological systems are unreasonably disturbed. Development shall be concentrated in wetlands of lesser ecological significance, in wetlands which have been irreversibly disturbed before July 1, 1972, and areas apart from wetlands. Counties, cities, and towns are authorized to adopt wetland ordinances with the following provisions:

(1) Permitted use include: The construction and maintenance of non-commercial catwalks, piers, boathouses, boat shelters, fences, duckblinds, wildlife management shelters, and other similar structures provided that such structures are so constructed on pilings as to permit the reasonably unobstructed flow of the tide and preserve the natural contour of the marsh, the cultivation and harvesting of shellfish and worms for bait, non-commercial outdoor recreational activities provided that no structure shall be constructed except as provided above, the cultivation and harvesting of agricultural or horticultural products including grazing and haying, conservation, repletion and research activities of the commission, the construction or maintenance of aids to navigation which are authorized by governmental authority; emergency decrees of health officials, the normal maintenance and repair on additions to existing roads providing that no waterway is altered and no additional wetlands covered, and, governmental activity on wetlands owned or leased by the state or a political subdivision thereof. (2) Any person who desires to develop any wetland within this jurisdiction other than for above purposes must first obtain a permit from the wetlands board of the political subdivision."

This is the most detailed list of statutory criteria for uses in coastal wetlands.

Regulatory Area/State/Statutory Cite	Standards	Comment

Prior non-conforming uses are exempted from regulation.

COASTAL AREAS

Coastal Zone

California
  Cal. Govt. Code
  §27402

Regional commissions regulate development in the coastal zone. No permit is to be issued unless the regional commission has first found both of the following: "(a) That the development will not have any substantial adverse environmental or ecological effect. (b) That the development is consistent with the findings and declarations set forth in Sections 27001 and with the objections set forth in Section 27302."
The "applicant" has the burden of proof on all issues.

These criteria are particularly specific with regard to environmental and ecological impact. Few acts prohibit outright particular uses.

Coastal Zone

Delaware
  Del. Code Ann. Tit. 7,
  §§7003; 7004
  (1975)

Act prohibits outright heavy industry in coastal zone. Quite detailed standards are provided for light industry.

Act prohibits heavy industry in coastal zone. Quite detailed standards are provided for light industry.

Beach Area

Florida
  Fla. Stat. Ann.
  §161.052
  (West 1972 &
  Supp. 1977)

Beach setback area for control of construction and excavaton includes land within 50 feet of mean high water. State regulation provides "No Person, Firm, Corporation, Municipality, County or other Public Agency shall construct any dwelling house, hotel, motel, apartment building, seawall, revetment, or other structure incidental to or related to facilities such as a patio, swimming pool, or garage, within 50 feet of the line between the medium high water at any riparian coastal location fronting the shoreline of the state, exclusive of bays, inlets, rivers, lays, creeks, passes, and the like."

A beach setback is also provided in Hawaii.

Coastal Area

North Carolina
  N.C. Gen. Stat.
  §113A-120
  (1975)

State is to adopt guidelines for local regulation of coastal areas including areas of "environmental concern." State is directed to identify areas of critical environmental concern.
  Coastal zone permits are to be denied if (1) in the case of coastal wetlands, that development would contravene a coastal wetland protection order, (2) in the case of estuarine areas, that the permit would not comply with statutory provisions applying to estuarine areas, (3) in the case of renewable resource areas, "that the development will result in loss or significant reduction of continued long-range productivity that would jeopardize one or more of the water, food or fiber requirements o(f) more than local concern," (4) in the case of a fragile or historic resource, "that development will result in major or irreversible damage to one or more historic, cultural, scientific, environmental or scenic values or

These are the most detailed criteria for uses in coastal areas of "particular concern."

Regulatory Area/State/Statutory Cite	Standards	Comment

natural systems . . ." , (5) in the case of waterways and lands under waters, that development will jeopardize the public rights or interests, (6) in the case of natural hazard areas, that development would occur in such a "manner as to unreasonably endanger life or property," (7) in the case of areas which are or may be impacted by key facilities, that "the development is inconsistent with State guidelines or local land use plans," or (8) "in any case, that the development is inconsistent with the State guidelines or local land-use plans."

SHORELANDS

Shorelands

Maine
Maine Rev. Stat. Ann., Ch. 424, §4811, *et seq.* (1974 and Supp. 1977-78)

The state adopts guidelines for municipal regulation of shoreland areas and can regulate such areas in the event local units fail to do so. Local regulations are to accomplish the purposes of the act which include to "further the maintenance of safe and healthful conditions," "prevent pollution," "protect spawning grounds, fish, aquatic life, bird and other wildlife habitat," "control building sites, placement of structures and other land use," and "conserve shore cover, visual as well as actual points of access to inland and coastal waters and natural beauty."

Comment: Shoreland zoning acts of Maine, Wisconsin, Michigan and Vermont set forth similarly broad criteria.

Shorelands

Minnesota
Minn. Stat. Ann. §105.485 (Supp. 1977)

The state is to adopt standards and criteria for county and municipal regulation of shoreland areas and to directly regulate such areas in the event local units fail to act. State standards and criteria are to apply to the "subdivision, use and development of shorelands" including: "(a) the area of a lot and length of water frontage suitable for a building site; (b) the placement of structures in relation to shorelands and roads; (c) the placement and construction of sanitary land waste disposal facilities; (d) the designation of types of land uses; (e) changes in bottom contours of adjacent public waters; (f) preservation of natural shorelands through restriction of land uses . . . "

Shorelines

Washington
Wash. Rev. Code Ann. §90.58.020 (Supp. 1977)

The state is to establish guidelines for local master programs and regulation of "shorelines" and "shorelines of statewide significance." The state is to directly regulate shoreland uses if local units fail to adopt satisfactory controls. State government in adopting guidelines and local governments in adopting master programs shall give preferences to "uses in the following order of preference which: (1) Recognize and protect the statewide interest over the local interest; (2) Preserve the natural character of the shoreline; (3) Result in long-term over short-term benefit; (4) Protect the resources and ecology of the shoreline; (5) Increase public access to publicly owned shorelines; (6) Increase recreational opportunities for the public in the shoreline . . ." The

Comment: This act sets forth the most detailed list of criteria and objectives among the shoreland statutes.

Regulatory Area/State/Statutory Cite	Standards	Comment

statute also provides that "uses shall be preferred which are consistent with control of pollution and prevention of damage to the natural environment or are unique to or dependent upon use of the state's shoreline.

Alterations of the natural condition of the shorelines of the state in those limited instances when authorized, shall be given priority for single family residences, ports, shorelines recreation uses including but not limited to parks, marinas, piers, and other improvements facilitating public access to shorelines of the state, industrial and commercial developments which are particularly dependent on their location on or use of the shorelines of the state and other development that will provide an opportunity for substantial numbers of people to enjoy the shorelines of the state."

SCENIC AND WILD RIVERS

Scenic and Wild Rivers

Minnesota
   Minn. Stat. Ann.
   §104.34 (1977)

The state is to designate wild, scenic, and recreational rivers and to establish standards and criteria for local regulations. The state may regulate shoreland areas directly in the event local units fail to adopt and enforce adequate controls. Standards and criteria may address topics covered by the state shoreland zoning act (see discussion above) and the goals and purposes of the scenic and wild rivers act.

Most scenic and wild rivers acts similarly permit the regulatory agency to exercise considerable discretion in controlling uses.

Natural Rivers

Michigan
   Mich. Comp.
   Mich. Comp.
   Laws Ann.
   §281.762
   (West Supp. 1977)

State designates natural rivers including wild, scenic, and recreational rivers and establishes development and use standards. Local units must adopt regulations meeting or exceeding those of the state within one year or the state is authorized to directly regulate areas. Regulations shall provide "for the protection of the river and related land resources consistent with the preservation and enhancement of their values and the objectives [of the act] . . . The ordinance or rule shall protect the interest of the people of the state as a whole. It shall take cognizance of the characteristics of the land and water concerned, surrounding development and existing uses and provide for conservation of soil, water, stream bed and banks, flood plains and adjoining uplands." It may control the type of use (*e.g.,* agriculture, forestry, recreation, residences), subdivision, location, and design of roads, and public utilities within 400 feet of the water's edge, the cutting of trees within 100 feet of the water's edge, and mining and drilling for oil and gas within 300 feet of the water's edge.

This act contains a particularly specific listing of standards.

Regulatory Area/State/Statutory Cite	Standards	Comment

WILDLIFE HABITAT AND ENDANGERED SPECIES

Wildlife Habitat and Endangered Species

Vermont Vt. Stat. Ann. Tit. 10 §6086 (Supp. 1975)	Permits for large scale development and subdivisions are to be issued by regional regulatory commissions only if a wide range of environmental and broader planning standards are met. The statute provides, in part, that a "permit will not be granted if it is demonstrated by any party opposing the applicant that a development will destroy or significantly imperil necessary wildlife habitat or any endangered species, and (i) the economic, social, cultural, recreational, or other benefit to the public from the development or subdivision will not outweigh the economic, environmental, or recreational loss to the public from the destruction or imperilment of the habitat or species, or (ii) all feasible and reasonable means of preventing or lessening the destruction, diminution, or imperilment of the habitat or species have not been or will not continue to be applied, or (iii) a reasonably acceptable alternative site is owned or controlled by the applicant which would allow the development or subdivision to fulfill its intended purpose.	Note, these standards operate through the large scale development permit requirements.

PRIME AGRICULTURAL LAND

Agricultural Districts

Hawaii Hawaii Rev. Stat. §§205-2; 205-3; (1968)	The state defines agricultural, rural, urban and conservation areas. Counties regulate agricultural areas consistent with overall statutory guidelines and those of the land use commission. The statute provides that "(w)ithin agricultural districts, uses compatible to the activities described in §205-2 as determined by the land use commission shall be permitted. Other uses may be allowed by special permits issued pursuant to this chapter. The minimum lot size in agricultural districts shall be determined by each county through its zoning ordinance, subdivision ordinance or other lawful means, provided that in no event shall the minimum lot size for any agricultural use be less than one acre." Section 205-2 provides that "(a)gricultural districts shall include activities or uses characterized by the cultivation of crops, orchards, forage, and forestry; farming activities or uses related to animal husbandry, and fish and game propagation; services and uses accessory to the above activities but not limited to living quarters or dwellings, mills, storage facilities, processing facilities, and roadside stands for the sale of products grown on the premises; and open area recreational facilities."	Only Hawaii directly zones agricultural lands.

Primary Agricultural Soils

Vermont Vt. Stat. Ann. Tit. 10, §6086 (Supp. 1975)	Permits for large scale development and subdivisions are to be issued by regional regulatory commissions only if they meet a wide range of environmental and broader planning standards. The statute provides, in part,	Note, this is not a sensitive areas act *per se* but rather incorpor-

Regulatory Area/State/Statutory Cite	Standards	Comment

that a permit "will be granted for the development or subdivision of primary agricultural soils only when it is demonstrated by the applicant that, in addition to all other applicable criteria, either, the subdivision or development will not significantly reduce the agricultural potential of the primary agricultural soils; or,

(i) the applicant can realize a reasonable return on the fair market value of his land only by devoting the primary agricultural soils to uses which will significantly reduce their agricultural potential; and

(ii) there are not nonagricultural or secondary agricultural soils owned or controlled by the applicant which are reasonably suited to the purpose; and

(iii) the subdivision or development has been planned to minimize the reduction of agricultural potential by providing for reasonable population densities, reasonable rates of growth, and the use of cluster planning and new community planning designed to economize on the cost of roads, utilities and land usage; and

(iv) the development or subdivision will not significantly interfere with or jeopardize the continuation of agricultural or forestry potential."

ates development standards under a large scale development site review act.

FORESTRY AREAS

Forest and Water Reserves

Hawaii
  Hawaii Rev. Stat.
  §183-41
  (1968)

State definition and regulation is provided for forest and water reserves. The Department of Land and Natural Resources is to define the boundaries of such districts and to establish subzones and regulations. The statute directs that "(i) establishing permitted uses in the subzones, the department shall give full consideration to all available data as to soil classification and physical use capabilities of the land so as to allow and encourage the highest economic use thereof consistent with requirements for the conservation and maintenance of the purity of the water supplies arising in or running or percolating through the land. The department shall also give full consideration to the preservation of open spaces and areas, as defined in § 201-2(7), so as to maintain, improve, protect, limit the future use of, or otherwise conserve open spaces and areas for public use and enjoyment."

The statute further provides that the department shall, "adopt such regulations governing the use of land within the boundaries of the forest and reserve zones as will not be detrimental to the conservation of necessary forest growth and the conservation and development of water resources adequate for present and future needs and the conservation and preservation of open space areas for public use and enjoyment.

"The department by means of the regulations may establish subzones within any forest and water reserve zone and specify the land uses permitted therein which may include, but are not limited to, farming, flower gardening, operation of nurseries or orchards, growth of commercial timber, grazing, recreational or hunting pursuits, or residential use. The regulations may also control the extent, manner, and times of the permitted

Only Hawaii has directly zoned forestry areas.

Regulatory Area/State/Statutory Cite	Standards	Comment

uses, and may specifically prohibit unlimited cutting of forest growth, soil mining, or other activities detrimental to good conservation practices."

Uses not consistent with regulations require variances.

Forestry and Agricultural Areas

Vermont
Vt. Stat. Ann. Tit. 10,
§6086
(1973)

Permits for large scale development and subdivisions are to be issued by regional regulatory commissions only if a wide range of environmental and broader planning standards are met. The statute provides, in part, that a permit will be "granted for the development or subdivision of forest or secondary agricultural soils only when it is demonstrated by the applicant that, in addition to all other applicable criteria, either, the subdivision or development will not significantly reduce the potential of those soils for commercial forestry, including but not limited to special forest uses such as maple production or Christmas tree production, of those or adjacent primary agricultural soils for commercial agriculture; or

(i) the applicant can realize a reasonable return on the fair market value of his land only by devoting the forest or secondary agricultural soils to uses which will significantly reduce their forestry or agricultural potential; and

(ii) there are no non-forest or secondary agricultural soils owned or controlled by the applicant which are reasonably suited to the purpose; and

(iii) the subdivision or development has been planned to minimize the reduction of forestry and agricultural potential by providing for reasonable population densities, reasonable rates of growth, and the use of cluster planning and new community planning designed to economize on the cost of roads, utilities, and land usage."

Note, these standards apply to development under the large scale development site review law.

GEOLOGICAL HAZARD AREAS

Geological Hazard Areas

Colorado
Colo. Rev. Stat.
§24-65.1-201 *et seq.*
(Supp. 1976)

Local units are to designate and regulate areas of state interest consistent with state guidelines including geological hazard areas: "In geologic hazard areas all developments shall be engineered and administered in a manner that will minimize significant hazards to public health and safety or to property due to a geological hazard. The Colorado geological survey shall promulgate a model geological hazard area control regulation no later than September 30, 1974."

California and Nevada require local units to identify and regulate seismic hazard areas.

MINERAL RESOURCE AREAS

Mineral Resource Areas

Colorado
Colo. Rev. Stat.
§24-65.1-201 *et seq.*
(Supp. 1976)

Local units are to designate and regulate consistent with state guidelines areas of state interest including mineral resource areas: "(1)(a) Mineral resource areas designated as areas of state interest shall be protected and

Only Colorado requires local regulation of mineral resource areas.

Regulatory Area/State/Statutory Cite	Standards	Comment

administered in such a manner as to permit the extraction and exploration of minerals therefrom, unless extraction and exploration would cause significant danger to public health and safety. If the local government having jurisdiction, after weighing sufficient technical or other evidence, finds that the economic value of the minerals present therein is less than the value of another existing or requested use, such other use should be given preference; however, other uses which would not interfere with the extraction and exploration of minerals may be permitted in such areas of state interest." . . .

"(c) The extraction and exploration of minerals from any area shall be accomplished in a manner which causes the least practicable environmental disturbance and surface areas disturbed thereby shall be reclaimed in accordance with the provisions of . . . (the statute).

"(d) Unless an activity of state interest has been designated or identified or unless it includes part or all of another area of state interest, an area of oil and gas or geothermal resource development shall not be designated as an area of state interest unless the state oil and gas conservation commission identifies such area for designation."

Mineral Resources

Vermont
   Vt. Stat. Ann. Tit. 10,
   §6086
   (Supp. 1975)

Permits for large scale development and subdivisions are to be issued by regional regulatory commissions only if environmental and broader planning standards are met. The statute provides, in part, that a "permit will be granted whenever it is demonstrated by the applicant, in addition to all other applicable criteria, that the development or subdivision of lands with high potential for extraction of mineral or earth resources, will not prevent or significantly interfere with the subsequent extraction or processing of the mineral or earth resources."

Note, these standards operate through the large scale development site review permit law.

RESOURCE PROTECTION CASES

The following cases illustrate judicial support for resource protection regulations.

FORESTRY AREAS

State v. Dexter, 32 Wash. 2d 51, 202 P.2d 906, *aff'd* 338 U.S. 863 (1949) (U.S. Supreme Court upheld a Washington statute requiring permits for tree-cutting and requiring landowner participation in a state reforestation program.)

Perley *et al.* v. North Carolina, 249 U.S. 510 (1919) (U.S. Supreme Court upheld North Carolina tree-cutting and slash disposal regulations for watershed areas.)

In re Opinion of Justices, 69 Atl. 627 (Ma. 1908) (Court held that proposed Maine statute regulating tree-cutting on wild land to protect water supply and reduce erosion would be valid.)

PRIME AGRICULTURAL LAND

Chevron Oil Company v. Beaver County, 22 Utah 2d 143, 449 P.2d 989 (1969) (Court upheld exclusive agricultural zoning for an area adjacent to a highway which was worth $20-$30 an acre without the zoning and $10,000 with the zoning.)

Gisler v. County of Madera, 38 Cal. App. 3d 303, 112 Cal. Rptr. 919 (1974) (Court upheld 18-acre minimum lot size agricultural zoning for land which had always been used for agricultural purposes.)

Steel Hill Development Inc. v. Town of Sanbornton, 469 F.2d 956 (1st Cir. 1972) (Court upheld rezoning of land for agricultural use with a six-acre minimum lot size.)

WETLANDS

Zabel v. Tabb, 430 F.2d 199 (5th Cir. 1970), *cert. denied* (Federal court upheld denial of a dredge and fill permit for a coastal area by the Corps of Engineers on environmental grounds. Denial was found to be authorized under NEPA and the Fish and Wildlife Coordination Act.)

P.F.Z. Properties, Inc. v. Train, 393 F. Supp. 1370 (D.D.C. 1975) (Court held filling of mangrove forest required a permit under the Federal Water Pollution Control Act.)

Candlestick Properties, Inc. v. San Francisco Bay Conservation and Development Commission, 11 Cal. App. 3d 557, 89 Cal. Rptr. 897 (1970) (Court upheld denial of a permit for filling in San Francisco Bay (estuarine area). Purpose of the regulation was to preserve existing character of the bay.)

Sibson v. State, 111 N.H. 305, 282 A.2d 664 (1971) (Court held that landowners could not recover damages from refusal of the state port authority to issue a permit for fill of coastal wetland.)

United States v. Joseph G. Moretti, Inc., 331 F.Supp. 151 (S.D.Fla. 1971) *modified*, 478 F.2d 418 (5th Cir. 1973) (Court held that filling of bay below high water for the purpose of creating lots was a "structure" requiring a permit from the Corps of Engineers and that the Corps had the power to order landowner to remove fill placed in bay without a permit.)

Potomac Sand & Gravel Co. v. Governor of Maryland *et al.,* 266 Md. 358, 293 A.2d 241 (Md. Ct. App. 1972), *cert. denied,* 409 U.S. 1040 (1972) (Court upheld a statute prohibiting dredging of coastal wetlands of Charles County. Court noted evidence of the natural importance of the area and failure of the landowner to show denial of all economic use.)

Golden v. Board of Selectmen, 358 Mass. 519, 265 N.E.2d 573 (1970) (Court held that state permit authority did not overrule a town's refusal of a permit for altering a coastal wetland since the town, as well as the state agency, had been granted power to consider permits.)

Sands Point Harbor, Inc. v. Sullivan, 136 N.J.Super. 436, 346 A.2d 612 (Super. Ct. App. Div. 1975) (Court upheld the New Jersey Coastal Wetland Act and an administrative order adopted pursuant to it as serving valid objectives and not discriminating between similarly situated landowners, despite differing treatment of some coastal wetlands, and declared it not a taking of property.)

Bernhard v. Caso, 19 N.Y.2d 192, 225 N.E.2d 521 (1967) (Court upheld denial of a permit for dredging a coastal area lying below the mean high water mark, based on a letter from the State Conservation Department requesting that no further dredging be done since the area could again become productive for harvesting of shellfish.)

New York City Housing Authority v. Commissioner of Environmental Conservation, 83 Misc. 2d 89, 372 N.Y.S. 2nd 146 (Sup. Ct. 1975) (Court held that a moratorium on alteration of coastal wetlands was valid and not a taking.)

Cal. Rptr. 93 (1972) (Court held that a county zoning ordinance that limited an area subject to severe flooding to parks, recreation and agricultural uses was a valid exercise of power rather than a taking, despite the fact that the area had been zoned in part to comply with Corps of Engineers requirements for construction of flood control works.)

Reuter v. Dept. of Natural Resources, Div. of Resource Dev., 43 Wis. 2d 272, 168 N.W.2d 860 (1969) (Court held that the state must consider possible impact on water quality in evaluating a permit application for dredge and fill of wetlands adjacent to a lake.)

Just v. Marinette County, 56 Wis.2d 7, 201 N.W.2d 761 (1972) (Court upheld state-supervised shoreland zoning for a wetland area despite the very restrictive nature of the controls on the theory that a landowner has no inherent right to destroy the natural suitability of the land.)

FLOOD PLAIN

Turner v. County of Del Norte, 24 Cal. App. 3d 311, 101 Cal. Rptr. 93 (1972) (Court held that a county zoning ordinance that limited an area subject to severe flooding to parks, recreation, and agricultural uses was a valid exercise of power rather than a taking, despite the fact that the area had been zoned in part to comply with Corps of Engineers requirements for construction of flood control works.)

Vartelas v. Water Resources Comm'n, 146 Conn. 650, 153 A.2d 822 (1959) (Court upheld a Connecticut state-level flood plain encroachment statute.)

Iowa Natural Resources Council v. Van Zee, 261 Iowa 1287, 158 N.W.2d 111 (1968) (Court upheld an Iowa state-level flood plain regulation statute but granted only part of the relief sought by the agency.)

Turnpike Realty Co. v. Town of Dedham, 362 Mass. 221, 284 N.E.2d 891 (1972) *cert. denied,* 409 U.S. 1108 (1973) (Court upheld zoning regulations that limited a flood plain to essentially open space uses despite testimony that the land was worth $431,000 before regulations and $53,000 after regulations and evidence that several hills above the regulatory flood elevation had been included in the flood plain district.)

Baker v. Planning Board of Framingham, 353 Mass. 141, 228 N.E.2d 831 (1967) (Court invalidated the refusal of a planning commission to approve a subdivision plat for a parcel of land that functioned as a natural flood storage area.)

Hamlin v. Matarazzo, 120 N.J.Super. 164, 293 A.2d 450 (Sup.Ct. Low Div. 1972) (Court held that NJSA 40:SS-1.20 authorizes a planning board to require that subdivisions have adequate drainage and protection from flooding and erosion.)

LAKES (See also wetlands)

Dennis v. Village of Tonka Bay, 64 F.Supp. 214 (D.C. Minn., 1946), *aff'd,* 156 F.2d 672 (1946) (Court upheld a zoning ordinance which restricted a shoreland site to residential uses in spite of claims that the ordinance rendered the property less valuable for residential use than for boat livery use and that the property had a different character because of the riparian rights involved.)

Poneleit v. Dudas, 141 Conn. 413, 106 A.2d 479 (1954) (Court upheld provisions of zoning ordinance which provided that filled-in lands were to bear zoning classification of adjacent zoned land (residential classification) in spite of claims of riparian owner, who wished to use property as a boat livery, that the residential classification deprived him of his riparian rights.)

Town of Lebanon v. Woods, 153 Conn. 182, 215 A.2d 112 (1965) (Court sustained town ordinance which regulated only limited aspects of uses and applied special provisions to shoreland areas.)

Ramapo v. Bockar, 151 Misc. 613, 273 N.Y.S. 452 (1934) (Court upheld a town zoning ordinance creating a residential district from which all commercial uses except farming and reservoirs were excluded and held town entitled to a permanent injunction against use of a lake, created by dam constructed in residential district, for public boating, swimming, and fishing.)

In re Lake Secor Development Co., Inc., 141 Misc. 913, 252 N.Y.S. 809 (1931) (Court upheld park area requirements for subdivision of lakeshore plat but held that the planning board could not require establishment of a water system.)

Brown v. Tahoe Regional Planning Agency, 385 F.Supp. 1128 (D. Nev. 1973) (Court held that the public welfare may require exceptionally restrictive land use classifications to protect the Lake Tahoe basin, but did not rule on the constitutionality of the regulations.)

In the Matter of Spring Valley Development, 300 A.2d 736 (S.Ct. Me., 1973) (Court upheld denial of a permit by the Environmental Improvement Commission to subdivide 92 acres near a pond because of the possibility of water pollution.)

Just v. Marinette County, 56 Wis.2d 7, 201 N.W.2d 761 (1972) (Court upheld state-supervised shoreland zoning and wetland conservancy regulation to protect water quality and natural suitability of the land.)

City of West Frankfort v. Fullop, 6 Ill. 2d 609, 129 N.E.2d 682 (1955) (Court upheld city ordinance prohibiting oil and gas well operations near a lake from which the city drew its drinking water.)

RIVERS

Namekagon Hydro Co. v. Federal Power Comm'n, 216 F.2d 509 (1954) (Court upheld an order of the Federal Power Commission denying a license for the construction of a dam and hydroelectric project on the Namekagon River in northern Wisconsin.)

Scott v. State, *ex. rel.* State Highway Comm., 23 Ore. App. 99, 541 P.2d 516 (1975) (Court upheld regulation freezing development for one year adopted under scenic waterways act.)

Application of Hemco, Inc., 283 A.2d 246 (1971) (Court upheld state denial of a dam permit to protect "sport fishing, undamaged stream bed and white water canoeing.")

Township of Grosse Ile v. Dunbar & Sullivan Dredging Co., 15 Mich. App. 556, 167 N.W.2d 311 (1969) (Court upheld a zoning ordinance which prohibited dike and fill for a public boating and fishing area in Detroit river which constituted fish and game habitat despite earlier fills at the site under a permit from the Army Corps of Engineers and a claim that a valid nonconforming use existed. Court based its decision in part upon the public trust in navigable waters.)

Simon v. Needham, 311 Mass. 560, 42 N.E.2d 516 (1942) (Court upheld a one-acre minimum lot size for an exclusive residential area near the Charles River.)

Board of County Com'rs v. Snyder, 186 Md. 342, 46 A.2d 689 (1946) (Court upheld a residential and farming classification for a section of river shoreland where appellants sought to construct a showroom, office, lounge, and storeroom for sale of factory-built motorboats.)

COASTAL AREAS (See also wetlands, flood plains, erosion areas)

McCarthy v. City of Manhattan Beach, 41 Cal. 2d 879, 264 P.2d 932 (1953) (Court upheld a beach zoning district that prohibited buildings in an area subject to storm damage.)

Godson v. Town of Surfside, 150 Fla. 614, 8 So. 2d 497 (1942) (Court upheld a zoning setback for buildings of 40 feet from the high water mark of the Atlantic Ocean.)

Walker v. Board of County Comm'rs of Talbot County, 208 Md. 72, 116 A.2d 393 (1955) (Court upheld an agricultural and residential zone for an area of Chesapeake Bay containing some coastal wetlands. In face of strong community opposition to a proposed oil refinery and the lack of features making the site uniquely appropriate, court held that loss of value is not a basis for a taking claim when the use proposed is detrimental to public health, safety, morals, welfare, *etc.*).

County Commissioners v. Miles, 246 Md. 355, 228 A.2d 450 (1967) (Court sustained 5-acre minimum lot sizes for coastal area.)

County Com'r of Anne Arundel County v. Ward, 186 Md. 330, 46 A.2d 684 (1946) (Court sustained a "partial" county zoning ordinance for a peninsula.)

Town of Marblehead v. Rosenthal, 136 Mass. 124, 55 N.E.2d 13 (1944) (Court sustained a partial zoning ordinance for a coastal village.)

In re Maine Clean Fuel, Inc., 310 A.2d 736 (Me. 1973) (Court upheld refusal of Environmental Improvement Commission to permit an oil refinery at a coastal site.)

California v. Superior Court, 115 Cal. Rptr. 497 (1974) (Court upheld denial of a permit by the state coastal commission for a project proposed in the 1,000-yard coastal zone, at least until the coastal zone plan was completed.)

Tom's River Affiliates v. Dep't of Environmental Protection, 140 N.J. Super., 355 A.2d 679 (1976) (Court upheld denial of permit to build a condominium complex under the Coastal Facility Review Act.)

PARKS

McCormick v. Lawrence, 83 Misc. 2d 64, 372 N.Y.S.2d 156 (S.Ct. 1975) (Court upheld denial of a permit for a boathouse on land regulated by the Adirondack Park Agency.)

Horizon Adirondack Corp. v. State—N.Y. Misc.,—388 N.Y.S.2d 235 (S. Ct. 1976) (Court upheld Adirondack Park regulations as applied to land within park.)

General Outdoor Adv. Co. v. City of Indianapolis, 202 Ind. 85, 172 N.E. 309, 72 A.L.R. 453 (1930) (Court upheld regulation of signs within 500 feet of park.)

People v. Sterling, 267 App. Div. 9, 45 N.Y.S.2d 39 (1943), *reh. and app. den.,* 267 App. Div. 852, 47 N.Y.S.2d 285 (Court upheld Park Commission ban of signs in Adirondack area.)

State v. City of Toledo, 75 Ohio App. 378, 31 Ohio Ops. 144, 62 N.E.2d 256 (1944) (Court held that municipality can limit the ingress and egress of an owner of land abutting a park or boulevard.)

MINERAL RESOURCES

Bandini Petroleum Co. v. Superior Court, 284 U.S. 8 (1931) (Court upheld a state statute prohibiting the "unreasonable waste of natural gas.")

Champlin Refining Co. v. Corp. Comm. of Oklahoma, 286 U.S. 210 (1932) (Court upheld a state statute regulating the extraction of oil and gas to prevent waste and insure a just distribution to all landowners of oil and gas from a single pool.)

Lindsley v. Natural Carbonic Gas Co., 220 U.S. 61 (1911) (Court upheld a state statute prohibiting the pumping of mineral waters to extract carbonic gas as an unreasonable and wasteful depletion of natural resources.)

Goldblatt v. Town of Hempstead, 369 U.S. 590 (1962) (Court upheld a town ordinance prohibiting quarrying two feet or more below ground water level despite a showing that little economic use remained for the land.)

Consolidated Rock Products Co. v. City of Los Angeles, 57 Cal. 2d 515, 20 Cal. Rptr. 638, 370 P.2d 342 (1962), *appeal dismissed,* 371 U.S. 36 (1962) (Court upheld an ordinance that prevented gravel operations in an area that, due to flooding, had few if any other economic uses.)

Famularo v. Board of County Commissioners, Adams County, Colo., 505 P.2d 958 (1973) (Court upheld a local mineral resource protection district.)

EROSION AREAS

Commonwealth v. Tewskbury, 11 Met. 55 (Mass., 1846) (Court upheld a statute prohibiting removal of sand and gravel from beaches to protect natural storm and erosion protective barriers.)

Oberst v. Mays, 148 Colo. 285, 365 P.2d 902 (1961) (Court upheld a statute authorizing counties to issue orders for land treatment to reduce blowing soil and to carry out such land treatment and assess landowners if such orders were not carried out.)

Spiegle v. Beach Haven, 46 N.J. 479, 218 A.2d 129 (1966) (Court upheld building setback and fence ordinances for a coastal flood and erosion area.)

BIBLIOGRAPHY

Many studies address individual sensitive areas, but few concern the broader context of sensitive area definition, standard-setting, and management. The following bibliography is divided into three sections. The first is annotated and contains "must" readings for any effort to broadly address sensitive areas. The second addresses individual areas. The third considers topics related to the design and implementation of sensitive area programs.

A. GENERAL REFERENCES

Bosselman, F. and D. Callies, *The Quiet Revolution in Land Use Control*, Council for Environmental Quality, U.S. Government Printing Office, Washington, D.C. (1971). Excellent description of the better known flood plain, shoreland, wetland, and coastal area programs.

Center for Natural Areas, Office of International and Environmental Programs, Smithsonian Institution, *Report Three, Planning Considerations for Statewide Inventories of Critical Environmental Areas: A Reference Guide*, prepared for the

U.S. Army Corps of Engineers, Washington, D.C. (1974). Step by step approach proposed for the definition of critical areas; focus upon data gathering and definition rather than subsequent management. Good appendix describing state definition efforts and selected data gathering programs.

Council of State Governments, *An Evaluation of Natural Resource Data Products by State Data Users*, Lexington, Kentucky (1975). Evaluation of selected federal natural resource data products by state planning, critical area, and other types of users; contains conclusions and recommendations.

Hill, D. and H. Thomas, *Use of Natural Resource Data in Land and Water Planning*, The Connecticut Agricultural Experiment Station, Bulletin 733, New Haven (1972). Excellent discussion of resource data and issues but limited discussion of critical areas *per se*.

Jones & Stokes Associates, Inc., Vols. 1 & 2, *Development Guidelines for Areas of Statewide Critical Concern*, State of California Office of Planning and Research, Sacramento (1974). Good discussion of the development standards for particular types of areas, matrices for development standards.

Kusler, J. *et al.* (3 parts), *Data Needs and Data Gathering for Areas of Critical Environmental Concern*, Part I: "Summary Report," Part 2: "Selected Papers from State Programs," Part 3: "Executive Statement," University of Wisconsin, Institute for Environmental Studies Reports 53, 54, and 55, Madison (1975). Survey of data used in existing critical area implementation programs for definition, standard-setting, administration purposes; includes twenty-seven recommendations for data gathering.

Niemann, B.J. *et al.*, *Recommendations for the Assessment, Inventory and Implementation of a Critical Resource Information Program (CRIP) for Wisconsin*, University of Wisconsin, Institute for Environmental Studies, Madison (1974). Extensive discussion of the values individual types of areas serve to society; focus upon data gathering and the definition of areas rather than subsequent management; matrices proposed for definition of areas. Good set of supporting documents, bibliography.

Special Environmental Subcommittee, *Report on Special Environments*, prepared for Office of Land Use, Department of Natural Resources, East Lansing, Michigan (1974). Proposes relatively detailed criteria for the selection of "special environments" including shorelands, geologic formations, wildlife habitat, natural rivers, wilderness, wild and natural areas, historic and archaelogical sites, and wetlands. Includes some discussion of implementation approaches.

Thurow, D., W. Toner and D. Erley, *Performance Controls for Sensitive Lands: A Practical Guide for Local Administrators*, American Society of Planning Officials, Planning Advisory Service Report 307, Chicago, Illinois (1975). Excellent general discussion of local regulatory approaches for sensitive areas, examples of local regulation.

United States Department of Interior, Office of Land Use and Water Planning, and U.S. Geological Survey, Resource and Land Investigations Program, *Primer, State Resource Management Programs, Critical Areas and Information/Data Handling*, U.S. Geological Survey, U.S. Department of Interior (1976). General discussion of critical area and information handling. A number of technical reports accompany this primer and discuss critical areas in greater depth. See *Technical Supporting Report C: Information/Data Handling Requirements for Selected State Resource Management Programs* (prepared by the American Society of Planning Officials) for an excellent discussion of data used in selected wetland, scenic and wild river, coastal zone, and comprehensive critical area efforts. See Draft, *Critical Areas: A Guidebook for Development of State Programs*, U.S. Geological Survey, Resource and Land Investigations Program (1975) for a general description of individual and comprehensive critical area programs, key issues, considerations in the design of programs, approaches for managing areas. See *Technical Supporting Report B: Case Studies*, for papers considering in some depth the Florida, Maine, and Oregon Programs. See U.S. Department of Interior, Office of Land Use and Water Planning and U.S. Geological Survey, Resource and Land Investigations Program, Draft, *Information Data Handling: A Guidebook for Development of State Programs*, U.S. Geological Survey, Resource and Land Investigations Program, Washington, D.C. (1975), for a detailed discussion of special information systems; however, little discussion of critical areas. See *Technical Supporting Report D: Information Systems, Technical Description of Software* and *Hardware and Technical Supporting Report E: Issue Papers* for general discussion of land use information system and data handling problems.

Virginia Division of State Planning and Community Affairs, *Critical Environmental Areas*, Richmond (1972). General discussion; proposed approach for defining and rating critical areas.

B. INDIVIDUAL TYPES OF AREAS

1. Agricultural Lands

a. Books and Special Reports

Miner, D., *Farmland Retention in the Washington Metropolitan Area*, Metropolitan Washington Council of Governments, Washington, D.C. (1976).

U.S. Department of Agriculture, *Perspectives on Prime Lands,* Seminar on the Retention of Prime Lands, July 16-17, 1975, U.S. Department of Agriculture, Washington, D.C. (1976).

U.S. Department of Agriculture, *Recommendations on Prime Lands*, Prepared at the Seminar on the Retention of Prime Lands, July 16-17, 1975, sponsored by the USDA Committee on Land Use, U.S. Department of Agriculture (1975).

b. Periodicals

Ellingson, "Differential Assessment and Local Governmental Controls to Preserve Agricultural Lands," 20 S.D. L. REV. 548 (1975).

Gale and Yampolsky, "Agri-Zoning," PLANNING 17 (Oct. 1975).

Hannah, "Legal Devices for Controlling the Use of Farmland," 38(4) VIRG. L. REV. 451 (1952).

"Legal Techniques for Promoting Soil Conservation," 50 YALE L. J. 1056 (1941).

"Preservation of Florida's Agricultural Resources Through Land Use Planning," 27 U. FLA. L. REV. 130 (1974).

"Property Taxation of Agricultural and Open Space Land," 8 HARV. J. LEGIS. 158 (1970).

Yannacone, "Agricultural Lands, Fertile Soils, Popular Sovereignty, the Trust Doctrine," Environmental Impact Assessment and Natural Law, 51 N.D. L. REV. 615 (1975).

2. Coastal Areas

a. Books and Special Reports

Bradly, E., Jr. and J. Armstrong, *A Description and Analysis of Coastal Zone and Shoreland Management Programs in the United States,* Sea Grant Program, University of Michigan, Ann Arbor (1972).

Brower, D., D. Frankenberg, and F. Parker, Vol. I, *Ecological Determinants of Coastal Area Management,* Sea Grant Program, N.C. State University, Raleigh (1976).

Godschalk, D., F. Parker, and T. Knoche, *Carrying Capacity: A Basis for Coastal Planning?,* University of North Carolina, Department of City and Regional Planning, Chapel Hill, N.C. (1974).

Brahtz, J.F. (ed.), *Coastal Zone Management: Multiple Use with Conservation,* John Wiley & Sons, Inc., New York (1972).

Clark, J., *Coastal Ecosystems*, The Conservation Foundation, Washington, D.C. (1974).

Hess, D., *Coastal Areas of Particular Concern: Part I: Eleven State Approaches,* Coastal Area Management Program, Connecticut Department of Environmental Protection, Hartford (1975).

Ketchum, B. (ed.), *The Water's Edge: Critical Problems of the Coastal Zone,* Massachusetts Institute of Technology, Cambridge (1972).

U.S. Department of the Interior, Federal Water Pollution Control Administration, *The National Estuarine Pollution Study*, 3 Vols., U.S. Department of Interior, Washington, D.C. (1969).

b. Periodicals

Ausness, "Land Use Controls in Coastal Areas," 9 WEST L. REV. 391 (1973).

"Coastal Controls in California: Wave of the Future?," 11 HARV. J. LEGIS. 463 (1973).

Dolezel and Warren, "Saving San Francisco Bay: A Case Study in Environmental Legislation," 23 STAN. L. REV. 349 (1971).

Morgan, "On the Legal Aspects of North Carolina Coastal Problems" (A Symposium), 49 N. CAR. L. REV. 857 (1971).

O'Flaherty, "This is My Land, the Doctrine of Implied Dedication and Its Application to California Beaches," 44 SO. CALIF. L. REV. 1091 (1971).

Peterson, P.S. and W. Walber, "Saving the Coast: The California Coastal of one Conservation Act of 1972," 4 GOLDEN GATE L. REV. 307 (1974).

Romero, R. and J, Schenkel, "Saving the Seashore: Management Planning for the Coastal Zone," 25 HAST. L. J. 191 (1973).

"The Concept of State and Local Relations Under the Coastal Zone Management Act" (A Symposium), 16 W. and M. L. REV. 717 (1975).

"The Delaware Coastal Zone Act," 21 BUFF. L. REV. 481 (1972) (note).

3. Erosion Areas

a. Books and Special Reports

Purpura, J. and W. Sensabaugh, *Coastal Construction Setback Line,* Florida Cooperative Extension Service, Marine Advisory Program (1974).

U.S. Army Corps of Engineers, U.S. Army Coastal Research Center, *Shore Protection Planning and Design,* Technical Report No. 3, 3rd ed. (1966).

Wahls, H.E., *A Survey of North Carolina Beach Erosion by Air Photo Methods*, Center for Marine Coastal Studies, North Carolina State University, Raleigh (1973).

b. Periodicals

Ferguson, "Nation-Wide Erosion Control: Soil Conservation Districts and the Power of Land-Use Regulation," 34 IOWA L. REV. 166 (1948).

4. Flood Plains

a. Books and Special Reports

Bureau of Outdoor Recreation, "Flood Plains for Open Space and Recreation," Report No. 39, Outdoor Recreation Action, Department of Interior, Bureau of Outdoor Recreation, Washington, D.C. (Spring, 1976).

Department of Natural Resources, *Guide for Flood Plain Management in Wisconsin,* Wisconsin Department of Natural Resources, Madison (1970).

Kusler, J. and T. Lee, *Regulations for Flood Plains*, American Society of Planning Officials, Planning Advisory Service Report No. 277 (1972).

Kusler, J., D. Yanggen, *et al., Regulation of Flood Hazard Areas to Reduce Flood Losses,* Vols. 1 & 2, U.S. Water Resources Council, U.S. Government Printing Office, Washington, D.C. (1970, 1971).

Murphy, F.C., *Regulating Flood-Plain Development*, University of Chicago, Department of Geography, Research Paper No. 56 (1958).

Office of the Chief of Engineers, U.S. Army Corps of Engineers, *Flood-Proofing Regulations*, U.S. Army Corps of Engineers, Washington, D.C. (1972).

Tennessee Valley Authority, *Flood Damage Prevention*, an indexed bibliography, Knoxville, Tenn. (1969).

White, G.F. and J.E. Haas, *Assessment of Research on Natural Hazards,* M.I.T. Press, Cambridge, Mass. (1975).

b. Periodicals

Abrams, "Flood Insurance and Flood Plain Zoning as Compatible Components: A Multi-Alternative Approach to Flood Damage Reduction," 7 NAT. RES. L. 581 (1974).

"County and Municipal Flood Plain Zoning Under Existing Wyoming Legislation," 7 LAND AND WATER L. REV. 103 (1972).

Deason, "Mandatory Federal Flood Insurance and Land Use Control," 49 FLA. B. J. 302 (1975).

Dunham, "Flood Control Via the Police Power," 107 U. PENN. L. REV. 1098 (1959).

"Ecological Aspects," 20 KANS. L. REV. 268 (1972) (Comment).

"Floodplain Zoning in California—Open Space by Another Name: Policy and Practicality," 10 SAN DIEGO L. REV. 381 (1973).

Hines, Howe, and Montgomery, "Suggestions for a Model Floodplain Zoning Ordinance," 5 LAND AND WATER L. REV. 321 (1970).

Plater, "The Taking Issue in a Natural Setting: Floodlines and the Police Power," 52 TEX. L. REV. 201 (1974).

5. Forest Areas

a. Books and Special Reports

Bingham, C., *Trees in the City,* American Society of Planning Officials, Planning Advisory Service Report 236, Chicago, Ill. (1968).

Solberg, I., *New Laws for New Forests*, University of Wisconsin Press, Madison (1961).

b. Periodicals

Arvola, "Forest Practice Regulation in California," 60 J. FORESTRY 872 (1962).

Ayer, "Public Regulation of Private Forestry: A Survey and A Proposal," 10 HARV. J. OF LEGIS. 407 (1972).

Galbraith, "Environmental Effects of Timber Harvest and Utilization of Logging Residues," 2 ENV. AFF. 314 (1972).

Grief, "Constitutional Law—Conservation—Extent of Police Power," 25 NOTRE D. L. 360 (1950).

Reich, "The Public and the Nation's Forests," 50 CALIF. L. REV. 381 (1962).

Siegel, "Environmental Law—Some Implications for Forest Resource Management," 4 ENVIR. L. 115 (1973).

"State Laws Limiting Private Owner's Right to Cut Timber," 17 WIS. L. REV. 186 (1952).

"Trees, Earth, Water and Ecological Upheaval: Logging Practices and Watershed Protection in California," 54 CALIF. L. REV. 1117 (1966).

6. Lakes and Shorelands

a. Books and Special Reports

Agency of Environmental Conservation, *Model Shoreland Zoning Report*, Agency of Environmental Conservation, State of Vermont, Montpelier (1974).

Borcher, E.J.R., *et al.*, Parts 1 & 2, *Minnesota's Lakeshore,* University of Minnesota, Department of Geography and Center for Urban and Regional Affairs, Minneapolis (1970).

Born, S., *et al., Inland Lake Demonstration Project*, University of Wisconsin Extension and Department of Natural Resources, Madison (1974).

Dunst, R., *et al., Survey of Lake Rehabilitation Techniques and Experiences*, Wisconsin Department of Natural Resources Technical Bulletin No. 75, Madison (1974).

Kusler, J., *et al., Strengthening Lake-Shoreland Management in Massachusetts*, University of Massachusetts Water Resources Center, Publication No. 68, Amherst (1976).

Michigan Department of Natural Resources, *A Plan for Michigan's Shorelands*, Michigan Department of Natural Resources, East Lansing (1973).

Minnesota Department of Natural Resources, *Shoreland Management, Classification Scheme for Public Waters,* Minnesota Department of Natural Resources, Division of Waters, Soils, and Minerals, Supplementary Report No. I, St. Paul (1971).

Minnesota Department of Natural Resources, *Elements and Explanation of Shoreland Rules and Regulations*, Minnesota Department of Natural Resources, Division of Waters, Soils, and Minerals, Supplementary Report No. 2, St. Paul (1971).

Minnesota Department of Natural Resources, *Procedural Guide for the Implementation of County Shoreland Ordinances*, Minnesota Department of Natural Resources, Division of Waters, Soils, and Minerals, Supplementary Report No. 3, St. Paul (1971).

University of Maine, Shoreland Zoning Project, *Municipal Guide for Shoreland Zoning*, Environmental Studies Center, Coburn Hall, University of Maine, Orono (1973).

b. Periodicals

Ayer, "Water Quality at Lake Tahoe: Dissertation on Grasshopper Soup," 1 ECOL. L. QUART. 3 (1971).

Craine, "Institutions for Managing Lakes and Bays," 11 NAT. RES. J. 519 (1971).

Kusler, "Artificial Lakes and Land Subdivisions," 1971 WIS. L. REV. 369.

Kusler, "Water Quality Protection for Inland Lakes in Wisconsin: A Comprehensive Approach to Water Pollution," 1970 WIS. L. REV. 35.

Kusler, "Carrying Capacity Controls for Recreation Water Uses," 1973 WIS. L. REV. 1 (1973).

7. Mineral Resource Areas

a. Books and Special Reports

Rogers, W., L. Ladwig, A. Hornbaker, S. Schwochow, S. Hart, D. Shelton, D. Scroggs and J. Soule, *Guidelines and Criteria for Identification and Land-Use Controls of Geologic Hazard and Mineral Resource Areas*, Colorado Geologic Survey, Department of Natural Resources, Special Publication 6, Denver (1974).

b. Periodicals

Annotation, "Constitutionality of Statute Prohibiting or Regulating the Location of Oil and Gas Wells," 3 A.L.R. 270 (1919).

Annotation, "Constitutionality of Statute Limiting or Controlling Exploitation or Waste of Natural Resources," 24 A.L.R. 307 (1923), 78 A.L.R. 834 (1932).

Annotation, "Constitutionality of Statute Regulating Petroleum Production," 86 A.L.R. 418 (1933).

Annotation, "Prohibiting or Regulating Removal or Exploration of Oil and Gas, Minerals, Soil, or Other Natural Products Within Municipal Limits," 10 A.L.R. 3d 1226 (1966).

Annotation, "Validity of Compulsory Pooling or Unitization Statute or Ordinance Requiring Owners or Lessees of Oil and Gas Lands to Develop Their Holdings As a Single Drilling Unit and the Like," 37 A.L.R. 2d (1954).

Binder, "A Novel Approach to Reasonable Regulation of Strip Mining," 34 U. PITT. L. REV. 339 (1973).

Clyde, "Legal Problems Imposed by Requirements of Restoration and Beautification of Mining Properties," 13 ROCK. MT. MIN. L. INST. 187 (1969).

Dawson, "Earth Removal and Environmental Protection," 3 ENV. AFF. 166 (1974).

Hammond, "The Wilderness Act and Mining: Some Proposals for Conservation," 47 ORE. L. REV. 447 (1968).

Kidd, "The Effect of Zoning and Land Use Control on Mineral Operations," 19 ROCKY MT. MIN. L. INST. 277 (1974).

Leisenring, "Western Coal—The Sleeping Giant," 19 ROCKY MT. MIN. L. INST. 1 (1974).

Moran, "Changing Concepts Relative to Land Use Controls and the Mineral Extractive Industries," 7 NAT. RES. J. 1 (1974).

Morison, "Land Use Planning and the Natural Resources Industry," 18 ROCKY MT. MIN. L. INST. 135 (1973).

Morton, "Strip Mining Reform—Some Political and Economic Ideas," 2 ENV. AFF. 294 (1972).

Place, "Problems and Opportunities Confronting Our Minerals Industry," 18 ROCKY MT. MIN. L. INST. 1 (1973).

Renkey, "Local Zoning of Strip Mining," 57 KENT. L. J. 738 (1969).

Sax, "Helpless Giants: The National Parks and Regulation of Private Lands," 75 MICH. L. REV. 239 (1976).

Schneider, "Strip Mining in Kentucky," 59 KENT. L. J. 652 (1971).

8. Areas Adjacent to Parks

a. Books and Special Reports

Kusler, J., *Public/Private Parks and Management of Private Lands for Park Protection*, University of Wisconsin—Madison Institute for Environmental Studies, Report 16, Madison (1974).

Little, C., *Green-line Parks: An Approach to Preserving Recreation Landscapes in Urban Areas*, Committee Print, Subcommittee on Parks and Recreation of the Committee on Interior and Insular Affairs, United States Senate, 94th Congress, 1st Session, U.S. Government Printing Office, Washington, D.C. (1975).

b. Periodicals

Broesche, "Land Use Regulation for the Protection of Public Parks and Recreational Areas," 45 TEX. L. REV. 96 (1966).

Davis, "Land Use Control and Environmental Protection in the Adirondacks," 47 N.Y.S.B.J. 189 (1975).

Horn, "Questions Concerning the Proposed Private Land Use and Development Plan for Adirondack Park," 24 SYR. L. REV. 989 (1973).

Forer, "Parks Lost to Urban Squeeze," 4 TRIAL 54 (1968).

Forer, "Preservation of America's Parklands: The Inadequacy of Present Law," 41 N.Y. UNIV. L. REV. 1093 (1966).

"Preserving Scenic Areas: The Adirondack Land Use Program," 84 YALE L. J. 1705 (1975).

Rabinowitz, "Martha's Vineyard: The Development of Legislative Strategy for Preservation," Vol. 3 (No. 2) ENV. AFFAIRS (396).

9. Scenic and Wild Rivers

a. Books and Special Reports

Bureau of Outdoor Recreation, "America's Wild and Scenic Rivers," Report No. 43, Outdoor Recreation Action, Department of Interior, Bureau of Outdoor Recreation, Washington, D.C. (Spring 1977).

b. Periodicals

Rich, "Managing Recreational Rivers," 8 AKRON L. REV. 43 (1974).

Tarlock, "Preservation of Scenic Rivers," 55 KENT L. REV. 745 (1967).

Tarlock and Tippy, "The Wild and Scenic Rivers Act of 1968," 55 CORN. L. REV. 707 (1970).

10. Wetlands

a. Books and Special Reports

Bean, M., *The Evolution of National Wildlife Law,* Council on Environmental Quality, U.S. Government Printing Office, Washington, D.C. (1977).

Bedford, B., *et al., The Wetlands of Dane County, Wisconsin,* Dane County Regional Planning Commission (1974).

Cowardin, L., *et al., Interim Classification of Wetlands and Aquatic Habitats of the United States,* U.S. Fish and Wildlife Service, Office of Biological Services, Washington, D.C. (1976).

Goodwin, R. and W. Neiring, *Inland Wetlands of the United States, Evaluated as Potential Registered Natural Landmarks*, U.S. Government Printing Office, Washington, D.C. (1975).

Helfgott, T., M.W. Lefor, and W.C. Kennard (eds.), *Proceedings: First Wetlands Conference*, Institute of Water Resources, The University of Connecticut, Report No. 21, Storrs (1973).

Larson, J. (ed.), *Models for Assessment of Freshwater Wetlands,* Water Resources Research Center, University of Massachusetts at Amherst, Publication No. 32, Amherst (1976).

Marcellus, K., G. Dawes, and G. Silberhorn, *Local Management of Wetlands, Environmental Considerations*, Special Report No. 35 in Applied Marine Science and Ocean Engineering, Virginia Institute of Marine Science, Gloucester Point (1973).

Shaw, S. and G. Fredine, *Wetlands of the United States, Their Extent and Their Value to Waterfowl and Other Wildlife,* Fish and Wildlife Service, United States Department of Interior, Circular 39, United States Government Printing Office, Washington, D.C. (1971).

b. Periodicals

Binder, "Taking Versus Reasonable Regulation: A Reappraisal in Light of Regional Planning and Wetlands," 25 UNIV. FLOR. L. REV. 1 (1972).

Biunno, "Environmental Law—Wetlands Fill Restrictions Do Not Constitute a Compensable 'Taking' Within the Meaning of the Fifth Amendment," 4 SETON HALL L. REV. 662 (1973).

"Coastal Wetlands In New England," 52 B. UNIV. L. REV. 724 (1972).

"Environmental Law—Zoning Ordinance Prohibiting Filling of Wetlands Adjacent to Navigable Waters Without a Permit is Constitutional Exercise of Police Power Not Requiring Payment of Compensation," 86 HARV. L. REV. 1582 (1973).

Gannon, "Constitutional Implications of Wetlands Legislation," 1 ENVIR. AFFAIRS 654 (1971).

"Land Use—Wetlands Regulation," 27 ARK. L. REV. 527 (1973).

Lefkowitz, "Jamaica Bay: An Urban Marshland in Transition," 1 FORD. U. L. J. 1 (1972).

"State and Local Wetlands Regulation: The Problem of Taking Without Just Compensation," 58 VIRG. L. REV. 876 (1972).

Stockholm, "Can New York's Tidal Wetlands Be Saved? A Constitutional and Common Law Solution," 39 ALB. L. REV. 451 (1975).

Welsh, "The Wetlands Statutes: Regulation or Taking?," 5 CONN. L. REV. 64 (1972).

11. Seismic Areas, Landslides, Etc. (Hazards Other Than Flood)

a. Books and Special Reports

Department of Housing and Urban Development, Federal Insurance Administration, *Report on Earthquake Insurance,* Department of Housing and Urban Development, Federal Insurance Administration, Washington, D.C. (1971).

Nichols, D. and T. Buchanan, *Banks, Seismic Hazards and Land Use Planning,* Geologic Survey Circular 690, U.S. Geological Survey, Washington, D.C. (1974).

Rogers, W., L. Ladwig, A. Hornbacker, S. Schwochow, S. Hart, D. Shelton, D. Scroggs, and J. Soule, *Guidelines and Criteria for Identification and Land-Use Control of Geologic Hazard and Mineral Resource Areas*, Colorado Geological Survey, Department of Natural Resources, Special Publication 6, Denver (1974).

Wallace, R., *Goals, Strategy, and Tasks of the Earthquake Reduction Program*, Geological Survey Circular 701, U.S. Geological Survey, Washington, D.C. (1974).

12. Scenic Areas (Aesthetics)

a. Books and Special Reports

Leopold, L., *Quantitative Comparison of Some Aesthetic Factors Among Rivers*, Geological Survey Circular 620, U.S. Geological Survey, Washington, D.C. (1960).

U.S. Environmental Protection Agency, *Aesthetics in Environmental Planning,* U.S. Environmental Protection Agency, Washington, D.C. (1973).

b. Periodicals

"Aesthetic Zoning: An Answer to Billboard Blight," 19 SYR. L. REV. 87 (1967).

Annotation, "Aesthetic Objectives or Considerations as Affecting Validity of Zoning Ordinance," 21 A.L.R. 3d 1222 (1968).

Annotation, "Validity and Construction of Zoning Ordinance Regulating Architectural Style or Design of Structure," 41 A.L.R. 3d 1397 (1972).

"Beyond the Eye of the Beholder: Aesthetics and Objectivity," 71 MICH. L. REV. 1438 (1973).

Cunningham, "Scenic Easements in the Highway Beautification Program," 45 DENVER LAW JOURNAL 168 (1968).

Eveleth, "New Techniques to Preserve Areas of Scenic Attraction in Established Rural-Residential Communities—The Lake George Approach," 18 SYR. L. REV. 37 (1966).

Magid, "Land Use Aesthetics, and the State Legislature," 19 WAYNE L. REV. 73 (1972).

Nance, "New Control of Advertisements," 120 THE NEW L. J. 55 (1970).

"Preserving Scenic Areas: The Adirondack Land Use Program," 84 YALE L. J. 1705 (1975).

Williams, "Legal Techniques to Protect and to Promote Aesthetics Along Transportation Corridors," 17 BUFF. L. REV. 701 (1968).

Zube, E.H., "Scenery as a Natural Resource: Implications of Public Policy and Problems of Definition, Description, and Evaluation," 63(2) LANDS. ARCH. 126 (1973).

13. Scientific Areas

a. Books and Special Reports

New England Natural Resources Center, *Protecting New England Natural Heritage*, Boston, Mass. (1973).

The Nature Conservancy, *The Preservation of Natural Diversity: A Survey and Recommendations*, Arlington, Va. (1975).

b. Periodicals

Tans, W., "Priority Ranking of Biotic Natural Areas," 13 MICH. BOTANIST 31 (1974).

C. PROGRAM DESIGN AND IMPLEMENTATION

1. Critical Area Data Gathering
(See Also General References)

(Note: Many of the following references apply generally to natural resource data and not specifically to critical areas.)

a. Books and Special Reports

Annotation, "Validity of Zoning Regulations, with Respect to Uncertainty and Indefiniteness of District Boundary Lines," 39 A.L.R. 2d 766 (1955).

American Society of Planning Officials, *Zoning Districts*, Information Report No. 136, Chicago, Ill. (1960).

Arthur D. Little Co., *An Evaluation of the San Francisco Bay Region Environment and Resources Planning Study*, Arthur D. Little, San Francisco, Cal. (1975).

Federal Insurance Administration, *Flood Map Preparation Standards,* Department of Housing and Urban Development, Washington, D.C. (1973).

Federal Mapping Task Force, *Report of the Federal Mapping Task Force on Mapping, Charting, Geodesy and Surveying,* U.S. Government Printing Office, Washington, D.C. (1973).

Gardner, J., *A Study of Environmental Monitoring and Information Systems,* Final Technical Report prepared for the U.S. Army Engineering Topographic Laboratories, Institute of Urban and Regional Research, University of Iowa, Iowa City (1972).

Kusler, J., C. Runge, and F. Alston (eds.), *Symposium Proceedings, A Survey of Programs for Statewide Land Resource Inventories*, University of Wisconsin Institute for Environmental Studies, Madison (1972).

Mesbenberg, M., *Environmental Planning: Environmental Information for Policy Formulation,* American Society of Planning Officials Advisory Service Report No. 263, Chicago, Ill. (1970).

Minnesota Department of Natural Resources, *Local Flood Data Collection*, Flood Plain Management Technical Report No. 3, St. Paul (1971).

Minnesota Department of Natural Resources, *Field Surveys for Flood Hazard Evaluation*, Flood Plain Management Technical Report No. 1, St. Paul (1971).

Minnesota Department of Natural Resources, *Use of Experienced Flood Data in Flood Plain Regulations,* Flood Plain Management Technical Report No. 4, St. Paul (1971).

Nichols, D. and J. Buchanan-Banks, *Seismic Hazards and Land Use Planning,* Geological Survey Circular 690, U.S. Geological Survey, Washington, D.C. (1974).

Rogers, W., L. Ladwig, A. Horbacker, S. Schwochow, S. Hart, D. Shelton, D. Scroggs, and J. Soule, *Guidelines and Criteria for Identification and Land-Use Controls of Geologic Hazard and Mineral Resource Areas,* Colorado Geological Survey, Department of Natural Resources, Special Publication 6, Denver (1974).

The Mitre Corporation, *Resource and Land Information Program: System Concept, Implications and Development Plan,* sponsored by the U.S. Geological Survey, Contract No. 14-08-0001-13297, Washington, D.C. (1972).

The Mitre Corporation, *Resource and Land Information Programs: Complementary Federal Data Programs and User Charge Policies,* sponsored by the U.S. Geological Survey, Contract No. 14-08-001-13559, Washington, D.C. (1973).

Tomlinson, R. (ed.), Vols. 1 & 2, *Geographical Data Handling,* International Geographical Union Commission on Geographical Data Sensing and Processing of the UNESCO/IGU Second Symposium on Geographical Information Systems, Ottawa, Can. (1972).

Tuerkheimer, F., *Legal Aspects of Water Pollution Detection Through Remote Sensing,* University of Wisconsin Institute for Environmental Studies, Remote Sensing Program, Report 15, Madison (1972).

b. Periodicals

Babcock, "Classification and Segregation Among Zoning Districts," 1954 ILL. L. FOR.

"Public Access to Government Held Computerized Information," 68 N.W.U.L. REV. 433 (1973).

"Use District Boundary Lines," 17 SYR. L. REV. 714 (1966).

2. Definition of Areas, Resource Assessment
(See General References Above)

a. Books and Special Reports

Battelle Pacific Northwest Laboratories, *An Inventory and Evaluation of Areas of Environmental Concern in Oregon,* Prepared for the State of Oregon Executive Department and Natural Resources Agencies, Richland (1973).

Bishop, A.B., *et al., Carrying Capacity in Regional Environmental Management,* Office of Research and Development, U.S. Environmental Protection Agency, U.S. Government Printing Office, Washington, D.C. (1974).

Brandes, C., *Methods of Synthesis for Ecological Planning,* Master's Thesis, Department of Architecture and Regional Planning, University of Pennsylvania, Philadelphia (1973).

California Office of Planning and Research, *State of California: Environmental Goals and Policy,* Office of the Governor, Sacramento (1973).

Carter, S., M. Frost, C. Rubin, and L. Sumek, *Environmental Management and Local Government,* Environmental Research Center, Environmental Protection Agency, U.S. Government Printing Office, Washington, D.C. (1974).

MacDougall, B. and C. Brandes, *A Selected Annotated Bibliography on Land Resource Inventory and Analysis for Planning,* Pennsylvania Department of Environmental Resources, Harrisburg (1974).

McHarg, I., *Design with Nature,* Doubleday, Inc., Natural History Press, Garden City, N.Y. (1971).

Missouri Department of Community Affairs, *Physical Characteristics and Constraints for Development, Part III: Areas Sensitive to Development in Missouri,* Office of Planning, Jefferson City (1973).

New England Natural Resources Center, *Protection and Management of New England's Natural Areas: A Report to the New England Regional Commission,* Boston, Mass. (1973).

Virginia Division of State Planning and Community Affairs, *Virginia's Critical Environmental Areas: An Update,* Virginia Division of State Planning and Community Affairs, Richmond (1973).

b. Periodicals

Finnel, "Saving Paradise: The Florida Environmental Land and Water Management Act of 1972," URB. L. ANN. 103 (1973).

Mandelker, "Critical Area Controls: A New Dimension in American Land Development Regulation," A.I.P. J. 21 (1975).

3. Natural Resources Protection, General

a. Books and Special Reports

Keyes, D., *Land Development and the Natural Environment: Estimating Impacts,* The Urban Institute, Washington, D.C. (1976).

Natural Resources Defense Council, Inc., *Land Use Controls in the United States* (E. Moss, ed.), The Dial Press/James Wade, New York, N.Y. (1977).

b. Periodicals

Carver, "Trend to State Protectionism in Natural Resource Management," 18 ROCKY MT. MIN. INST. 253 (1973).

Doub, "Technical Regulation and Environmental Law," 26 AD. L. REV. 191 (1974).

"Protection of Environmental Quality in Non-Metropolitan Areas by Limiting Development," 57 IA. L. REV. 126 (1971).

4. Statutory Enabling Authority for Local Regulation

a. Books and Special Reports

American Law Institute, *Model Land Development Code,* Tentative Drafts 1, 2, 3, Chicago, Ill. (1968, 1970, 1971).

Anderson, R. and G. Rosweig, *Planning, Zoning and Subdivision: A Summary of the Statutory Law in the 50 States,* New York Federation of Official Planning Organizations, Albany (1966).

Solberg, E. and Pfister, *Rural Zoning in the United States: Analysis of Enabling Legislation,* Economic Research Service, U.S. Department of Agriculture, Miscellaneous Publication No. 1232, U.S. Government Printing Office, Washington, D.C. (1972).

Strauss, E. and J. Kusler, *Statutory Land Use Control Authority in the Fifty States With Special Reference to Flood Hazard Regulatory Authority,* United States Department of Housing and Urban Development, Federal Insurance Administration, Washington, D.C. (1976).

5. Environmental Litigation

a. Books and Special Reports

Sax, J., *Defending the Environment: A Strategy for Citizen Action,* Alfred A. Knopf, New York, N.Y. (1971).

b. Periodicals

Herman, "Procedural Short-Circuits in Natural Resources Cases," 19 LOY. L. REV. 599 (1973).

Hershey, "The Protection of Environmental Interests by Non-Public Action," 73 W. VA. L. REV. 231 (1971).

Leventhal, "Environmental Decision-Making and the Role of the Courts," 122 U. PA. L. REV. 509 (1974).

Oakes, "Environmental Litigation: Current Developments and Suggestions for the Future," 5 CONN. L. REV. 531 (1973).

Moskowitz, "How to Use Experts Effectively in Land Regulation Proceedings," REAL ESTATE L. J. 359 (1975).

Sax, "The Public Trust Doctrine in Natural Resource Law: Effective Judicial Intervention," 68 MICH. L. REV. 471 (1970).

Sax and Conner, "Michigan's Environmental Protection Act of 1970: A Progress Report," 70 MICH. L. REV. 1004 (1972).

Sive, "Securing, Examining, and Cross-Examining Expert Witnesses in Environmental Cases," 68 MICH. L. REV. 1175 (1970).

"The Florida Environmental Protection Act of 1971: The Citizens Role in Environmental Management," 2 FLA. ST. U. L. REV. 736 (1974).

6. Population

a. Periodicals

Lamm, "Legal Control of Population Growth and Distribution in a Quality Environment, The Land Use Alternatives," 49 DENVER L. J. 1 (1972).

"The National Land Use Environmental Problem: Legal and Pragmatic Aspects of Population Density Control," 43 U. CINN. L. REV. 377 (1974).

7. Comprehensive Plan

a. Periodicals

Hart, "Comprehensive Land Use Plans and the Consistency Requirement," 2 FLA. STAT. U. L. REV. 766 (1974).

"State Control Over the Location of Development in the Absence of a Comprehensive Plan As a Valid Exercise of the Police Power," 22 KAN. L. REV. 127 (1973).

Sullivan and Kressel, "Twenty Years After—Renewed Significance of the Comprehensive Plan Requirement," 9 URB. L. ANN. 33 (1975).

Tarlock, "Consistency with Adopted Land Use Plans as a Standard of Judicial Review: The Case Against," 9 URB. L. ANN. 69 (1975).

8. Governmental Immunity From Regulations

a. Periodicals

"Balancing Interests to Determine Governmental Exemption from Zoning Laws," 125 U. ILL. L. F. 125 (1973).

"Governmental Immunity from Local Zoning Ordinances," 84 HARV. L. REV. 869 (1971).

9. Tax Incentives

a. Books and Special Reports

Council on Environmental Quality, *Untaxing Open Space,* U.S. Government Printing Office, Washington, D.C. (1976).

b. Periodicals

Heller, "The Theory of Property Taxation and Land Use Restrictions," WIS. L. REV. 751 (1974).

"State Taxation—Use of Taxing Power to Achieve Environmental Goals: Vermont Taxes Gains Realized From the Sale or Exchange of Land Held Less Than Six Years," 49 WASH. L. REV. 1159 (1974). Vt. Stat. Ann. tit. 32, secs. 1001-10 (1973).

Zimmerman, "Tax Planning for Land Use Control," 5 URB. L. ANN. 639 (1973).

10. State Constitutions and the Environment

a. Periodicals

Kirchick, "The Continuing Search for a Constitutionally Protected Environment," 4 ENVIR. AFF. 515 (1975).

Howard, "State Constitutions and the Environment," 58 VA. L. REV. 193 (1972).

Tobin, "Some Observations of the Use of State Constitutions to Protect the Environment," 3 ENVIR. AFF. 473 (1974).

11. Development Rights

a. Periodicals

Baker, "Development Rights Transfer and Landmarks Preservation—Providing a Sense of Orientation," 9 URB. L. ANN. 131 (1975).

Carmichael, "Transferable Development Rights as a Basis for Land Use Control," 2 FLOR. ST. UNIV. L. REV. 35 (1974).

"Compensable Regulation: Outline of a New Land Use Planning Tool," 10 WILL. L. J. 451 (1974).

Costonis, "Development Rights Transfer: An Exploratory Essay," 83 YALE L. J. 75 (1973).

Rose, "A Proposal for the Separation and Marketability of Development Rights as a Technique to Preserve Open Space," 2 REAL ESTATE L. J. 635 (1974).

12. Easements

a. Books and Special Reports

Wisconsin Department of Resource Development, *Proceedings of Conservation Easements and Open Space Conference,* Wisconsin Department of Resource Development, Madison (1971).

b. Periodicals

Brown, "State Land Use Laws and Regional Institutions," 4 ENVIR. AFF. 393 (1975).

Cunningham, "Scenic Easements in the Highway Beautification Program," 45 DENV. L. J. 168 (1968).

Gannon, "The Scenic Easement in New York," 33 REAL ESTATE APPR. 12 (1967).

Jordahl, "Conservation and Scenic Easements: An Experience Resume," 39 LAND ECONOMICS (1963).

Silverstone, "Open Space Preservation Through Conservation Easements," 12 OSGOODE HALL L. J. 105 (1974).

13. Environmental Impact Assessment

a. Books and Special Reports

Dikert, G. and K.R. Domeny (eds.), *Environmental Impact Assessment: Guidelines and Commentary,* University Extension, University of California, Berkeley (1974).

Ditton, R.B. and T.L. Goodale (eds.), *Environmental Impact Analysis: Philosophy and Methods,* Proceedings of the Conference on Environmental Impact Analysis, Green Bay, Wisconsin, University of Wisconsin Sea Grant Program (1972).

Leopold, L.B., F.E. Clarke, B.B. Hanshaw, and J.B. Belsey, *A Procedure for Evaluating Environmental Impact,* U.S. Geological Survey Circular 645, U.S. Geological Survey, Washington, D.C. (1971).

Warner, M. and E. Preston, *A Review of Environmental Impact Methodologies,* U.S. Environmental Protection Agency, Washington, D.C. (1974).

b. Periodicals

Cramton and Berg, "On Leading a Horse to Water: NEPA and the Federal Bureaucracy," 71 MICH. L. REV. 511 (1973).

Tissen, "Environmental Policy Acts: Analysis and Application," 10 WILL. L. J. 336 (1974).

14. Air and Water Pollution (As Related to Land Use)

a. Books and Special Reports

Aspen Systems Corporation, *Compilation of Federal, State and Local Laws Controlling Nonpoint Pollutants,* Office of Water and Hazardous Materials, U.S. Environmental Protection Agency, Washington, D.C. (1975).

Endicott, E., E. Selig, *et al, Legal and Institutional Approaches to Water Quality Management Planning and Implementation,* U.S. Environmental Protection Agency, Washington, D.C. (1977).

b. Periodicals

Annotation, "Validity and Construction of Anti-water Pollution Statutes or Ordinances," 32 A.L.R. 3d 215.

"E.P.A. Regulation of 'Indirect Sources': A Skeptical View," 12 HARV. J. LEG. 111 (1974).

Mandelker and Rothschild, "The Role of Land-Use Controls in Combating Air Pollution Under the Clean Air Act," 3 ECOL. L. QUART. 235 (Spring, 1973).

15. Performance Standards, Special Permit Controls

a. Periodicals

Heyman, "Innovative Land Regulation and Comprehensive Planning," 13 SANTA CLARA LAW 183 (1972).

"Industrial Zoning and Beyond: Compatibility Through Performance Standards," 46 J. URBAN L. 723 (1969).

McDougal, "Performance Standards: A Viable Alternative to Euclidean Zoning?," 47 TUL. L. REV. 255 (1973).

Morris, "Environmental Statutes: The Need for Reviewable Standards," 2 ENVIR. L. 75 (1971).

Sternlieb, Burchell, and Hughes, "Planned Unit Development: Environmental Suboptimization," 1 ENVIR. AFF. 694 (1971).

Stirne, "The Use of Conditions in Land-Use Control," 67 DICK. L. REV. 109 (1963).

York, "Controlling Urban Noise Through Zoning Performance Standards," 4 URB. LAW 689 (1972).

16. Taking of Property

a. Books and Special Reports

Bosselman, F., D. Callies, and J. Banta, *The Taking Issue,* U.S. Government Printing Office, Washington, D.C. (1973).

b. Periodicals (See also Wetlands, Flood Plains)

Kusler, "Open Space Zoning: Valid Regulation or Invalid Taking," 57 MINN. L. REV. 1 (1972).

Michelman, "Property, Utility and Fairness: Comments on the Ethical Foundations of 'Just Compensation' Law," 80 HARV. L. REV. 1165 (1967).

Sax, "Takings and the Police Power," 74 YALE L. J. 36 (1964).

Sax, "Takings, Private Property and Public Rights," 81 YALE L. J. 149 (1971).

GLOSSARY

Aquifer. A body of rock or soil that contains sufficient saturated permeable material to conduct groundwater and to yield economically significant quantities of groundwater to wells and springs.

Barrier island. A detached portion of a barrier bar, usually formed through wave deposits. It lies offshore and is usually parallel to the shore.

Blanket data gathering. Aerial surveys, field surveys, or other investigations conducted for an *entire* locality, region, state, *etc.* Surveys or investigations may address: (1) a single data element such as topographic contours; (2) a single type of area (*e.g.,* all wetlands); or (3) two or more types of area (*e.g.,* flood plains, wetlands). Such surveys usually produce a photomosaic or map.

Bog. A term commonly applied to forested wetlands formed in deep, steep-sided lakes with small watershed areas and poor drainage. High acidity is typical. Decomposition rates are characteristically slow resulting in extensive deposits of peat. Floating mats of *Sphagnum* moss, sedges, and heath shrubs such as leatherleaf and cranberry are common along with black spruce, northern white cedar, Atlantic white cedar, and larch.

Case-by-case data gathering. Aerial surveys, field surveys, or other investigations conducted on an individual basis for a particular project (*e.g.*, a subdivision) or particular area (*e.g.*, Big Cypress Swamp). Surveys may pertain to a particular data element such as topography or to many elements. Case-by-case data gathering is extensively used for areas lacking maps at sufficient scale for regulatory purposes and to supplement blanket data gathering. Typically, the gathered data are used directly by the decision-maker and not reduced to map or other formats for inclusion in a data file.

Critical. Of special importance, requiring high-priority treatment. Webster defines critical (in part) to mean "of, relating to, or being a turning point or specially important juncture . . . b. relating to or being a state in which or measurement or point at which some quality, property, or phenomenon suffers a definite change, crucial, decisive . . . d. indispensible for the weathering, solution, or overcoming of a crisis . . ." The present report applies the term to resource areas of special importance in state and local programs due to their usefulness, hazards, or development threats.

Data. Air photos, maps, field investigations, field notes, graphs, written descriptions, direct visual inspections, and other types and sources of information which may be used in the definition, planning, regulation, acquisition, or other management of areas. No precise distinction is drawn in the present report between "information" and "data," since all data potentially useful in sensitive area management may be considered "information."

Definition of area. The designation of a type of area or particular area for regulatory purposes including (1) the formulation of criteria and procedures for designation of the area, and (2) the actual inventory and mapping of the area. Webster provides, in part, that "define" means "1a: to fix or make distinct in outline, 2a: to determine the essential qualities or precise meaning of . . . b: to discover and set forth the meaning of." Criteria and procedures for identifying lands may take varying levels of specificity, including: (1) simple listing of types (*e.g.*, agricultural lands, flood plains, coastal areas); (2) more specific written definitions setting forth not only types but objectives, tests, and procedures for determining gradations in areas (*e.g.,* the 50-year and 100-year flood plains); and (3) precise, detailed descriptions for particular lands.

The actual inventory and mapping of lands may also take place with varying levels of specificity ranging from small-scale, generalized maps of areas to large-scale maps showing not only area boundaries but also subzone boundaries. Although maps are the most suitable approach for defining particular areas, metes and bounds description and other techniques may be used (*e.g.*, a flood profile to define flood plain areas).

Ecology. The study of interrelationships between plants and animals and their environment.

Ecosystem. The system of interrelationships within and between a biological community and its physical environment.

Enabling statute. A statute delegating power to local units of government or a state agency to adopt and administer regulations or issue special permits for development consistent with more general statutory goals and procedures.

Estuary. The mouth of a river where the current of the river meets the tide and where salt and fresh waters mix.

Eutrophication. An increase in concentration of nutrients in rivers, estuaries, and other bodies of water. This increase may be due to natural causes, man's influence, or a combination of both.

Food chain. The means by which energy and material are transferred from a producer (a green plant) to a herbivore and to one or more carnivores. A typical example of a food chain is a green plant, a plant-eating insect, and an insect-eating bird.

Georeferencing system. A system of points, grids, or other descriptive parameters used to describe systematically and accurately the geographical location of particular soils, topography, structures, or natural or cultural features in a manner which will allow retrieval, analysis, and display on spatial criteria. The locator may take the form of simple nominal code designation, public land survey, state plan coordinate system, various projections of latitude and longitude, universal transverse mercator (UTM), *etc.*

For an extensive discussion of geoinformational systems, see R.F. Tomlinson (ed.), *Geographical Data Handling,* Volumes 1 and 2 (International Geographical Union Commission on Geographical Data Sensing and Processing for the UNESCO/IGU Second Symposium on Geographical Information Systems: Ottawa, August 1972).

Groin. A shore protection structure built (usually perpendicular to the shoreline) to trap sand and other material moving along the shoreline, thus retarding erosion of the shore.

Land use regulations. Statutes, rules, ordinances, or guidelines controlling the type, mode, design, or other aspects of a use of land. Land use regulations are local legislative acts (ordinances), state legislative acts (statutes), and formally adopted orders and rules of administrative agencies (administrative rules and regulations).

Nomination procedures. A technique for defining sensitive areas or gathering data for them whereby landowners, citizens, interest groups, local governments, regional planning agencies, state and federal agencies, or other parties are asked to suggest or "nominate" potential areas to the agency responsible for designation or data gathering. Such an approach has often been informally applied to identify areas on an initial basis and is formally incorporated in the Florida and Minnesota critical area efforts.

Ordinance. A locally adopted regulation.

Performance standards. Standards establishing maximum permissible outputs or impacts for uses on natural resources or adjacent uses or prescribing a degree of protection from natural hazards. These standards relate to the ultimate effect or performance of uses, not to their specific design. Standards may relate to outputs such as air pollution, sewage, noise, vibration, or glare or to impacts such as blockage of flood flows or destruction of wildlife. They may establish hazard protection requirements such as "protection to or above the 100-year flood elevation." Their principal goal is to maintain or preserve natural processes and minimize the impact of development.

Resolution (data). The observable or represented detail of a map, aerial photo, or other data or information product. Resolution depends on the minimum distance between features, the contrast between features, and the specificity of characteristics observable or represented by those features.

Scale. The relationship between a measurable distance on a map, air photo, or other data or information product and the corresponding distance on the earth. Scale is expressed as an equivalence such as 1 inch = 200 feet or as a numerical fraction or ratio (1:24,000). *Larger scale* data or information products are those with features represented at a size corresponding more closely to their actual size than the same features represented on *smaller scale* data or products. For the purpose of this report, *small scale* maps or products are those with ratios of 1:24,000 to 1:50,000. *Large scale* includes ratios of 1:1,200 to 1:24,000. Data or products at even larger scales are generally referred to as "very detailed" or "at very large scale." These scales appear to be rarely practical for regional or statewide mapping but may be helpful for local efforts.

Standard-setting. The establishment of rules or guidelines to restrict the type, design, location, mode of construction, mode of operation, or other aspects of sensitive area uses. Sensitive area standards may take the form of inflexible rules for direct application to particular uses, performance guidelines for direct application to particular uses, minimum inflexible or performance guidelines for local land use regulations, or standards for delegating discretionary decision-making responsibility to a state or local regulatory board or agency.

Use standards usually consist of written lists of prohibited, permitted, and conditionally permitted uses for an area with minimum specifications or conditions. Use standards may apply to both structural and nonstructural (*e.g.,* fill, mining operations).

Sensitive areas. Areas where *natural resource* values (soils, minerals, vegetation) or hazards (floods, erosion, *etc.*) play a primary role in determining land use suitability or capability. These include, but are not limited to, flood plains, wetlands, coastal areas, shorelands, erosion areas, prime agricultural lands, scenic areas, areas of special recreation interest, and areas of scientific interest. For the purposes of this report, sensitive area is used interchangeably with critical resource area. It should be noted that sensitive areas are to be distinguished from broader "critical areas" which may be identified pursuant to the enabling statutes of Florida, Minnesota, and other states modeling their legislation after the American Law Institute land development code. These broader areas include not only resource areas but also sites of major new developments or areas impacting on public facilities where natural resource values or hazards may play an insignificant role in determining the suitability or capability of the land.

Sensitive areas include many areas with special natural resource characteristics which have been variously described as "fragile areas," "areas of particular concern," "areas of state concern," "areas of critical environmental concern," and "natural resource zones."

Statute. A legislative act adopted by Congress or a state legislature.

Special permit uses. Uses neither prohibited nor permitted as of right by regulations but instead permitted only upon issuance of a special permit by a regulatory board or agency after fact-finding to determine the particular natural resource values and hazards at a site, the impact of the specific proposed use, and the compliance of the use with general or special standards. The regulatory agency often exercises considerable discretion in evaluating proposed uses in light of general regulatory goals and standards and attaches conditions to permits to minimize impact.

Water table. The upper surface of the free groundwater in a zone of saturation except when separated by an underlying layer of unsaturated material.

Wetland. Land where an excess of water is the dominant factor determining the nature of soil development and the types of plant and animal communities living at the soil surface. It spans a continuum of environments where terrestrial and aquatic systems intergrade.

INDEX